THE BIG STORY

David Grzybowski

THE BIG STORY

THE ORAL HISTORY OF PHILADELPHIA TV NEWS

TEMPLE UNIVERSITY PRESS
Philadelphia | Rome | Tokyo

TEMPLE UNIVERSITY PRESS
Philadelphia, Pennsylvania 19122
tupress.temple.edu

Published 2024

Library of Congress Cataloging-in-Publication Data

Names: Grzybowski, David, 1991– author.
Title: The big story : the oral history of Philadelphia TV news / David Grzybowski.
Description: Philadelphia : Temple University Press, 2024. | Includes bibliographical references and index. | Summary: "This book provides an oral history of television news broadcasting in Philadelphia from the late 1970s into the 2020s. In over 200 interviews, journalists in front of and behind the camera reflect on what it was like to cover major news stories and how they built trust with viewers"— Provided by publisher.
Identifiers: LCCN 2024006694 (print) | LCCN 2024006695 (ebook) | ISBN 9781439921821 (cloth) | ISBN 9781439921845 (pdf)
Subjects: LCSH: Television broadcasting of news—Pennsylvania—Philadelphia—History. | Television journalists—Pennsylvania—Philadelphia. | Reporters and reporting—Pennsylvania—Philadelphia—History. | Philadelphia (Pa.)—History. | LCGFT: Oral histories.
Classification: LCC PN4899.P5 G79 2024 (print) | LCC PN4899.P5 (ebook) | DDC 070.4/30974811—dc23/eng/20240525
LC record available at https://lccn.loc.gov/2024006694
LC ebook record available at https://lccn.loc.gov/2024006695

♾ The paper used in this publication meets the requirements of the American National Standard for Information Sciences—Permanence of Paper for Printed Library Materials, ANSI Z39.48-1992

Printed in the United States of America

9 8 7 6 5 4 3 2 1

To the loves of my life, Jodi, Quinn, and Drew.

In loving memory of Joanna Grzybowski and Daniel Gilbert.

We love and miss you!

CONTENTS

A BRIEF HISTORY OF PHILADELPHIA'S TV NEWS STATIONS

KYW

Channel 3 is one of the oldest television stations in the country. It began as W3XE in 1932, owned by Philadelphia's Philco Corporation. In 1941, Philco was granted a commercial license and rebranded as WPTZ-TV. It would later become one of the first affiliates of the NBC television network. After Westinghouse Broadcasting (later known as Group W) purchased the station in 1957, the call letters were changed to WRCV and then changed again to WKYW; the station became known as KYW. One of the more popular shows on Channel 3 was *The Mike Douglas Show*, which aired from 1965 to 1978.

In 1957, Marciarose Shestack became Philadelphia's first female television anchor, coanchoring KYW broadcasts. KYW was at the top of the ratings books in 1965 under the news team of Vince Leonard, Tom Snyder, Marciarose Shestack, Malcolm Poindexter, and Trudy Haynes. KYW made history, as Haynes and Poindexter, who were hired by longtime KYW news director Al Primo, were the first African American TV reporters in Philadelphia. With this news team came the birth of the *Eyewitness News* format, created and planned by Primo. The *Eyewitness News* format leverages the visual element of television broadcasting and features reporters on the scene, firsthand accounts of events happening, and newscasts that emphasize authenticity in their reporting.

KYW moved to a new state-of-the-art building on Independence Mall East in July 1972 and stayed there until 2007, when it moved to a new building at 1555 Hamilton Street, in the Center City neighborhood of Philadelphia.

In 1995, Group W, the successor to Westinghouse Broadcasting, was acquired by the CBS Corporation. As a result, KYW-TV became a part of the CBS Television Stations group. KYW-TV was effectively separated from its radio counterpart in November 2017, when CBS Radio merged into Entercom, which is now known as Audacy.

Notable KYW past and present news team members include Allen Scott, Bill Bradley, Pete Boyle, Wally Kinnan, Lee Dexter, Marciarose Shestack, Tom Snyder, Bill Kuster, Al Meltzer, Vince Leonard, Malcolm Poindexter, Trudy Haynes, Mort Crim, Tom Lamaine, Larry Kane, Orien Reid, Diane Betzendahl, Steve Bell, Diane Allen, Marc Howard, Andrea Mitchell, Maury Povich, Steve Baskerville, Walt Hunter, Jack Jones, Robin Mackintosh, Larry Mendte, Jessica Savitch, Dick Sheeran, Pat Ciarrocchi, and current on-air talent Ukee Washington, Stephanie Stahl, Kate Bilo, Joe Holden, Chandler Lutz, Don Bell, Pat Gallen, Natasha Brown, and Jim Donovan.

WPHL

Channel 17 first hit the airwaves as WPCA-TV from 1960 to 1962, the city's first commercial UHF (ultrahigh frequency) station. The call letters stood for "People's Church of the Air." The channel went dark until new owners Len Stevens and Aaron Katz flipped the switch on WPHL Channel 17 as an independent station on September 17, 1965.

WPHL produced numerous local television shows, including children's shows *Wee Willie Webber Colorful Cartoon Club*, *Dr. Shock's Horror Theater*, and the 1980s teen dance hit *Dancin' on Air.*

In the 1970s, WPHL offered public-affairs shows hosted by longtime director Dorie Lenz, who hosted shows on Channel 17 called *Delaware Valley Forum* and *New Jersey Forum* and worked on segments that spoke about women's issues and other Emmy-winning television projects.

In 1975, WPHL moved from its original studio facility at 1230 East Mermaid Lane in Wyndmoor to its current studio on Wynnefield Avenue in the Wynnefield section of Philadelphia. WPHL's marketing promotions branded the station as "The Great Entertainer." Throughout

Channel 17's tenure, the station aired games of various Philadelphia teams, including the Phillies, the 76ers, the Flyers, Big 5 basketball, and other sports. WPHL was the home of the Phillies from 1971 to 1982 and 1993 to 1998, and in affiliation with Comcast SportsNet until 2014.

In 1995, WPHL became an affiliate of The WB Television Network, catering to a younger audience with such shows as *Buffy the Vampire Slayer* and *Dawson's Creek*.

WPHL had success in the Philadelphia television market with the shows *Inquirer News Tonight* and *WB17 News at Ten*, but the station eliminated the entire news department in September 2005, letting go more than thirty people on the news staff due to costs and low ratings. WPHL aired the Philadelphia Mummers Parade from 1995 to 2022, an annual parade taking place every New Year's Day in Philadelphia. As of 2024, WPHL has a revamped news program that includes *PHL17 Morning News* and a features and entertainment show, *Weekend Philler.*

Notable WPHL past and present news team members include Steve Highsmith, Toni Yates, Mike Dardis, Jim Sinkovitz, Mary Stoker Smith, and current news teams Jennifer Lewis-Hall, Jenna Meissner, Kelsey Fabian, Jason Lee, and Monica Cryan.

WTXF

Channel 29 signed on as WIBF-TV on May 16, 1965. The call letters were the initials of owners William, Irwin, and Benjamin Fox, two brothers and their father, who also owned radio station WIBF-FM/103.9 in the Philadelphia suburb of Jenkintown. In 1969, the Taft Broadcasting Company acquired WIBF-TV and changed the station's call letters to WTAF. This purchase was the highest price paid for a stand-alone UHF to date, costing $1.4 million to purchase all shares of WIBF Broadcasting.

In 1986, WTAF launched the Philadelphia area's first primetime 10:00 P.M. weekday and weekend newscasts. A year later, the TVX Broadcasting Group acquired WTAF-TV from Taft Broadcasting. This move meant another rebranding for the station, as its call letters became WTXF in 1988. In the early 1990s, WTXF went through ownership changes from Paramount Communications Inc., to Viacom Inc., to Fox Television Stations, LLC. WTXF's station headquarters sits at 4th and Market Streets in the heart of Old City in Philadelphia.

On April 1, 1996, Fox 29 entered Philadelphia's weekday morning news programming with the launch of *Good Day Philadelphia*, a daily morning news program.

Notable WTXF past and present news team members include Don Tollefson, Sheinelle Jones, Dave Huddleston, Joyce Evans, Clayton Morris, Bill Vargus, John Bolaris, George Mallet, Dorothy Krysiuk, Kerri-Lee Mayland, Dave Schratwieser, Grover Silcox, Lee McCarthy, Jill Chernekoff, Bruce Gordon, Tracey Matisak, Dawn Stensland-Mendte, Colleen Wolfe, and current on-air talent Mike Jerrick, Alex Holley, Jennaphr Frederick, Karen Hepp, Steve Keeley, Thomas Drayton, Jennifer Joyce, Kathy Orr, Sue Serio, and Bob Kelly.

WCAU

In 1946, the *Philadelphia Evening Bulletin* named its proposed television and radio stations WPEN-TV and WPEN Radio. Channel 10's call letters did not last long, as a year later, WPEN-TV's name was changed to WCAU.

WCAU went on the air on May 23, 1948, broadcasting from 1622 Chestnut Street in Center City. The station's transmitter was located on top of the PSFS Building, one of Philadelphia's most iconic structures. In 1958, WCAU became the first affiliate of the CBS Television Network. Anchor John Facenda was the face of WCAU from 1958 to 1973, known for his stylish voice and delivery. In 1952, Channel 10 moved to a new station headquarters at City Avenue and Monument Road in Bala Cynwyd, but after sixty-six years, in 2018 it eventually relocated to Center City, in the Comcast Technology Center.

WCAU offered diverse television programming that included *The Big Top* with Ed Mahon, *Action in the Afternoon*, Jane Norman's *Pixanne*, Gene London's *Cartoon Corners*, and *Grand Chance Roundup* and *Mr. & Mrs.*, both hosted by longtime WCAU talent Gene Crane.

In 1965, WCAU followed Channel 3's lead in racially integrating its staff by hiring Edie Huggins, who worked at the station for more than forty-two years.

In September 1995, KYW and WCAU switched networks, with KYW joining CBS and WCAU joining NBC.

Notable WCAU past and present news team members include John Facenda, Herb Clarke, Tom Brookshier, Bill Campbell, Gene Crane, Renée Chenault-Fattah, Jillian Mele, Al Meltzer, Terry Ruggles, Mike

Strug, Brian Williams, Bill Baldini, Steve Levy, Aditi Roy, Jesse Gary, Glenn "Hurricane" Schwartz, Denise Nakano, Monique Braxton, Lu Ann Cahn, Vai Sikahema, Amy Freeze, and current on-air talent Jacqueline London, Erin Coleman, Keith Jones, Tracy Davidson, Bill Henley, Rosemary Connors, Matt DeLucia, Deanna Durante, Tim Furlong, Ted Greenberg, Cydney Long, and John Clark.

WPVI

WFIL-TV was born from WFIL AM/FM radio, which started out as an affiliate of the DuMont Television Network, a network that went on the air in August 1946. DuMont was one of the first three TV networks in the United States. Channel 6 went on the air as WFIL-TV in 1947; the station's first facility was located at 46th and Market Streets in Philadelphia. In 1963, Channel 6 moved to a new building at City and Monument Avenues in Bala Cynwyd. In 1971, Capital Cities Communications purchased the station and changed its call letters to WPVI-TV.

Channel 6 had aired entertainment and children's programming, such as *Bandstand* (eventually called *American Bandstand*), *Romper Room* with Miss Connie, *Chief Halftown*, and *Popeye Theater*, a late-afternoon cartoon show featuring Philadelphia's sweetheart, Sally Starr.

In 1996, WPVI-TV became a part of the Walt Disney Company when Disney acquired Capital Cities. In 2009, WPVI moved into a brand-new state-of-the-art facility next door to its Bala Cynwyd studios.

In 1976, anchor Jim Gardner joined WPVI and served as the lead anchor of the station until his retirement in 2022. For more than four decades, Gardner anchored the 6:00 P.M. and 11:00 P.M. newscasts in Philadelphia, one of the longest anchoring tenures in the country. From the 1970s to the present, WPVI has remained a ratings powerhouse and is arguably one of the most successful television stations in the country.

Notable WPVI past and present news team members include Larry Kane, Jim Gardner, Jim O'Brien, Vernon Odom, Gary Papa, Monica Malpass, Lisa Thomas-Laury, Scott Palmer, Dave Roberts, Rob Jennings, Siani Lee, Dave Frankel, and current on-air talent Rick Williams, Brian Taff, Cecily Tynan, Ducis Rodgers, Adam Joseph, Sarah Bloomquist, Sharrie Williams, Alicia Vitarelli, Nydia Han, Walter Perez, Chad Pradelli, Jamie Apody, Katherine Scott, Karen Rogers, Tamala Edwards, and Matt O'Donnell.

THE BIG STORY

PART I

Innovating on Air

ANCHORS AWAY

Larry Kane and Jim Gardner

Larry Kane began his broadcasting career in 1957 in Miami, Florida, at WQAM radio. As a young radio reporter in 1964, Kane gained recognition from national media after being the only American correspondent to travel with the Beatles on their North American tour. In 1966, at just twenty-three years old, Kane arrived in Philadelphia, Pennsylvania, becoming WFIL's radio afternoon drive anchor. In 1969, Kane transitioned into television, working at WFIL-TV and later helping launch the highly successful Action News *format, leading Channel 6 to local ratings crowns in the early 1970s. Following its acquisition by Capital Cities, WFIL changed its call letters to WPVI-TV in April 1971.*

On June 1, 1976, Jim Gardner (born James Lawrence Goldman) joined WPVI as a reporter and anchor of Action News at Noon. *After graduating from Columbia University, Gardner worked at WINS radio and WFAS radio in White Plains, New York. In 1974, Gardner began a new career as a television broadcaster at WKBW-TV (a Capital Cities–owned station) in Buffalo, New York, before departing alongside producer Alan Nesbitt for Cap Cities' newly acquired station in Philadelphia.*

In May 1977, after Kane left Philadelphia for New York City, Gardner took over his 6:00 P.M. and 11:00 P.M. solo anchor assignments at WPVI. Kane joined WABC-TV in New York City on June 13, 1977, where he anchored the 11:00 P.M. newscast and handled other network coverage. Kane anchored the news in New York but still lived in Pennsyl-

vania with his family and commuted daily to the Big Apple. Kane hired and paid an ex-Philly cop to drive him to and from New York each day during the week, but New York critics blasted Kane for his commute. When Kane left Philadelphia, he signed a six-year contract with WABC but did not stay with the station until anywhere close to the end of that term. When Kane left WPVI, he was reportedly the highest-paid anchorman in Philadelphia, earning close to $100,000 a year. Kane made close to $225,000 to $250,000 in New York in 1977. WPVI's Jim O'Brien, Don Tollefson, and Steve Levy also auditioned for the top anchor spot at Channel 6 after Kane's departure. Gardner became a centerpiece of the Action News *team, with a supporting cast of weathermen Jim O'Brien and Dave Roberts and sports anchors Don Tollefson, Gary Papa, and Scott Palmer.*

Kane's tenure in New York did not last long, as he returned to Philadelphia less than a year after leaving. (WABC made a deal with Kane that he would not anchor any national network broadcast until 1982.) Upon returning to Philadelphia in 1978, Kane anchored the 6:00 P.M. and 11:00 P.M. newscasts at WCAU-TV. Curiosity ran high as to whether he could take his new station to the top of the news ratings, but twenty months after Kane arrived at WCAU, the news ratings at Channel 10 had improved only marginally, with WPVI and Gardner still on top.

In 1993, Kane joined KYW-TV, then an NBC affiliate, to become the lead anchor and host a weekly produced program called The Bulletin with Larry Kane. *Kane anchored the 6:00 P.M. and 11:00 P.M. newscasts at KYW until his retirement in December 2002, when his seat was filled by Marc Howard, also formerly of WPVI. Kane spent thirty-six years on the air in Philadelphia and is the only person in the city to anchor and work at three stations—WPVI, WCAU, and KYW—in a top-five television market.*

Despite all the station changes for Kane, Gardner remained at WPVI until his retirement in December 2022, being replaced on the 6:00 P.M. newscast by Brian Taff and the 11:00 P.M. newscast by Rick Williams.

"We have long had an unstated agreement, you and I. I like to say that we formed a covenant years ago. We give you respect and our commitment to reporting in a no-nonsense way those things that are important to you and making sure that what we tell you is accurate and fair," Gardner said in his final newscast in 2022.

Gardner worked at WPVI for forty-six years, solo anchoring the 6:00 P.M. and 11:00 P.M. newscasts.

The following interviews were completed prior to Gardner's retirement in 2022.

Larry Kane, Anchor, WPVI, WCAU, and KYW:
I arrived [at WFIL] in September of 1966 as a radio newsman. I'd never been on TV before. About a year into my tenure there, I realized that [WFIL] had a TV station, which I knew about, but I didn't know much about it. Someone suggested I'd start doing some reporting for them, I guess in early 1967. They had me on a schedule where I would do afternoon-drive radio for WFIL. Believe it or not, during the height of its success, it still had a half-hour newscast at 6:30 at night on the radio called *Assignment 56*. In many ways, it was really the forerunner of *Action News*. I eventually did that, and they would send me out a couple of nights to do some TV reporting, which I knew very little about. Remember, this was the film era, so you had to get back [from your field assignment] by a certain time to get the film processed in a lab downstairs. That was a big deal. For example, if you were out at five o'clock and you could get back by 5:30 with the film, you might be able to get thirty seconds on the air at six o'clock, if you were fortunate. There *were* cameras, believe it or not.

Neal Zoren, TV Columnist:
In 1977, Larry [Kane] had made a great name for himself in Philadelphia. He has changed news in various ways, not only for being young and brash and different from other newscasters. First of all, he was the first journalist. The others were basically broadcasters who were given an anchor job. Larry Kane is a news person who comes from radio. There's a lot of things that he does that goes beyond just reading the news. Larry Kane loves the news. He loves to talk to people and loves to get the story and know something about the story that nobody else knows. He really is sharp that way.

Kathy Gerrow, Producer, Writer, and Assistant News Director, KYW and WCAU:
For one thing, [Larry Kane] was the most plugged in and informed anchor I'd ever worked with. He knows everybody. Before there was social

media, Larry Kane invented his own social media, and it was his telephone. A newsroom at night after everyone leaves after the day when you have to put on an eleven o'clock show—there's not many people in the newsroom. He would work the phone all night. That's what he did. He would talk on the phone all night. He just talked to people, leaders, politicians, and he wasn't necessarily tracking down a specific story, but he was just always a news gatherer. When something would happen, whatever it might be . . . in his brain, he [has] reams of information that are stored there from his years and years of phone calls.

Bill Shull, Producer, WCAU and WTXF:
Larry Kane was the man. He was the guy who took the mantle from John Facenda, Vince Leonard, and some of the men who came before him and who were still there when Larry came along. Larry was young, and he was brash. Somebody called him "Shotgun Larry" because of the way he delivered the news in that fast style. It was something TV news hadn't seen before. He had almost instant success. They [WFIL] were number one for the first time in just a year.

Ed Rendell, Former Philadelphia Mayor and Pennsylvania Governor:
Larry Kane was the big anchorman in the market. He made Channel 6 what it was and what it remained all these years.

Mike Strug, Reporter, WPVI, KYW, and WCAU:
Action News had turned the city around. In a sense, [Larry Kane] was the guy that made it happen, along with Jim O'Brien and Joe Pellegrino and all of the people that were a part of *Action News* from the beginning. For him to go up [to New York]: Hey, congratulations. That was a big deal. We wished you all of the success.

Larry Mendte, Anchor, WCAU and KYW:
There is no place else in the country like [Philadelphia] that has the relationship between the audience and the anchors, especially. Larry Kane was a god, and when he went to New York, he broke people's hearts.

Ned Warwick, Assignment Editor and News Director, WPVI:
[Larry Kane's leaving] was a big deal. There was lots of newspaper coverage. There were television critics writing every day about local televi-

sion news. Everybody was under scrutiny. Larry Kane's going to New York and leaving PVI was a big deal. Replacing him was—what—I guess Jim [Gardner] was about twenty-six years old? It was a huge gamble, but my god, it turned out to be absolutely once again the right move. It came as a result of a lot of agonizing, a lot of thinking about the best way to go. It was taken very seriously. The question really was, there wasn't so much confidence that this [replacement] would work. It was every bit of a sense that this could be a big risk. This could end in failure, but something had to be done. We had to replace Larry Kane, and Larry Kane was a big fixture. A big future of the market.

Bob Feldman, Producer and Assistant News Director, WPVI:
[Jim Gardner] came as a noon anchor, knowing very well that Larry Kane had left and that we were going to look for someone to replace him. He made all the difference.

Here's the difference about Jim Gardner, and I'm not sure if he does it to this day, but I would be surprised if he doesn't. After every show, he would take our aircheck tape, which we did in the newsroom, and he would take it into the edit rooms and watch himself to see how he could be better. That's the kind of person he was. He didn't tell anyone about it—he just did it. He wanted to be sure he did it as well as he could, and he could learn. If he ever made a mistake, he could correct it. That's very unusual for an anchor. They don't do that.

Jim Gardner, Anchor, WPVI:
I had no goal. I was scared to death to anchor the news in Philadelphia and to be a reporter in Philadelphia. My goal was to do that and to somehow do it well and somehow become comfortable with it. I was intimidated. I turned people off. I don't know if it was compensation or whether it was a function of a couple of us who were from Buffalo and came down here at the same time, virtually at the same time, particularly Alan [Nesbitt] and I. We saw some things that we thought were disappointing and that we could kind of show them [how to do better]. Well, people didn't want two new guys, including a twenty-eight-year-old, to come down and show them anything. I felt like I had Alan's support. He would say, "Jim, show them!" I did, and people didn't like that. It took me quite a while to figure that out, a lot longer than it should have.

Ned Warwick, Assignment Editor and News Director, WPVI:
You know what happened as a result of that change? There was something about the cast of characters in that newsroom that just made it. And there was a sense of fun. We wanted to be successful, and we fought hard, took no prisoners, and it was all a glorious battle day in and day out with the other television stations.

Jim Gardner, Anchor, WPVI:
I've always joked with Alan [Nesbitt] that they didn't really want me for the six and eleven [o'clock news], and they wanted this guy John Hambrick. There were three brothers, the Hambrick brothers. John was in San Francisco. There was a Hambrick in Baltimore. They were the local anchor Hambrick brothers. They were very much in fashion at the time.

All the consultants would say, "Watch John Hambrick. He is the guy." They talked to him. He was in town, I think. Alan called me up one night and said, "We are over at the Marriott with John Hambrick, playing poker. Why don't you come over?" I can't remember why I didn't, but I didn't. I thought that they really wanted him because he was a huge deal in the landscape of local news, and maybe they wanted me there to do the 5:30 [broadcast] or something like that. I've kidded Alan ever since that that was what they really wanted. Alan said, "Absolutely not. Larry wanted you, and that's the way we went." I never tried out for [the anchor position], and it never occurred to me that this would be something that was [an option]—it just seemed absurd. Why would I get that job? I had just gotten there five minutes ago. I hadn't earned my stripes.

Neal Zoren, TV Columnist:
When Larry Kane left, they didn't look for a star anchor from another market. They used their newcomer, Jim Gardner, who had been on radio and who had been on the air to see what he could do. They would go from there, but Gardner proved to be comfortable and popular because it's the Channel 6 format that works. It doesn't matter who the personality is. It's not the people. The people count, and the longevity of the people count, but basically it's the formatting. You can plug anybody you want into it, and Channel 6 is keen about knowing who works and who doesn't work in that format.

Mike Strug, Reporter, WPVI, KYW, and WCAU:
Channel 6 still does this—they bring people in, and they work for a long time. You become totally familiar with them. To this day, I know more people at Channel 6 than I do at any other stations, despite the fact that I haven't worked there since 1979 or 1980. There are still people there that I've met over the years, and they keep them there. When somebody leaves, they move that person, and they bring someone new in from Iowa. They move that person into [the vacant slot]. So they had prepared the city for Jim [Gardner] to take over. So when Larry [Kane] left, Jim took over, and it couldn't have been a more natural [transition]—"Hey, it's Jim," who was working all along anyway.

Jim Gardner, Anchor, WPVI:
It never occurred to me. In fact, it wasn't even on my radar to think that I might do the six and eleven o'clock news. It didn't occur to me. But obviously, it was occurring to [station management], and they did interview a whole bunch of anchorpeople from around the country. For whatever reason, they eventually settled on this twenty-eight-, twenty-nine-year-old kid. If I had been on the outside looking in, I would've thought, you know, "What the hell are they doing—it's absurd!" But that's the way they went. So they asked me to do the six and eleven [o'clock news], and that was that.

Larry Kane, Anchor, WPVI, WCAU, and KYW:
I did a very good job, I think, preparing and supporting him.

Steve Sacks, Producer, WPVI:
It wasn't a bad deal because Larry [Kane] wanted to go to New York. The way I understood it, and the way the crew understood it, was that Larry wanted to go to New York. Obviously, it made sense bringing in Jim [Gardner]. Jim wasn't doing anything to hurt Larry. There was no problem in that respect. Larry was a pretty easy guy to work with. Most of the anchors, especially at Channel 6—I don't know about other places, but the people that wound up anchoring there become really well known. When you meet them offstage, they do know what they are talking about.

Bob Kravitz, Photographer, WPVI:
It was weird because some of us didn't think it would work. We didn't know [Jim] Gardner. It worked. People really caught up to Jim.

Neal Zoren, TV Columnist:
People will say Larry Kane did not do well at WABC. That's not true. He got teased in the New York media for taking limousines, for not living in New York, but his show was top-rated in New York. The show was not one and done, and it was not a failure. It was just that he was not the star he was here.

Steve Capus, Producer, KYW:
It's very easy and unfair to overlook what Larry Kane has represented in the Philadelphia market. He brought *Action News* to life back in the day and was so good at it that New York picked him up to help WABC.

New York didn't particularly take to Larry in part because he loved the [Philadelphia] area so much that he didn't move and [instead] commuted. That didn't go over well in New York. I understand that. Larry Kane is also an immensely talented guy, and it was good to work with him. I feel fortunate I got to work with him both at Channel 10 and later at Channel 3 when he came over.

Art Moore, Publicity Director, WPVI:
I know Larry [Kane], and I think he's an incredibly talented man, so this is in no way disparaging of him, but I think when he left, there's a percentage of people in Philly who sort of resented that. Especially with his going to New York. Having it not work out in New York and come back, [the city's attitude] sort of was that he left us, so, well, we really aren't gonna be there for him. He never was number one again, coming back again. *Action News* always maintained that [position]. That sounds overly simplistic, but there's something about that mark and those viewers who take so many of those things personally. On a small scale, it may not seem like much, but it's a collective unit. You have a lot of eyeballs who are saying, "I'm not going to watch there and stay here because these people stayed with me."

Larry Kane, Anchor, WPVI, WCAU, and KYW:
I think when I came back, [Jim Gardner] may have taken that as an affront. My job was not to come back and beat him. My job was to come back and do the news and do it well. There is no animosity, but I think that he's always been very sensitive about it. He will deny this, but I began it all. We haven't had much of a relationship, but we see each other, and we are courteous.

Steve Capus, Producer, KYW:
When you have competitors like Jim Gardner or Larry Kane when he was at Channel 10, when you have players of that caliber, you had better try to up your game and do everything you can to compete, or you're gonna get your clock cleaned. It doesn't happen automatically. You can't just roll over and say, "Well, nobody's going to beat Jim Gardner, so we're not gonna do a newscast tonight." You have to try to do what you can. Every news director who's worked in Philadelphia that has gone up against Jim Gardner has tried to figure out the secret formula to defeat the guy. Every single one of those news directors and producers—including me—has failed. It hasn't worked. You name it, they have tried it. That's why when he finally leaves the anchor chair, there will be heartfelt applause for his brilliant career, but there will also be some people across town [breathing] a sigh of relief because maybe now they can try to knock off the mighty WPVI *Action News*.

Larry Kane, Anchor, WPVI, WCAU, and KYW:
It's a silent competition. We are not friends. We do respect each other. All you have to know about how Jim Gardner feels about me is to walk into their Hall of Fame in their building and not see a picture of me there.

Jim Gardner, Anchor, WPVI:
Competition between me and Larry [Kane]? Larry was the guy. There was no competition. I was just trying to be a noon anchorman. The idea of there being a competition between me and Larry Kane to PVI is laughable from my point of view.

Larry Kane, Anchor, WPVI, WCAU, and KYW:
I think we both had an impact in different ways. There's no question that the original *Action News* changed the face of television around the

country and was very successful. There is nobody that has his tenure on the air anywhere. He's battled through my return to Philadelphia, Jim O'Brien's death. You have to give him a lot of credit for that.

Ed Rendell, Former Philadelphia Mayor and Pennsylvania Governor:
I never thought Larry [Kane] would or could be replaced, but Jim Gardner took over, and over the course of time, Jim has created an even better following and even better ratings for Channel 6. He was much like the Walter Cronkite of Philadelphia. People trust him to tell them the truth. They say it doesn't happen unless Jim Gardner says it happens. I think that's pretty true.

Neal Zoren, TV Columnist:
It was basically an accident of somebody's ambition, somebody taking over a post and then keeping the post for forty years.

Dave Roberts, Meteorologist, WPVI:
I don't think anybody can top Jim [Gardner] or will ever top him in terms of authenticity. The man was driven to be professional and to do the job.

I knew what he was thinking, and he knew what I was thinking. By that, I mean when we covered a story. The intermix of the three people on the air is really important. If there was a real serious story he was covering, we knew we had to blend in. We knew when to be light, when to be airy about something, and when to be serious. All he had to do was look at me, and I got the message, like, "Dave, we have to deal with this very carefully and cautiously, be careful of what we say." In addition to the story, there's transitions between segments and so forth. My bottom line is, both of us knew what the other one was thinking. We knew how to handle it. At times, we had a lot of fun. I don't know how many times I've heard from people how much they always enjoyed the banter.

Don Polec, Features Reporter, WPVI:
[Jim Gardner's] the last of journalistic integrity, I think. In a world where there is an increasing amount of flash and trash on the air, he keeps it real. He takes his job very seriously. We had some flashes over the years because I would be very flippant and very cavalier.

Whenever he thought I was over the line, he'd let me know. It was a good balance.

Stu Bykofsky, TV Columnist:
I took Jim Gardner out to dinner along City Avenue, and it was like playing handball and you slapped the ball into the wall, but instead of a hard ball, it was pudding. I slapped the ball into the wall, and it just stopped there. I would ask him a question, and nothing would come back, I mean nothing but one-word answers. I avoid asking questions that could be answered "yes" or "no." I ask "how" questions and the "why" questions. This was the early 1980s: '81, '82. Maybe by then, I guess, I had gotten a reputation of being a tough critic. I guess I was, but fair, I think.

[Channel 6 was] not firing anchors every other week. They were not getting new reporters. Some of the reporters there have died of old age. They would not get rid of them because—and here's the promotion part—they were your friends. They were your family. They were everywhere. That news van is everywhere. They didn't in their promotional efforts talk about how good their news was—although they could have. They really couldn't talk about how many Emmys they had won because they wouldn't allow their people to participate.

Cecily Tynan, Meteorologist, WPVI:
When I eventually moved up to the desk to sit next to [Jim Gardner] when Dave Roberts was retiring, I was very intimidated. I realized that he has a tremendous sense of humor: very dry, witty sense of humor. He can sing pretty much any Broadway tune there is. He's a Broadway aficionado. After the fact, as I got to know him, [I wondered] why I was intimidated by him. He's a really nice guy, and he really does care about our product and about the viewers. He just doesn't get up there and read what people write. He pretty much writes the newscasts, the six and eleven [o'clock], with our producer. He's just grounded. He doesn't have a tremendous ego. He's pretty private. He's not somebody who talks about his personal life as much on the air or on social media. He doesn't think the news is about him. The news is about our community and our world, and he is just [broad]casting that along to people.

The most interesting thing to watch, for him, is when there is breaking news. He basically just takes over in directing the newscasts. When there is breaking news, there are no scripts, and sometimes he is dealing with different chopper shots or different cameras in different locations, and he will be saying to the director, "Can we take Chopper 6 for this view?" or "Can we go to Dann Cuellar, who is on the scene?" It's interesting to watch when you are there with him, kind of fly on the wall, watching how he really just starts to direct the show from the anchor desk.

Brian Taff, Anchor, WPVI:
[Jim Gardner] is voracious in consuming the news. He wants to talk to you about it. He and I have had countless discussions about the state of politics or the play of the day. He doesn't just come in, bang it out, and go home. He lives and breathes it. I will tell you: As much as I respect that, it taught me the importance of emulating it. You are not going to make it in this town or this business at that level unless that's what you are willing to deliver on a daily basis. I don't think he would disagree with me if I said this: To some extent, Jim is like Philadelphia. When I first arrived, I think he kept me at arm's length too. He wanted to feel me out: Is this guy anything more than a voice or a guy who can talk or this and that? I remember being on the set—we used to do special reports at eleven o'clock, and I would sit with him on the set. When the story was over, I would have this little knot of fear in my throat because I knew he was going to ask me a question about it, and I didn't know what the question was going to be. Very often, although his questions are always tailored to give the audience something different, I think he was kind of testing me: What can I ask you about the story that you wouldn't expect to know? That's a really good preparation technique. If you are also preparing to answer Jim's question, then you know the story through and through.

Jamie Apody, Sports Anchor and Reporter, WPVI:
In my head, Jim [Gardner] is a wannabe sportscaster. He doesn't want to say that, but he loves sports, and it's his favorite thing. He comes in every day to hang out in the sports office. It's his hiding spot, and he loves it. He and I were very close from the get-go. People—to this day—are intimidated and afraid to talk to him, and I think he is the warmest, smartest, most amazing human being on the planet. He's like a second father

to me. He was at my wedding. I was at his kid's wedding. The day I had my first child, I had a C-section for [my son] Tanner, and Jim's texting my husband: "When can I come to the hospital and see him?" [I say,] "Can you tell him to come tomorrow?" He shows up the next day, and he was there for all three of the births of my kids in the hospital to meet them, which is insane. He's so good at what he does. A lot of people can't say they were a producer in a bigger market, because I was a producer in L.A. first, so I've seen anchors in bigger markets than this even. What sets him apart is he works his tail off. Not to say other people don't, but he writes almost every word he says. If he didn't write it, he will make sure to review it. He's one of a few anchors in a major market that does that. Most of them stroll in for an eleven o'clock show at ten thirty and read what everyone wrote for them. He doesn't do that.

If there's a big story, he asks to come in. He doesn't want to miss a thing. He writes and reads through all of his stuff. He's the smartest person in this building, and he's the best writer in this building. Along the way, he teaches—my gosh, how many countless young producers has he probably had an effect on in forty-five years? Good Lord.

It was a weekend when he told me I'm never leaving. He said to me, "You gotta get rid of your agent—you aren't going anywhere," and he told my parents that. I knew that he accepted me at that point. I have so many Jim stories.

In the first month or so I was here, I did a radio interview with another sports talk station. He came in while I was on. He comes in screaming and saying some off-color jokes. I'm motioning to him that I'm on the radio. Gary [Papa] tells him I'm on the radio. He literally goes in my line of sight and starts doing very unsightly things with a football that I can't even begin to admit. I start cracking up, and the guy on the radio says, "Oh, is Gary making you laugh?" I'm like, "Not exactly. . . ." God forbid I ever let anyone know who it was because he comes across so seriously, but boy, 90 percent of the crack-ups on the air are his doing, and he doesn't want you to know about it. He has a lot to do with that.

Charles Barkley, NBA Superstar and Broadcaster, TNT:
[Jim Gardner] is the godfather. I think he is the godfather of Philadelphia media for my generation. Anytime I am around him, which is not a lot, I feel like I'm around greatness.

Rick Williams, Anchor, WPVI:
[Jim Gardner] wanted to make sure that every reporter in his show had their act together. When I first met him, he did welcome me to the newsroom and welcomed me to Philly. He gave the impression that if I was going to be on his show, my reports were going to have to be strong. I tried to make them so. There was a long line of reporters there who were very, very competent, and I just wanted to emulate them: from Vernon Odom, Cathy Gandolfo, people who had been there for years and who knew Philadelphia, knew the *Action News* way, and knew how to tell a story and put a package together that had substance. I emulated them and just hoped that if and when my pieces ended up in Jim's show, they would be acceptable.

Gail Shister, TV Columnist:
Part of the reason news becomes popular and personalities become popular is because viewers think they are the [anchor's] friends. They are inviting them over every day at the same time. Obviously, the relationship there is very different from any other medium. It's visual. "Jim Gardner is my friend." That's also the way local stations promote themselves, as "We are your friends." Especially PVI.

Jim Gardner, Anchor, WPVI:
I view 90 percent of what I do [as being] in the newsroom and 10 percent in the studio. I think there are probably some anchorpeople out there who see themselves [as doing] 90 percent of their job in the studio and 10 percent in the newsroom. I don't feel that way. Was I nervous at the beginning about my work in the studio? Sure. Very, very nervous. But I never lacked confidence about my ability in the newsroom as a writer, as a reporter. I think I was a good reporter, and I think I am a good reporter. I don't mean to sound, you know, presumptuous here, but I think I'm a good reporter. I think I am a good writer, and I think I am seen as a good writer. I think I'm a really good collaborator with producers on getting the best data in a newscast. That's always been a strength and something I really enjoy doing. When you are done with that, you have to do it in the studio and tell people what you've done. I don't know that I'm particularly good in the studio. I guess I am good enough. I've never had any coaching. I've never had any stuff like that. A lot of people do

that work with consultants and all that. I don't know if people at our station do, but I know a lot of people do. I've never had that experience. So the studio has always been a place where we tell people about all the work we have done. That's how I see my job. In terms of my sort of comfort [regarding] my place in this consultation with people at Channel 6, yeah, it definitely took at least several years for me to be comfortable for that.

THREE MILE ISLAND

On March 28, 1979, Three Mile Island, a nuclear power plant located in Middletown, Pennsylvania, close to the state capital of Harrisburg, suffered one of the worst civilian nuclear power plant accidents in U.S. history. The accident began when a pressure valve in the plant's Unit 2 reactor failed to close. Cooling water, contaminated with radiation, drained from the open valve into adjoining buildings, and the reactor core began to overheat and melt.

Following the accident, news spread quickly throughout Pennsylvania, leading neighbors to worry about their safety from leaked radiation. In the ensuing years, investigations and lawsuits have claimed that above-average rates of cancer and birth defects followed the accident in the surrounding Pennsylvania area. No deaths occurred during the incident itself in 1979.

Jim Gardner, Anchor, WPVI:
Back in those days, we had the [Associated Press] machines. They spit out paper, and they had a bell system: Three bells was you might find this interesting, five bells was something else, seven bells was urgent, and ten bells was whatever. I think it was around four o'clock or four thirty, somewhere around there, and all of a sudden the news machines started ringing off the table. It got everybody's attention. We walked over and saw that there was concern about an accident at Three Mile

Island. At that point, not many people had heard of Three Mile Island. What was Three Mile Island?

Jim Sinkovitz, Anchor and Reporter, WPHL:
The accident was actually discovered by a traffic reporter in an airplane—he said one of the cooling towers wasn't producing steam. There was no announcement made that anything was shutting down. Some phone calls were made, and finally someone [at the plant] hung the phone up, saying, "We can't deal with you now." That's when we found out basically that something was definitely wrong. The next day, of course, we found out that there had been an incident, but it wasn't being called an accident yet, and it certainly wasn't being called a meltdown. It took a while before we got some legitimate information. Even [Governor] Dick Thornburgh and Bill Scranton, the lieutenant governor at the time, had a news conference saying that we had been misled by Metropolitan Edison, the operator of the plant at the time. It was very difficult (a) to understand exactly what was going on and (b) to comprehend what was going on because few of us knew anything about radiation or what potential disaster was pretty much diverted by having a containment building.

Bob Feldman, Producer and Assistant News Director, WPVI:
It was scary as hell. No one had any idea what was going on. We made a decision very quickly when we heard that there was a possible meltdown and there could be radiation released from Three Mile Island that we oughta be there. I put together a team of two or three reporters, and we literally took a van and two crews and drove to Harrisburg. Within about eight hours, we were in Harrisburg. They didn't have microwaves, they didn't have satellites then. We had landlines for video. I booked out what turned out to be the only video line from Harrisburg to Philadelphia at that time. We had a way of getting a picture from Three Mile Island back to Philadelphia.

Larry Kane, Anchor, WPVI, WCAU, and KYW:
Basically, we sent a whole bunch of people there. We had limited live capability. I know we had a live microwave, but the microwaves didn't go that far. I think we sought some satellite time. I'm not quite sure. The satellite times in those days were $5,000 a minute. We all thought we

were gonna get killed, that this big mushroom cloud was suddenly floating over Pennsylvania. So when we reported the episode, it was really a panic. I was in the newsroom. It was around two o'clock in the afternoon. We proceeded to cover the hell out of it for about three or four weeks and then indefinitely.

Mike Strug, Reporter, WPVI, KYW, and WCAU:
It was very tense. We look at it now, and you say, "Oh, there was a big event there." We didn't know at that point. I remember Marge Pala, who was a reporter, spoke to someone at the nuclear agency down in Washington, D.C., who said they didn't know if there may be an explosion and that we could have all hell over Pennsylvania. I remember walking out with the guy who was the operations manager, with whom I was very friendly. We were standing out there talking about sending our families to Florida because nobody knew what was going to happen, early on. The other thing is, we were sending crews there, and nobody knew how much radiation there was from it. I think at that point, I got in touch with Hahnemann or Jefferson Hospital, and we got those little radiation tags you see X-ray technicians wearing. We had to make sure each of the crews had one of these things.

Bob Feldman, Producer and Assistant News Director, WPVI:
We were there for, I want to say for almost a week, and we weren't given a lot of information. We were able to report from there that there didn't seem to be any explosions, there didn't seem to be any panic, but no one knew what was being blown up out of the towers. [The radiation] was definitely coming from west to east. Our job really was to find out if it was coming to Philadelphia.

Bob Kravitz, Photographer, WPVI:
When we were doing standup in front of the capitol in Harrisburg, there was this white snowy stuff that started falling from the sky. I had no idea what it was.

Bill Baldini, Reporter, WCAU:
Some reporters would not go for fear that they would be sterilized. To go there, you had to volunteer. When we went there, it was like a movie set. By the time we got there, there was no one on the streets. The streets

were evacuated, and it was like a science-fiction movie. I remember walking down the street, and there was no one around. It was abandoned. We didn't know whether we were getting irradiated or not. When CBS got involved, their attitude was incredible. I remember a battery went in a camera, and their attitude was, "Don't even replace the battery, just leave the camera and the sound stuff as it is, and we will supply a new one." I remember they had a bus running 24/7 to evacuate [people] with space suits that they would have on hand. It was insane. You look back and say, "Did I really do that?" Yeah, I did it for two weeks. It was crazy.

Chris Wagner, Anchor, WPVI:
I covered it the first day. I went out with the camera crew, and we were really nervous and really scared. We were wondering what we were gonna find and if radiation was being put out into the air. I only covered it that one day because I was young, and I wanted to have children, and I was afraid of getting irradiated. I asked them not to send me back. I only covered it the first day. Ironically, that was the day the radiation was let out.

Rob Jennings, Anchor, WPVI:
We had no idea how serious it was and wouldn't know the full story for several days. The plant's owner, General Public Utilities, was trying to keep a lid on details, undoubtedly hoping to avert a Hiroshima in the American Heartland.

I had just seen a movie called *The China Syndrome* and at first had no inkling that a similar nuclear meltdown could be happening a hundred or so miles from Philadelphia, that we might be on the verge of our own China Syndrome.

Vernon Odom, Reporter, WPVI:
It was very frightening. Tremendous uncertainty. Lack of faith in the credibility of the operators of Three Mile Island. They didn't know what they were talking about and were all over the place. Earlier in my career, I had worked in Atlanta and covered Jimmy Carter and his rise in political fame and fortune. I saw him down there, and I knew Jody Powell, his press secretary. I knew them all very well because they were in Atlanta for many years when he was governor. I came to Philly the year he

got elected president. I asked them how bad it was, and they said they didn't know and they weren't getting any straight answers. When I got that same statement from Governor Thornburgh, I got really concerned. It was frightening.

Jim Gardner, Anchor, WPVI:
My reaction was, "Let's take it easy, let's make sure we know what we are talking about," and we did our best to say what we knew at six o'clock. None of us really knew what nuclear energy was or the nuclear physics behind what was going on. I thought it might be a really good idea to have a nuclear physicist come into the station, just to give us all a seminar that night. In fact, we did invite a guy from Temple [University]. I don't remember his name, but he came in, and for a couple of hours we talked with this guy about nuclear physics, what was happening, what was it that we should be concerned about, and we all had this crash course. It made us all feel a little bit more comfortable, that we could understand what was going on and we could talk to an audience without faking it. We at least had a baseline knowledge that [made us feel] like we were being reasonable television journalists. I do remember after the eleven o'clock news, I went to this place where I went on occasion with some friends down in Old City, wondering which way the wind was blowing. We just told everybody that it was very unlikely that this could ever have been what everybody was scared about, but I myself sat there wondering, "Is the wind blowing thirty miles per hour from Middletown, Pennsylvania, to Philadelphia? Is this something that should be of concern?" Over the next couple of days, we gained a very realistic picture of what was going on.

Terry Ruggles, Reporter and Anchor, WCAU:
Every day, there were briefings at the Middletown High School two times a day with a guy by the name of Dr. Denton, who worked with the Nuclear Regulation Commission, and we didn't know what was going on. One night, we went to the state house for a press conference by Governor Thornburgh, and there were sixty cameras there. People came from all over the world—they were there from Japan, Germany. The BBC was there—a guy there by the name of Martin Bell and I became good friends because the story lasted so long.

Andy Doane, Photographer, WPVI:
That weekend, I was home in my apartment with my girlfriend. We were just laying around, and I never answered my phone on the weekends because I figured it was the job. The phone rang, and I don't know why, but I picked it up. It was my boss, Alan Nesbitt. I'm like, "Oh man, it's Alan," which is never a good thing on a weekend. He said to me, "What you are doing?" I said, "Well, I'm here with my girlfriend, not doing too much of anything." He said, "Can you do me a favor? [President Jimmy] Carter is flying in to Three Mile Island. All I need you to do is go up there, shoot him going in, and come back." He said that was all I needed to do. I was ready to leave and take my girlfriend to Connecticut to get away from this nonsense, but I said okay. I got there, and he was waiting for me outside the station, asking what took me so long. I told him I was doing him a favor, remember? We got in the car with my photographer and [anchor] Marc Howard. We got up to Three Mile Island. We got there, the chopper flew in, Carter got out of the chopper with a moon suit on and walked into the reactor. He was in there for, like, thirty-five to forty minutes, came out, got back on the chopper, and flew out. I said, "Okay, we got our story." We called Alan back in Philadelphia and said, "Look, we got Carter going in and out, and we are ready to leave." He said he was having a hard time finding someone to replace me. He knew that in the first place! He just wanted us to get there. We stayed there for another five days. Let me tell you, I was nervous and scared because I didn't know what was going on and what was happening at that time.

Ed Schimmel, Executive Producer, WPVI:
As I recall, we were a little bit slow to recognize the seriousness of it. I remember the Saturday night after it began was the night that President Carter came to tour Three Mile Island. Just before we went on the air, we added a story about that. Our anchorperson was running down the back stairs to go on the eleven o'clock newscast and somehow dropped that page out of his script. So when we got on the air that night with the newscast, we kind of missed that page. I was expecting him to read about the president's visit, and next thing I knew, he was on to the next page. I was like, "What the hell is going on?" Then, I discovered after the fact that he had dropped his script on the way down to the studio, and that's how that newscast got screwed up.

Andy Doane, Photographer, WPVI:
We stayed [near Three Mile Island] for five days. I had to buy clothes because I didn't have any clothes. I didn't realize how much danger I was in until I got back from there after I covered that story, and I watched *The China Syndrome.* Once I saw the movie, I said, "Really? This was what I dealt with!"

Bob Kravitz, Photographer, WPVI:
I called the assistant news director because I needed clothes. "You can't buy clothes. It's not in the budget," he told me.

Marc Howard, Anchor, WPVI and KYW:
I interviewed a lot of people, and they were all frightened and nervous. Looking back on it, not one person died from any cause related to that. It's interesting, yet it ended the nuclear power business. [The meltdown happened] the same week as the movie *The China Syndrome* [came out], which is talking about a meltdown. That movie and Three Mile Island really stuck a knife in that industry.

Dick Sheeran, Reporter, KYW:
I went to a place called Kuppy's Diner. I was big on talking to regular folks; that was my thing. I always sought out diners in small towns and neighborhoods. A lot of people were not at the plant. The gist of it was that they weren't concerned—at least, they said they weren't. Then, two days later, we went all the way out there, came back, and did the story. There was then a more serious announcement, as I recall, a couple days later, on Friday. Then, we went out there and stayed there for a week to ten days, and it was touch and go there for a while. You depended on the people who worked at the plant for information because they knew the subject. One of the clips that I see was on my retirement reel was me asking Governor Richard Thornburgh, "What are you going to tell the people that live around here about what's going on?"

Terry Ruggles, Reporter and Anchor, WCAU:
There was this migration of people leaving, but there wasn't a panic situation. You would go down the street, and here would be people packing up. You would stop and [they would] say, "We are going to Elmira, New

York," or "We have friends in Baltimore," that kind of thing. There were only two hotels that were staying open—one was the Holiday Inn Downtown, and the other was a Sheraton on the other side of the river. We went in, and WHP-TV was the CBS affiliate, and Channel 10 was a CBS-owned station at that time. We went into WHP, and there were myself, [reporter] Bill Baldini, [reporter] Ralph Penza, and all of us had crews with us. We stayed at the Holiday Inn Downtown, which was deserted. The only people there were the media coming into town.

Rob Jennings, Anchor, WPVI:
I went to Three Mile Island several times to cover the story. At-risk residents were being evacuated from Middletown. Each day, a little more of the seriousness of the escalating crisis was being revealed, and each day, I began to get a little more worried about the effects of the radiation being vented from the Unit 2 reactor and whether the meltdown in the unit's core could be stopped before it burned a hole toward China. What would happen to the people in central Pennsylvania? How about their homes and businesses? Would Middletown be turned into a ghost town, or even be erased from the map? Fortunately, TMI's runaway reactor was cooled in time and permanently sealed, but that harrowing event was a chilling first for a young *Action News* anchor and reporter named Rob Jennings.

Terry Ruggles, Reporter and Anchor, WCAU:
What heightened it was the unknown. It was the same summer that Michael Douglas and Jane Fonda made a movie called *The China Syndrome*, which was about a nuclear meltdown and a reactor going through the core of Earth. So with that as a background, it was a very tense spot because we didn't know what was going on. Within one hundred miles of Three Mile Island were Philadelphia, Baltimore, and Washington, D.C. They were talking about closing down the [Pennsylvania] Turnpike to prevent any traffic from going back and forth past the reactor towers. That didn't happen, but it was a long time before they knew exactly what was going on. It was a story for years and years to come because they had to do the cleanup of the reactor and get all the material out of there and store it. It was a tense time for about two weeks, and then after that, it was a source of stories for easily two or three years.

POPE JOHN PAUL II VISITS PHILADELPHIA

Pope John Paul II arrived in Philadelphia, Pennsylvania, on October 3, 1979, becoming the first pope to visit the City of Brotherly Love. Pope John Paul II celebrated Mass at Logan Circle in the Center City neighborhood of Philadelphia in front of more than one million people. The stage for the Mass was constructed on top of the Swann Memorial Fountain at Logan Square, with a 360-degree view for spectators to watch every angle. The stage was built in seventeen days and required four thousand pieces of wood and more than 450 gallons of paint.

During his forty-eight-hour stay in the city, Pope John Paul II dined at the residence of Archbishop John Cardinal Krol, visited Saint Charles Borromeo Seminary to chat with more than 170 seminarians, visited Saint Peter's Episcopal Church and the tomb of Saint John Neumann, and made a stop at the Ukrainian Cathedral of the Immaculate Conception. Philadelphia was not the only U.S. city the pope visited on his weeklong trip to the United States in 1979, as he also stopped in Des Moines, New York, Chicago, and Washington, D.C.

KYW broadcast the Mass at the Ukrainian Cathedral of the Immaculate Conception and produced a special called Prime Time Sunday *devoted to the pope's visit. WCAU aired a news special on the pope's visit to Philadelphia as well. All three channels broadcast live the pontiff's arrival at Philadelphia International Airport, speeches at the Cathedral Basilica of Saints Peter and Paul, and the Mass on the Parkway at Logan Circle.*

Terry Ruggles, Reporter and Anchor, WCAU:
We had done a whole lot of stories on the pope coming, and it was the first time the pope was coming to Philadelphia. It was a really big deal. The reason he was coming to Philadelphia was there was a national conference of priests and nuns that was in town, and he was coming to address them. The first thing that happened is he comes into the airport, and I am in the motorcade on a flatbed truck, which is right in front of the Popemobile as it goes up Broad Street.

Larry Kane, Anchor, WPVI, WCAU, and KYW:
I was the anchor for all the events. We had a priest from the archdiocese with me. You won't believe this, but very few people know this: John Facenda joined me. That's when I learned John was a great broadcaster but really not a news person, as such. He had to ad lib for a couple of hours. He did a very good job. He had not worked for the station in years. We thought it would be great to bring in a great Catholic kid like John Facenda, and it was great coverage. The most dynamic part of the coverage was the evening when the pope spoke and delivered a Mass at Logan Circle, or Logan Square, as they call it in Philadelphia. It was a beautiful fall night in October. We broadcast all of it live.

Bob Kravitz, Photographer, WPVI:
It was just a lot of urgency. That's one thing about being a news photographer: Urgency was the big thing. Being at the right place at the right time. You had to know what to do with the camera. You didn't play with the camera.

Marc Howard, Anchor, WPVI and KYW:
We did something unique then. [The pope] was in a parade up Broad Street, and we had a truck with cameras on in front of it, so you could get video of him kissing babies and all of these things. We were the only station at the time that was able to do the following: We put a dish on the top of the truck and a receiving dish at city hall. We had a technician on the truck who kept the dish pointed at city hall, so we were live with the pope going up Broad Street. I think that was the first time anybody in Philly had done a live moving shot of an event, which was rather interesting. Live TV was not new, but it was interesting to do it on a moving truck.

Ed Schimmel, Executive Producer, WPVI:
All the different locations that the pope was visiting, and we had live shots and hard lines at different places. We were able to follow him as he was making his way around the city.

Andy Doane, Photographer, WPVI:
They set up relay systems, something we called a "golden rod," which was a rod that we transmitted signals from back to the station. They would have it around the city to bounce [the signal] back to the Roxborough tower, which would send [the signal] back to City Line Avenue to the station.

Greg Meyer, Photographer, KYW:
I was on top of Saint Agnes Hospital with a golden rod microwave transmitter. When the pope drove by, those guys were down on the street with the camera attached to my transmitter, and [the signal] got shot up toward city hall or wherever it went.

I went out to adjust the microwave as the pope was going by. He was going by slowly. At that point in time, somebody in the Philadelphia police force saw me up there adjusting this microwave transmitter and thought it was a gun. At that point in time, pedal to the metal, the entire convoy—they zipped up Broad Street.

Cathy Gandolfo, Reporter, WPVI:
I was stationed on Broad Street down around Marconi Plaza. My job that day really was to interview people who were watching, waiting for the procession to come up Broad Street after [the pope] landed at the airport. We were out there for hours and hours. It was a big crowd, of course. I never found out [if it was] because he was running late or there was some fear or rumor that there was a security issue. But instead of driving up Broad Street slowly so everyone could get a good look, they came up Broad Street probably at fifty miles per hour. Everybody just watched as the car zipped by. Everybody was like, "Oh, geez—he really went by fast, didn't he?"

Dick Standish, Reporter, KYW:
My role was to be sort of a person in the field giving you various highlights. The day the pope arrived, I was at Saint Agnes [medical center].

We waited and waited, with everyone looking down Broad Street. All of a sudden, the pope and his car came flying through, maybe going thirty or forty miles an hour. You can't be going too slow for security reasons.

Harvey Clark, Reporter, WCAU:
It was interesting. My coverage of Pope [John] Paul's arrival there was the security end of it. We went up on top of a building with the Secret Service, and everybody was looking down on the stage and everything else. It was interesting because there's so much security that goes on behind the scenes that nobody ever sees and nobody knows about.

Dick Standish, Reporter, KYW:
The next morning, the pope was scheduled to speak at the old Convention Hall around 11:00 A.M. You talk about huge crowds! It was packed all the way around, waiting for him to arrive. Malcolm Poindexter, one of the best people I have ever worked with, and I were out there in the field. Vince Leonard was anchoring. It was one of those cases when you have a long live period, and you have to fill that space. Malcolm stood on a pile of police barricades that were thrown there. He was shorter than me, and the producers wanted us closer together. In the shot, you see the two of us, and you don't realize that Malcolm is standing on these shaky police barricades. They were not set up, and they were just kind of stacked there. He did a great job. You would have never known it at all. For my part, I am talking up to this photographer on top of the truck. You couldn't see it as a viewer, but right behind me, I'm being punched in the back by a fellow who has his hand doubled up, like a knuckled kind of thing. It wasn't like being punched to the ground, but I could certainly feel it. The most unusual thing about that was later, once I got finished, I did the report while being punched in the back. [The guy] was dressed like a Roman Catholic priest. I'm sure he was not. I never heard of any kind of a security problem with a pretender that day.

Robin Mackintosh, Reporter, KYW:
I was assigned to be on the street in front of the cardinal's residence at the end of the parade as [the pope] came through over by Saint Joseph's University. I was on the street, the car came by, and that's the only time

I saw him. Everybody, of course, was thrilled and throwing kisses and waving and so forth. It was a pretty exciting day. Then, they had lights on the car, and he was standing up inside a convertible, and there he was.

Bob Feldman, Producer and Assistant News Director, WPVI:
We ended up being able to cover it every single step of the way. [The pope] stayed at the cardinal's home on City Avenue overnight, about a half mile from the station. We literally put a truck there. We put a truck and a crew outside every site that was scheduled. They had a motorcade several times when they moved several places.

Rob Jennings, Anchor, WPVI:
I did a live shot outside [the shrine to] Saint John Neumann. The area was mobbed. A sea of people, all straining to catch a glimpse of the pope. You would have thought the Beatles had arrived! It was both exciting and chaotic, people screaming and waving at him. I got a brief glimpse of the pope's head as he entered the church. The Mass on the Parkway was a highlight in Philadelphia history.

Dick Sheeran, Reporter, KYW:
I had grown up in Philadelphia, covering different crowd stories, but that was the biggest crowd I had ever seen. It was at Logan Square, around 19th Street and the Parkway, and there were people from the west all the way to the art museum and to the east all the way down to city hall, and all filled in on the Parkway. I had never seen anything like that. It was a gigantic crucifix, a cross set up in the square, and that is where he conducted a Mass.

Andy Doane, Photographer, WPVI:
What they did was everyone was located in one area and never really moved from that one area. They had other crews in different areas wherever [the pope] would go. I was outside the basilica with the crowds and all, shooting with another photographer at the time with a reporter. Once he left the basilica and did his Mass, he would leave there and go somewhere else, and some other crew would pick him up from there. It was kind of hard to get around the city at the time because everything was shut down.

Larry Kane, Anchor, WPVI, WCAU, and KYW:
I subsequently met [Pope] John Paul on three separate occasions. I interviewed him in 1985, and when I mean *interview*, I mean a real interview at the Vatican about Cardinal Krol's thirtieth or twenty-fifth anniversary as the archbishop of Philadelphia. I traveled with Cardinal Krol to Alaska in February of 1981, I believe. We flew in on a Learjet to Anchorage, Alaska, with Jim Murray of the Philadelphia Eagles, and he brought his Ron Jaworski jersey to give to the pope. The guy that was with me was Ed Pesak. We only spent, like, a day and a half there. We covered the Mass, and we met the pope again as he got off the plane, and the cardinal took me over to him. I met him one more time. It was quite an experience.

Terry Ruggles, Reporter and Anchor, WCAU:
We got a tip that night that the next day, [the pope] was going to come and bless the children in the cancer ward at Children's Hospital. We were the only ones who had that tip, so I went down there with a crew, and I knew the public relations director there pretty well. So, I am up on the floor, and again, I am happy as a Cheshire cat, because we are the only ones who have this story. My friend Bill Baldini was over on 5th and Girard, which is where Bishop John Neumann was [buried] before he was a saint; there was a church there. That was where the pope was going first. The crowds were so big at 5th and Girard that the pope was running late because he was shaking hands and talking to people. I am up on the sixth or eighth floor of Children's Hospital with others, looking down. The motorcade pulls up, and the pope looks up, and he [makes] the sign of the cross. I look at the public relations director and say, "You know the pope is not going to come up here now." She said, "How do you know that?" I said, "I know that because he is forty-five minutes late and because he just looked up and blessed the church." My cameraman said, "If you took some of these kids down there, he couldn't help but cross the street to see them." I'm just going about my business interviewing people, and I looked down from the sixth floor, and where the emergency room used to be, there was a roundabout where the ambulances pulled in. It was right across the street from the old Civic Center. I look down, and here is the public relations director with a dozen kids. They are in gurneys and wheelchairs and have IVs. I've got this

press pass on, so I go running down without my cameraman, and I stick the press pass in my shirt, and my tie covers it so you can't see the pass. These huge pope's henchmen come across the street, and they start asking us in this group what's his or her problem and who's with each of them. They go through, and I am standing next to a kid by the name of Jimmy Daily from the northeast. Jimmy's on an IV, and next to him is a nurse with two babies who have some blood disorder, and she has them in a stroller. This henchman comes across and says to Jimmy Daily, "Who are you with?" and I said, "He is with me," and I grab Jimmy's IV, and we go walking across the street. The nurse with the two kids came walking, and what they did was at the doors to the Convention Center, they had wooden sawhorses keeping the crowd back. In between the sawhorses were those kinds of theater red velvet cords that they used to direct people for lines. Sure enough, we hear the thing ending, and the doors open, and the procession comes out. The pope comes out, and he immediately comes over to this group that I'm with and starts blessing the children. I'm standing next to Jimmy Daily, and he blesses him, and I look over, and there is a nurse with these two little infants, and she can't pick them both up, so I pick one up, and Jimmy Daily is on my right—I have the infant on my left arm—and after he is done with Jimmy Daily, I just hand the baby to the pope, and he blesses the baby and hands him back to me.

Vernon Odom, Reporter, WPVI:
A lot of people were thrilled to have [the pope visit], and it was a big deal for the city. Frank Rizzo was the mayor then, and he was a devoted Catholic. Philly has a huge Catholic population. It was a big, big deal. People were coming from far and wide. It was quite a spectacle.

Frank Goldstein, Photographer, WCAU:
I had the helicopter duty instead when John Paul went to the Ukrainian church. My job there was to get him leaving the church. He came out, stopped at my camera, winked at me through the camera, and walked on. That was really the only direct contact I had with him.

Jim Gardner, Anchor, WPVI:
That was a very big deal for me. We did eleven hours of unscripted television, and it was 1979. I was anchoring for two years, and I was thir-

ty-one. It was my first real test of unscripted television. I'm Jewish, and I didn't know as much about Catholicism and Catholic ritual as I thought I needed to know. I went to the Penn Bookstore and bought a pile of books. I lived at 2nd and Bainbridge Street. I was a thirty-one-year-old bachelor, so my dining room table had never had anything on it. I came home with a pile of books and dumped them onto the table and read them. I felt like I was back in college, taking notes and doing outlines because I felt I really needed to be prepared. I was told that we did a really good job. That was maybe one of the more satisfying experiences in my early television career because I think as a station, we did a really good job. I thought that I did a good job, and it was a situation where I really had to learn a lot to feel confident going into the event. I always told my kids that preparation is the most important part of any task. I thought I prepared well. There were moments during the coverage that were special for Channel 6.

Ned Warwick, **Assignment Editor and News Director, WPVI:**
Channel 6 knew how to cover events, but there had never been an event like the pope's visit. The thing that is so indelible in my mind is we had a reporter whose name was Hank Sperka, who was sort of a large, tall guy with silver hair who would stop at nothing to get a story. He was a force of nature when given an assignment. Whoever he trampled or ruffled, he would still get there. Sperka spoke Polish. As the pope was getting off the plane, Hank Sperka, who wasn't shy in front of anybody, shouted at the pope in Polish. The pope turned and talked to Hank Sperka.

Bob Kravitz, **Photographer, WPVI:**
I was a sound man at the time. I was working with Hank Sperka. Hank talked Polish. He yells in Polish to the pope, "It's nice to see you here in our city, Pope!" The pope blessed Hank and looked down at me and blessed me. It gave me one hell of a chill. It was really weird. I'm Jewish.

THE PASSING OF WPVI'S JIM O'BRIEN

Jim O'Brien was born James Franklin Oldham in Galveston, Texas, on November 20, 1939. O'Brien had various radio and television jobs in the United States and Canada before arriving in Philadelphia in 1969, starting as the morning-drive disc jockey on WFIL AM. O'Brien would later hold a series of weather and news reporting positions at WPVI after officially joining the television station in 1971.

O'Brien hosted Dialing for Dollars, *which aired at 10:00 A.M. on weekdays on Channel 6. O'Brien transitioned to the anchor desk in 1977 with* Action News at Noon *and then the 5:30 P.M. newscasts, and he was paired with anchors Lisa Thomas-Laury and Marc Howard in 1981.*

O'Brien had a passion for skydiving and completed well over eight hundred jumps. On September 25, 1983, O'Brien was involved in a skydiving accident in Gilbertsville, Pennsylvania, that resulted in his sudden death. As O'Brien jumped from 8,500 feet in the air, his parachute became entangled with the lines of the parachute of another skydiver, Doug Sellix, of Bethlehem, Pennsylvania. O'Brien extricated himself by pulling a handle that released his main chute. After freeing himself, O'Brien pulled another handle that released his reserve chute, but the reserve chute did not fully open before he struck the ground in a plowed field.

WPVI anchor Chris Wagner announced the death of Jim O'Brien on the evening newscast on September 25, stating in her opening remarks,

"Our top story tonight is one that has devastated all of us here at Action News. *Our friend, our news anchor, our weatherman, Jim O'Brien, died today." Wagner then tossed to WPVI reporter Vernon Odom, reporting live from the scene of the accident and talking to O'Brien's parachute club friends. Wagner was then joined by anchor Jim Gardner to discuss the tragic news of O'Brien's death.*

Gardner began: "Jim and I usually did most of our philosophizing a few minutes before the newscast. It was just Friday night when we were talking about what proved to be a false rumor about the imminent death of a relatively young public official in Philadelphia," Gardner stated on air. "The conversation prompted Jim to say, 'Jim, don't waste time; get the most out of life that you can and do it now.' He said, 'You just don't know what fate has in store for you.' That was less than forty-eight hours ago. That was Jim's credo. 'Get the most you can out of life.' And he did."

Gardner continued his remarks, holding back tears, stating how much he and the Action News *team would miss O'Brien's presence. WPVI decided to hold a news conference with members of their* Action News *team—WPVI's general manager Larry Pollock, Jim Gardner, Chris Wagner, Don Tollefson, and publicity director Art Moore—making remarks to the local Philadelphia media. WCAU's top story at 11:00 P.M. was O'Brien's death, with Terry Ruggles anchoring, tossing to reporter Bill Baldini, who covered the story from the scene of the accident in Montgomery County. WCAU featured Larry Kane discussing his relationship with O'Brien and thoughts on his passing.*

Twenty-four hours after the accident, WPVI aired a thirty-minute Tribute to Jim O'Brien *hosted by Jim Gardner, featuring interviews with WPVI employees Marc Howard, Lisa Thomas-Laury, Scott Palmer, Gary Papa, Chris Wagner, Dave Roberts, Don Tollefson, news director Alan Nesbitt, general manager Larry Pollock, and former colleague Larry Kane.*

After the death of O'Brien, WPVI selected Dave Roberts to be their new meteorologist for the 5:00 P.M., 6:00 P.M., and 11:00 P.M. newscasts. Harry Martin replaced Roberts on AM Philadelphia.

In 2001, WCAU ran not one but two ratings sweeps pieces on Jim O'Brien. One tribute to O'Brien was told by Steve Levy, a former Channel 6 colleague who had left for WCAU in the early 1980s. The segment included footage of O'Brien on Channel 6's newscast and man-

aged to avoid mentioning WPVI at all. The second sweeps piece on O'Brien highlighted his daughter, actress Peri Gilpin, who spoke about her memories of her father. WCAU described O'Brien as "the late local TV legend" and "the weatherman we all remember."

O'Brien was known for his energy-charged delivery, grace, and humor during his tenure at WPVI, at one point being the highest-paid television personality in Philadelphia. O'Brien is still remembered as one of the most beloved Philadelphia broadcasters of all time.

Jim Place, United Parachute Club, Friend of Jim O'Brien:
Jim and I and a couple of people were good friends. We jumped together a lot. On that particular day, Jim and I made a jump, as I recall. We then went to a restaurant, which is at the front of the property at that airport. He and I were having coffee—we figured we already made a jump. We went in there to drink coffee and sign each other's log books. We figured we had an hour until our next jump, at least. We weren't even finished with our coffee, and somebody came in and said, "Let's go, we are up next." For some reason, we were going to be jumping sooner than we had thought. We went out, got in the plane, and jumped. That was the last time I ever saw Jim O'Brien alive.

Vernon Odom, Reporter, WPVI:
I went up there. A lot of these guys who were his parachute club buddies—and he would bring them to the station, and I recognized some of them—they came up and told me what had happened. They told me he had already jumped many times that day. They jumped out and apparently got caught, or their ropes or whatever you call them got tangled. O'Brien said to the guy to cut him away. O'Brien saved [that guy's] life and sacrificed his own. Those were direct quotes. That's exactly what happened that day. It was shocking. I knew O'Brien very well, and I worked with him every day. He was quite a character. It was shocking to be there on the scene. Within a few hours, I was still up there, putting together a piece for our news. Our news director Alan Nesbitt drove up there with somebody else from the news department. He said, "Did you go to where he fell?" and I said, "Yeah." He said, "Is there anything out there?" I said, "No, everything is gone." I remember a lot of newspaper

reporters wanted to interview me since I'd been out there, and they wanted to ask me questions.

Chris Wagner, Anchor, WPVI:
Rob Jennings, who was the regular weekend anchor, was off. I was anchoring that weekend. My assistant news director called me in the morning and said, "Sit down." I said, "What?" and he said, "Jim O'Brien is dead. He was parachuting this morning, and his parachute didn't open, and he died." I was just in shock. He said, "Do you think [you] can anchor?" I said, "Hell yes, I can do it." I went to the station as soon as I got myself ready. Everybody came to the station that day—the entire newsroom came to the station. Everybody was crying. We were just in shock. He was such a huge part of the *Action News* team. He was so hilarious and so outrageous. Probably the best communicator I've ever seen in my life.

Dave Roberts, Meteorologist, WPVI:
It was probably the most upsetting day in my broadcasting career. A friend who had called me, who was a good friend of [Jim] O'Brien's, was called upon to go in and recognize and verify and view the body. He called me and informed me of that. We called in to the station, went in, and just tried to talk about it a little bit. It was a Sunday, and Monday was just a horrendous day, and it just continued. Everyone was in complete shock. The weather board with the clouds that he used to write on was still there. No one went on the site. [Station management] said to me that they wanted me to do the weather. I said, "I'm not ready to step on that [weather] set in less than twenty-four hours after the man was killed." To attempt in any way to do a show was still too raw for all of us. For [Jim] Gardner and myself. I said, "You gotta give me some time here," and they respected that. They just read the forecast. I went in on Tuesday, and I took that cloud down. On the cloud, he had written *brilliant* in terms of what the weekend was going to be like, but I think he spelled it BRIALYANT. He knew how to spell, but he did things differently so it caught attention. I took that cloud down, and I went and put it in my locker. That cloud stayed in my locker until I left. When I left, I gave it to Mike Monsell [vice president of marketing at WPVI]. I told him, "I feel this should be passed down in some fashion." I did an *AM Philadel-*

phia show that morning that was all about O'Brien, as he had been on our show a number of times. We showed some of that and showed pictures. It was just devastating and very, very emotionally drudging. We all struggled with it.

Eliott Rodriguez, Reporter, WPVI:
It was one of the saddest days of my life. Jim [O'Brien] was one of the nicest people to me when I started working there. I was an outsider, and I didn't know anyone in Philadelphia, and Jim couldn't have been nicer. I remember he came up to me to ask me for a pronunciation of something in Florida. It was one of the Keys, and I forget which one, but he had asked me to pronounce something from Florida. He came up to me and even said on the air, "Hey, I heard it from the Florida guy." He was just one of the warmest, most talented, nicest people I have ever worked with through all the years and was really the person who made the biggest impact on the viewers that I had ever seen.

Jim Gardner, Anchor, WPVI:
I was having breakfast at the famous delicatessen at 4th and Bainbridge. We had, at the time, a table in the back of the deli that was sort of the regulars table. We would assemble back there on Sunday mornings, sometimes Saturdays—talk politics, by and large. There was no cell phones, obviously. So, the phone rang in the deli, asking for me. There was a phone on the ledge near the window right by the table. I picked it up, and it was Kenny Plotnik. Kenny was an assignment manager at WPVI at the time. He went on to become news director at WABC in New York. We were pretty good friends. He said, "Are you sitting down?" I said, "Yeah." "Jim O'Brien is dead"—that's how he put it. Kenny was one to screw around a lot. We had a lot of joking around with Kenny, Eddie Schimmel, and myself back in those days. I said, "Yeah, right." He said, "No. He had a skydiving accident, and he is dead." Everybody's immediate reaction was to come to the television station. Where else would we go? It sounds like a cliché, but it was one of those moments.

Scott Palmer, Sports Anchor and Reporter, WPVI:
I was not working that day. It was a beautiful September day, and I was outside, raking leaves. Kathy, my wife, said there was a phone call for

me. I came in, and the assistant news director who gave me the news said that I needed to go to Veterans Stadium because Don [Tollefson] was too emotional to continue working and asked me if I would do it. So, I did, after becoming emotional and crying for a while. I pulled myself together and drove to the Vet and sat in the Channel 6 seat for the Eagles game against the St. Louis Cardinals. I remember as the news started breaking—no one knew when I first sat down. I really just kept to myself. I didn't want to talk to anyone. I didn't know what people knew or what they didn't know. One by one, journalists started looking at me with a kind of pale face. I tried not to return their glance. I just kept trying to look straight at the game. After the game was over, they just asked me to do interviews with the Eagles about Jim. It was so strange. So we did that, and I remember driving back to City Avenue and seeing people listening to news radio and whatever they were listening to, and they would just break down crying.

Don Tollefson, Sports Anchor and Reporter, WPVI and WTXF:
I was in the press box, and I got a call from one of the news executives, and he told me the news. So, I was obviously stunned and in silence for a couple of minutes. He then said, "Larry Pollock (our general manager) is in the stands, and you need to find him." There were no cell phones, and I knew where his seats were, so I didn't have him paged or anything. I went down to his seats, and I was the person who told him. We went into the first-aid room to kind of compose ourselves. The first-aid room was a place where players' wives hung out. They didn't have these player lounges [then]. It was a place where I had gotten to know the staff. As we were walking from his seats into the first-aid room behind home plate, there was this murmur. You could hear this murmur in the stands. It was one of the eeriest moments of my life because people who were listening on the radio heard the news, and it started to spread throughout the Vet. We consoled each other as much as we could. I had to drive Larry back to the station. It was the longest twenty-minute drive. The game was still going on, and he was very, very concerned about how anybody on the air could compose themselves well enough to announce this beloved colleague's death.

Art Moore, Publicity Director, WPVI:
It was very difficult to wear both hats because it was emotional, and at the same time, I had to be at the station and deal with the press and

questions and all of that. It was probably one of the most difficult days of my life just because of the personal side of it.

Lisa Thomas-Laury, Anchor, WPVI:
My husband and I were over at the Deptford Mall. We were shopping, and my assistant news director Bob Feldman called me, and he said, "I have some really sad news." I almost fell down. I remember the next store we were near was Bailey Banks & Biddle, and I had to go next door and sit down. I just couldn't believe it because I had seen him that previous Friday. He had told Marc Howard and myself that he was going to skydive. And he said, "You know, Lis, you could be really good at it, and you guys have to do it with me one day." We both told him, "No, we don't think so." After it settled in, I told my husband, "I have to go to the station." It was just very quiet in the car, and he was going to take me to the television station. It was one of those surreal days where you just couldn't believe what you just heard. Chris Wagner was filling in that weekend at the anchor desk. I remember when I went up to the newsroom and saw her, I remember how red her eyes were.

Rob Jennings, Anchor, WPVI:
[Right before the accident,] I had anchored for Jim Gardner and taken Jim O'Brien home for a home-cooked meal. We drove back to the station and did the eleven [o'clock news]. That was the last time I saw him. I went on vacation and was at Busch Gardens in Virginia. I thought I heard Jim's name on the morning news there but decided I must have been hearing things. When I got back to Philadelphia, someone ran up to me and said, "Jim O'Brien was killed." I sat stunned and speechless, numb. Jim O'Brien was one of the most talented people I have ever known. He insisted that you never tell him what you were going to say in your toss to him at the weather set. He wanted to be spontaneous. He was all that and more. And that great, deep voice. I can still hear him say, "Hey, Robbie!"

Larry Kane, Anchor, WPVI, WCAU, and KYW:
I found out about that Sunday afternoon. We reported it on the air as a major story on Channel 10.

Tom Lamaine, Sports and Weather Anchor, KYW:
I was covering the Eagles football game that morning. Jim [O'Brien] had asked me several times to join his skydiving club. I said to Jim, "In the Navy, I was told not to jump out of a perfectly good airplane unless I had to eject from a jet fighter." I said, "You know, Jim, I know you are big on it, but it's not something I'm interested in." That morning, when I heard that Jim had been killed, I knew exactly where he was because it was a Sunday morning skydiving thing for Jim. Even before I was told how Jim lost his life, I more or less put two and two together and knew where he would be on a Sunday morning.

Steve Highsmith, Anchor and Reporter, WPHL and WCAU:
When I started skydiving, I learned from the man who taught him. I did not know that until I happened to go to this man and his jump zone in Lakewood, New Jersey. Jim had many, many more jumps than I have. He was far superior to me in his ability to do that and what his experience was. We learned from the same person.

I called my jump instructor, and he told me what happened and how it happened, and I helped report on how the accident happened. I went to Channel 6 that night, where they held a sort of news conference. It was sort of a conversational open environment in which they welcomed reporters so that they could have the people who knew Jim O'Brien best talk about him. They were very gracious and very professional. Another lasting moment for a lot of reasons. One, because I understood a little bit of what Jim O'Brien liked about [skydiving], I understood how to explain what happened, which is often misunderstood if people don't know something and misreport it. I think of how the Channel 6 family responded to a very tragic event in which they could have shut down and said nothing. They realized three things: It was worth it for their own good to be able to talk about it, but more importantly than thinking about themselves, they thought about Jim and what should be said. They also thought about their responsibilities as news people. They put all of that together, and they did a very good job.

Bill Baldini, Reporter, WCAU:
It always hits you harder when you know the person. It was extremely sad and very difficult to do. When you have to cover someone you know,

it is extremely difficult. You do what you have to do, and then you think, "I'm better off doing it than somebody that doesn't know him." At least you can add that personal touch and show people who this guy really was behind the scenes.

Terry Ruggles, Reporter and Anchor, WCAU:
I was the weekend anchorman at Channel 10 the day it happened. I was in there around three or four o'clock, and we started getting these reports that Jim O'Brien had died in a parachute accident. You have to remember, Jim O'Brien was the biggest thing in television in Philadelphia at that time. I went on the air, and I certainly didn't go to the airport or the scene. I was very impressed with Jim Gardner's writing on the death, how close they were and what good friends they were.

Jim O'Brien was an interesting guy. He came into our place to fill in as a weatherman, and he was a disc jockey at WFIL. We used him as a weekend weather fill-in. He was talking about good guys and bad guys, good friends and bad friends, and everything like that. We opted not to call on his talents and passed him by, and he went on to be one of the biggest things in Philadelphia broadcasting history.

Bob Feldman, Producer and Assistant News Director, WPVI:
Every station in town led their newscasts with Jim O'Brien's death. The competition leading with that story was unusual. The outpouring of the citizens, the viewers of Channel 6, was amazing. Besides the fact that we got flooded with phone calls, we received almost fifty thousand letters and mentions of condolences. People dropped things off at the station, condolence cards, as if we had lost a member of our family. The way the station handled that, besides acknowledging it on air, was that every single person who wrote or sent something to the station received a letter back thanking them, which I thought was just an amazing thing for the station to do. When you have thousands and thousands of people, you can't normally respond to them, but we did.

Jim Gardner, Anchor, WPVI:
It was tough, but we had newscasts to do. It was interesting how in the midst of all of this emotion, we knew how to do that. We knew how to

get information. We knew how to parse through what we needed to do and what we needed to know to put a newscast on the air. We functioned well, and we did what we were supposed to do. It was brutal.

Andy Doane, Photographer, WPVI:
The only time I ever saw Jim Gardner cry was that day. He actually cried. You have to understand, at Channel 6 in those days—in the seventies, early eighties—it was like a family. Everybody hung out with each other. We partied, we drank together.

Jim Gardner, Anchor, WPVI:
Jim [O'Brien] was a fascinating guy. There's no way people watching our newscasts probably could know who Jim really was. He was driven, had a volcanic personality; as funny and brilliant as he could be, he could get angry and frustrated. He just demanded of himself and everybody else a certain commitment and a certain sense of perfection, which I did too. It was an interesting mix.

When I started doing the six and eleven o'clock news, I think Jim was very concerned that it was going to be okay. He had a thing with Larry [Kane], and they had great chemistry. *Action News* was already a thing. You know, when this twenty-nine-year-old kid took over, I think he was anxious about our survivability, and for the first four or five months, he didn't provide me with a great deal of support. We were good on the air, and he was great to me on the air. Off the air, he pulled back. I guess he was waiting to see whether we were going to survive this transition. When it became apparent that we were, he relaxed, and we became good friends. We would hang out a little bit, and we would go out after the show. He taught me a lot about a lot of different things, television and otherwise. Those first several months were tough.

Chris Wagner, Anchor, WPVI:
If people would give [Jim O'Brien] shit about the forecast or something, and if he would get a lot of calls and stuff, he would pull up a chair to the camera and get about a foot away from the camera and say, "Now look, people, I'm just relaying the information that I am getting about the weather. Don't put it on me." He was hilarious. People didn't do things like that.

Steve Sacks, Producer, WPVI:
Every word that [Jim O'Brien] used on the [weather] cloud, you would see he had written down on the back of the set. That's an assumption of mine that [it was so] he would not use the same word twice. I don't remember seeing the same word there. That list of words was all sorts of words. It could even be made up, like, "Oh ay, what a day" or something. What was on that cloud was written behind that set.

Marc Howard, Anchor, WPVI and KYW:
When a forecast was wrong, [Jim O'Brien] would call AccuWeather "AccuGuess" on the air. Those were some of his funny things. The other line he used to use was "I shoveled three inches of partly cloudy off my driveway this morning."

Scott Palmer, Sports Anchor and Reporter, WPVI:
I can tell you that Jim [O'Brien]—early on together, I would say, "What if I say this?" and he said, "Never tell me what you are going to tell me before." Because it wouldn't be magic. I remember that clear as day. He would say, "Don't ever tell me what you are gonna talk about in the toss." He would tell me, "There is nothing that you can get us into that I can't get us out of."

Eric Schoenfeld, Executive Producer, WPVI:
When I was in Baltimore, I worked with Oprah Winfrey, Brent Musburger, Chris Berman, Robin Roberts, and all of these people and Jim Gardner. There has never been a broadcaster, there has never been a communicator, better than Jim O'Brien. He was the most amazing broadcaster I have ever seen. Not that I have ever worked with—I have ever *seen.*

Don Tollefson, Sports Anchor and Reporter, WPVI and WTXF:
I came to work about a week later, and Jim [O'Brien]'s girlfriend at the time had left me something that was kind of a memento of my time with Jim. It was wrapped, and I unwrapped it. It said, "Jim would want you to know how much he loved you." That's all it said. It was just a moment where I paused at my desk, and I said both as a professional and also as a person, I hope I can live up to the standard he set, an incredibly high bar. That would be the great tribute to his legacy.

Harvey Clark, Reporter, WCAU:
Steve Levy was Jim O'Brien's brother. They took vacations together. They skied and did everything. We had Steve in the newsroom, so when Jim died, we kind of mourned for Steve as well as Jim because it really, really knocked Steve on his butt for a while. It's a small club, so when anything terrible happens to somebody in that club, you feel like it happened to you personally or it happened to part of your family.

Steve Levy, Anchor and Reporter, WPVI, KYW, and WCAU:
We used to tell each other that we were closer than brothers. He and his wife are godfather and godmother to my daughter. So the loss is still, to this day, very personal, and it's still very emotional. I spoke to his mom every two to three weeks for all of those years because that's what we were. That's not a news story. That's part of your life.

Rob Guarino, Chief Meteorologist, WTXF:
I was watching him through my grade school and high school years. I have loved the weather since I was eight. Jim [O'Brien] just had a flair about him. These were the days when they had a smiley-face cloud for high pressure and a little gray set piece for low pressure. It was really cartoony, technically. Jim O'Brien was just an entertainer, and he made weather fun. He didn't get into so much science, but he made you understand it and have fun with it, with all of his sayings and phrases.

Stu Bykofsky, TV Columnist:
[Jim O'Brien made] the almost unbelievable achievement of going from the hippy-dippy funny weather guy, [a job that] he basically started with no experience. He was a DJ before that. He transitioned to being a serious anchor, something even some of his friends and admirers at PVI didn't think he would be able to do, but he did. He had this wonderful loving personality because he was so nice. In fact, he was a very dark person. He was moody. He was not a pleasant person to be around. That was real life. That wasn't TV life. All that matters to the viewer is TV life, and Jim had this way of projecting this friendly, aw shucks, good ol' boy personality that Philadelphia really came to love.

Don Tollefson, Sports Anchor and Reporter, WPVI and WTXF:
Jim [O'Brien] was an incredible stickler for [talent] paying attention to one another on the air. If you got caught not listening to something he said, and then he asked you a question about it, he would get very angry. He was the leader in the clubhouse.

Ned Warwick, Assignment Editor and News Director, WPVI:
The idea of taking a radio disc jockey doubling as a weatherman? Who then imagined that [Jim O'Brien] would make a great news anchor? I'm not sure I would have seen that. I'm not sure I would have made that decision. It was a brilliant one. It was a successful one. It was amazing, and he was a real force of nature. Back in our old newsroom at WPVI, which was a concrete bunker with a bunch of second-hand desks in it, Jim O'Brien was working one day at the desk, writing at a typewriter. He went to stand up, and some spring or something from a busted chair kind of tore his pants. He was so angry, he picked up a chair and smashed it against the desk. In the sort of superheated atmosphere of that cramped and unpleasant newsroom, [that] was one more incident, one more piece of vivid color that that place seemed to produce. He was something. He really helped make that *Action News* presence. He was part of the definition of it.

Gail Shister, TV Columnist:
I was amazed at the depth of the reaction. It was as if a beloved mayor had been assassinated or something. I had no idea of the breadth of his popularity. I do remember several on-air people at PVI got very teary about it on air. That was certainly unusual. I remember also that PVI covered it in what I thought was really over the top, in the sense that this story never stopped. It felt like the stories never stopped. I just thought after the first day or two, it was—pardon the pun, but it was a little bit of overkill because you are talking about someone in your own shop. Despite his popularity, at a certain point, you have to ask yourself, "How many stories do we need to continue to do every day?" and "How long do we need to continue this depth of coverage?" The station was sorta in shock. I remember that. I also remember trying to talk to them the day after, and it may have been even beyond that, trying to talk to talent to get reactions, and I couldn't get to anybody. The station spokesmen kept saying, "No comment, no comment." No one wanted to talk

about it for publication, and that's how deep it hit. I think another reason it hit Philadelphians so hard is the way he died. Just the idea that anybody would die in a parachute accident is very unusual and also very unusually gruesome. I think that added to the shock.

Chris Wagner, Anchor, WPVI:
On the third day, the news director said, "Okay, that's it, we are done. Now, we have to get back to business. No more Jim O'Brien." And then we got back to business. We really mourned with the Delaware Valley, and I think they appreciated that because I think people felt like they knew him. He was such an incredible communicator that people felt they knew him, and they would sob on the streets. They would come up to us while we were out doing stories, and they would be crying. I don't think it was too much that we let our grief show for a couple of days because the regular *Action News* viewers were grieving as well.

Cecily Tynan, Meteorologist, WPVI:
I was coming to my interview, and I was on the plane, talking to people about Philadelphia, asking them what station they watched. I got in my taxi to come to the station for my interview, and I asked the taxi driver what he watched. Pretty much everyone said Channel 6. He was the one who told me about Jim O'Brien, and he said how it was such a shame what had happened to him. I had thought it was recent, the way he was talking about it, and then realized it was so many years before. [Jim O'Brien] crafted our weather forecast. It's not until recently that we got rid of the clouds with the sayings, and when I came here, we were still using the magnets and the smiley faces, which in the nineties was pretty low tech. He developed that, and viewers loved it.

Larry Kane, Anchor, WPVI, WCAU, and KYW:
I believe it was 1981. It was a really bad blizzard. Our studio was located in the lobby of Channel 10, overlooking the street. They put me outside to do a cut-in on the weather in between one of these soap operas or something on the air. I went out there, and I was on the lawn. City Line Avenue was dead, and nothing was moving. All of a sudden, I heard galloping and some screaming. It was [Jim O'Brien]. He saw me on the air and ran out of the newsroom and ran across City Line Avenue. I saw him coming and said, "I think we have a guest on the air." He tackled me to

the ground. We came back on, and we did a little interview. He said, "I miss you, buddy," and we just chatted, and that was it. I said, "This is Jim O'Brien. Jim, do you want a job here?" I was kidding with him. He said, "I don't think [WCAU weatherman] Herb Clarke would appreciate that." I said, "Of course, just kidding." We chatted a little bit, and that was it.

Lisa Thomas-Laury, Anchor, WPVI:
When I came there [to WPVI], I had worked with Jim [O'Brien], and he really took me under his wing. I was very young and very green in the business, and he really helped me, as I had a really rough start, as the station wanted to change my hair, and they didn't like my Appalachian twang or my accent. I was going through a little rough period when I first came there. I remember thinking to myself how lucky I was to be working with someone like him, who really was looking out for my interests and someone with a little bit more experience in the business. People saw him as the goofy, wacky weatherman, but quite frankly, I came to know that Jim cared more about that place than the people in it and our success more than about anybody there. After about two or three months with him working with me and pronouncing various suburbs and cities—Conshohocken and things that were tripping me up—he told me to focus on what I was doing, and not let the management distract me from what I came to do. I began to really thrive there. I felt I owed it mostly to him.

Howard Eskin, Sports Reporter and Anchor, KYW, WCAU, and WTXF:
I was an engineer at WFIL radio. That's where I first met Jim [O'Brien]. I worked with George Michael at one point, and then Jim O'Brien in the morning. Jim O'Brien was a person that would always help somebody that he could see would help themselves. If he saw you weren't helping yourself, he would get all over you, but he wouldn't waste his time trying to help you. We really got to know each other. We became friends. We rode motorcycles at times, and we made some trips. Jim was great to me. When I left WFIL, I was doing talk radio at WWBD in the late seventies and early eighties. Channel 3 called me about me being their main sportscaster in 1982. I told Jim about it, and I didn't want the job.

I wasn't confident I would do a good-enough job. He said, "If [you] don't take this job, I am going to kick your ass because you will never get this opportunity again in your life." So, I went to an audition and talked to him about it. Without his urging, without his tips and advice . . . I went through with it and got the job. My audition tape was terrible. He would call me maybe once or twice a week to give me tips while he was working at Channel 6 and I was working at Channel 3. He helped me get better. He told me a year and a half before it actually happened [for me]. He told me I belonged doing television, doing TV sports, and he told me how much better I could be than anyone else who was on the air. I remembered that when the opportunity came about. He pushed me into doing everything I could to get the job.

Deborah Knapp, Anchor and Reporter, WCAU:
[Jim O'Brien] was a real risk-taker, and actually PVI was trying to get him to stop, and he just refused. I think his previous contract tried to get him to stop skydiving. He liked riding motorcycles. He just liked living life to the fullest, doing what he wanted to do. He was a bigger-than-life personality.

Dick Standish, Reporter, KYW:
This will give you an idea of the ratings power of Channel 6 and Jim O'Brien. Sometime in the late 1980s or early 1990s, Channel 10 ran a ratings piece on the death of Channel 6's Jim O'Brien. I forget how they did it exactly or what the grounds were as to why they would be doing it.

Paul Gluck, Executive Producer and News Director, WCAU and KYW:
As a matter of fact, and I recall it, Channel 10 rolled over one block of *60 Minutes* with a special report about Jim O'Brien's death, which I thought was extraordinary, and it was also wonderfully executed. It was not a ratings stunt. It was a chance for the people who knew him to express how they felt about him and do it in the most journalistic fashion.

Marc Howard, Anchor, WPVI and KYW:
Most interesting is that we all thought *Action News* was over [because he was gone], and people would quit watching because they loved him

so much. Believe it or not, the ratings went up in the weeks and months after he died because it was almost like they tuned in to watch the family. I never realized until he died why *Action News* was so popular, and it was because people viewed us as part of their family. I remember for months, for at least six months after he was killed, people would stop me on the street, take my hand, and say, "I am so sorry for your loss." I realized that these people felt like they knew him and were a part of our family. I never realized that so graphically until he died. That really is why *Action News* was and still is so dominant.

THE MOVE BOMBING

MOVE is a controversial Philadelphia-based "back-to-nature" Black liberation group founded in 1972 by John Africa (born Vincent Leaphart). The MOVE group has advocated for animal rights and anarcho-primitivism, with Black nationalist and Pan-African inflections. In 1978, most of the MOVE members moved into a row house in the Powelton Village section of West Philadelphia, a predominantly African American neighborhood, where the group organized various public demonstrations against the Philadelphia Police Department.

On August 8, 1978, when police arrived at the MOVE compound to execute a court eviction order, a shootout erupted, during which Philadelphia police officer James Ramp was fatally shot in the back of his neck. MOVE denied responsibility for Officer Ramp's death. During the standoff, bystanders, police officers, firefighters, and some MOVE members were injured. Nine MOVE members were convicted of third-degree murder in the death of Officer Ramp.

In 1981, MOVE relocated to 6221 Osage Avenue in the Cobbs Creek section of Philadelphia, another predominantly African American community. MOVE turned its main headquarters into a bunker, broadcasting profane messages over bullhorns on a daily basis, calling for the release of the jailed MOVE members, and keeping a wide range of animals around the house. The group's neighbors wanted action from the city and alleged poor conditions for the children being raised in the compound.

On May 13, 1985, then-Mayor Wilson Goode dispatched police to execute warrants for the eviction and arrest of residents of the MOVE *compound. When the police tried to evict* MOVE *members on charges of possession of explosives and harassment of neighbors, they refused to comply, and a gun battle ensued. From a helicopter, police dropped a bomb on the house to destroy the rooftop bunker, starting a fire that eventually spread to sixty-one homes. Eleven died, including five children. More than two hundred people were displaced from their homes, and the fire damage was estimated at $5 million. Only two* MOVE *members escaped the bombing: Birdie Africa and Ramona Africa.*

Goode appointed an investigative commission, whose report denounced the city's decision to bomb a row house as "unconscionable." In 1996, a federal jury awarded Ramona Africa and the relatives of two people that were killed in the bombing a total of $1.5 million in damages in a civil suit judgment. The jury also determined that Philadelphia officials had authorized the use of excessive force and had violated the Fourth Amendment protection against unreasonable search and seizure.

The New York Times *reported that the City of Philadelphia paid more than $27.3 million in legal fees and the cost of rebuilding the houses that were destroyed in the bombing. The* MOVE *group itself was also paid $2.5 million to settle wrongful death suits brought on behalf of the five children who died.*

Every Philadelphia TV station reported informatively on the event, but WCAU devoted more on-air time than any of its Philadelphia TV competitors. WCAU's overnight Nielsen ratings showed that it had more viewers than WPVI. From the time the Philadelphia Police helicopter dropped a device on the MOVE *compound at 5:28* P.M.*, WCAU dominated the local Nielsen ratings consistently throughout the evening. For the first time since 1981, the same year the overnight Nielsen ratings assessments began, Channel 10 had more viewers than Channel 6's evening newscasts.*

Key TV viewing times occurred from 8:00 to 8:30 P.M. *when KYW and WCAU provided live coverage of the inferno around the* MOVE *compound. Meanwhile, 6abc cut away after fifteen minutes to show the beginning of ABC's* Hardcastle and McCormick. *During that thirty-minute block, 35 percent of the people watching TV in Philadelphia tuned in to WCAU, 30 percent watched KYW's coverage, and WPVI had only 19 percent of viewers.*

Harvey Clark, Reporter, WCAU:
I knew MOVE, and [its members] respected me. At the time, I was interested in racism in the city. I was born and raised in Chicago under Mayor Richard J. Daley, who ran Chicago with an iron fist. I remember [Mayor] Frank Rizzo when I arrived [in Philadelphia]. I never had any real respect for Frank because in my estimation, Frank was truly a racist, and he was truly a pig and a guy who told me some of his greatest people that he admired were Richard J. Daley and J. Edgar Hoover and all of that. Coming from my generation and my background, I'm suspicious of these guys from the time I meet them to the time I leave.

MOVE 1985['s attempted eviction] was technically going to happen in 1984. That's the word that we had. I used to go, even on my days off. I would go out to Osage Avenue and hang out with the neighbors and hang out with MOVE. I would go sit on the porch and talk to Ramona Africa and try to get her to explain to me what the hell their philosophy was. I never got to that point, but she would talk and talk and talk. I would talk to John Africa, and I would talk to all of those people before '85. The neighbors knew me, and I knew them. I sat on the porch and talked in my free time. I used to do this.

I got a call, and someone said to me over the phone, a friend and a cop, that [I didn't] want to be out there this morning by 6:00 A.M. I got up and got out there at 3:00 A.M. I called the station, and we were all set up. At six o'clock, just like a stopwatch, is when the shooting started. The sun just started to come up, and [firefighters] started to put water on the house and all of this.

Tom Kranz, Executive Producer, WCAU:
I didn't have any actual fear of our people until the day it actually happened on May 13. MOVE was a story that was with us from 1978 to 1985, seven years, a story that kind of never went away. The 1985 interaction never became real for us until the bunker appeared on top of their house. We had been reporting on the complaints of the neighbors: Bullhorn was going off, and they were cursing them out on Christmas Eve, and all of this stuff. In the greater scheme of things, with TV being the visual medium that it is, I don't think we really cared until we saw the structure they had built on top of the building. . . . I grew up in a row home neighborhood in Philadelphia. The street I grew up on was exactly like Osage Avenue. It's a narrow one-way street with small two-story

homes all next to each other. In a very big way, I felt like I was covering the storm at home in my hometown. I could really commiserate with the people who lived there. If you have a bad neighbor in a neighborhood like that, you are totally fucked. There is nothing you can do. People are in close quarters. If your next-door neighbor is bad, that's bad, but if you have a neighbor up the street who is causing trouble, these guys would literally patrol on the rooftop with a gun, looking at their neighbors. I kind of put myself there as a resident. We knew when they evacuated the street, it was not going to be good.

Chris Wagner, Anchor, WPVI:
I went down after the noon news the day that they bombed it. We had not been there at all in the morning. It was the only decision our news director ever made while I was there that I thought was completely screwed up. He didn't want to provoke anything even though the police were down there, so he didn't send us. Channel 10, Channel 3 were there. Everyone was there, and we were not. I was the first reporter from our station to get down there at one o'clock in the afternoon. As soon as I got done with the noon news, I went down there. They kept us really far back. There was a lot of gunfire. At five o'clock, a helicopter goes overhead, and they dropped the bomb on [the house]. I was literally speaking on the air when the kaboom went off, and that's when they bombed it. All hell broke loose. They made us get way back, so we ran down the street, and some kids said, "Hey, you can come on our roof." So it was as close as the cops would let us get. I had gone to work that day dressed for anchoring, so I had on high heels and a dress. They only had a ladder that went up to the top of the first floor. We went up the ladder, and there were wires that went along the side of the house. I had to get between the house and wires so I didn't get electrocuted. The guys were up on top, and they pulled me up to the rooftop. Diane Allen was up there with her crew with Channel 3. We just live shot until two in the morning. It looked like the city was burning down. It was horrific. It just seemed so unreal that in Philadelphia in 1985, we could be burning out this huge section of the city.

Eliott Rodriguez, Reporter, WPVI:
Channel WCAU had done a better job than we had, quite frankly, on that story. We were behind. That day, they had video of the helicopter

dropping the satchel on [the house]. We didn't have that video. We didn't have as many crews there. I remember being out there and feeling like we had been outgunned on that story.

Larry Kane, Anchor, WPVI, WCAU, and KYW:
We were the only station that stayed on the air continuously. We even preempted the *CBS Evening News*. We stayed on the air. I was on the air from about eight o'clock in the morning until about two the next morning. It was just unreal. The whole thing was breaking and developing. We tried to report it responsibly. Channel 6 made one of its biggest mistakes that night: They ran a movie called *Murder in Miami*. This is the only reason I remember that, because of that night. We stayed on the air, and we were hands down the number-one station that night, which was rare. It was just an incredible story. I woke up the next morning, and I thought it was all a dream, and it was a bad dream. The story was very active. It was very hard, and we had to maintain calm. In my career, it was probably one of the most traumatic stories I've ever done. When the bomb dropped, we were one of the only people with the actual video of it. It became a major piece of evidence in the hearings that ensued.

Marc Howard, Anchor, WPVI and KYW:
We were on live, I think, at eight o'clock at night. I think we interrupted the network to be live to cover it more. I went to city hall, and Mayor [Wilson] Goode was there. I got in and talked to him live on the news. Of course, he had done nothing wrong, he said, and he felt he was forced to take action because of what [the MOVE members were] doing. In those days, I used to anchor the five o'clock news and then go out and be a reporter for the 11 [o'clock news]. That particular night, I remember going to city hall and getting a live interview with Mayor Goode.

Pat Ciarrocchi, Anchor and Reporter, KYW:
For me, it was intense trying to pay close attention. The thing that was really important that I found during the course of doing live broadcasts on breaking stories and anchoring live broadcasts on breaking stories is that you have to really pay attention to the live reporter who is in the field. You have to take notes on what they say so that when you debrief them, you can advance the story. Or, if you then go to somebody else in

the field, you can make a comparison to what somebody else has said at another point along the way.

Robin Mackintosh, Reporter, KYW:
They sent me to the local hospital, Misericordia Hospital, down in Southwest Philly. They figured anyone that was injured in this would be sent there. I sat there all day long, and nobody asked me to come out and cover the thing. It's about 11:30 [P.M.], and an ambulance shows up, and its Ramona Africa and Birdie, who were both burned in the thing and were sent over there. We got shots of [Ramona] coming out. I forget what she said, if anything, but we did get that. The MOVE thing came to me the next day when [the station] decided that they wanted people to get in there. Like, Press Pass no. 10 to get down to Osage Avenue and see for myself what was going on. It was a war zone: still smoky, still smelly, dead animals all over the place. They had tons of cats in that place. Dead bodies were all over the place at the scene of the house. It was a tragic scene. All of these [other] people had lost their houses.

Bob Feldman, Producer and Assistant News Director, WPVI:
We ended up not having the best view of the site as one of the competition. We did not get video of the bomb package being dropped on the house. Except for that camera angle, we had everything else.

Everyone was kept far away. We had one camera person in a house down the block with a view of the front side of the house or a slightly side view. We didn't have a live picture because we couldn't get a microwave truck there. We were kept back. We had to send tapes back and forth. The one camera that got really close, we didn't want anyone to know—including police—that we were that close. So, we kept filming and kept shooting tape, but we couldn't get it to air until afterward.

Terry Ruggles, Reporter and Anchor, WCAU:
The only reason Channel 10 got the shots of the helicopter was because we put a camera up on top of the mast of the microwave. That was our shot.

Cherie Bank, Health Reporter and Anchor, WCAU:
We were the only ones to get the bomb going off. Horrible as that is, it was the evidence that was needed in court. Steve Levy was on the air for,

like, six hours straight in the studio. He was a really good ad lib-er, so he really helped move everything along. It was great coverage.

Liz Matt, Reporter, WPVI and WTXF:
The second MOVE [confrontation], we were live on the air at *AM Philadelphia*, and we just gave over our airtime to *Action News*. We were live on the air during a morning talk show, and this was breaking news, so we just said, "We are suspending our daily program, and we are going to give the rest of our airtime to be handled by *Action News*."

Randy Covington, News Director, KYW:
In the morning, I thought we were very strong—perhaps the best out of any of the Philly stations. But in the afternoon, WCAU had the money shot. They had the shot of the helicopter dropping the C-4 [explosive]. It was an extremely competitive day in Philadelphia television news. Philadelphia is a competitive TV market, but on a story like this, you do everything that is humanly possible to serve your viewers well and, in the vernacular of TV news, win. The battle I thought swung to CAU, but the story wasn't over. We had, I believe, the first shot of Birdie Africa after he escaped the house. As I think back, it was perhaps the most surreal story I was ever involved in.

Steve Schwaid, News Director, WCAU and WTXF:
It was totally surreal because—I'll never forget—they told us the day before, an employee [from the police department] told us the day before, they were going to go to the MOVE house that Sunday, that Mother's Day weekend, as I recall, and we're all sitting there thinking, "This is crazy." I remember being there that night. I think it was Mother's Day night when it was lit up like a Hollywood set. Police brought in all these lights and looked like they were going to shoot a movie, and of course, we're like, "This isn't real, this isn't real." The following morning, we're all live, and they all start shooting each other. Two of our chief reporters were Walt Hunter and Jack Jones. Walt was amazing. Jack was frighteningly, scary amazing. We had live shots with Jack Jones lying on the ground next to cars to avoid getting hit by bullets. I remember the scene. We had video at one point of police cars coming in with more ammunition. This was out of control. I wasn't at CAU, I was at KYW, and they dropped the bomb at one point. We all didn't know what was going on,

to be honest with you. Eventually, we knew Osage Avenue was on fire, and we're like, "This can't be real." At one point, we said, "Send the chopper up; let's get some aerials," and [the police] said that all choppers couldn't go to that area. No choppers were allowed in that area. The next thing you know, there was WPVI's chopper up in the area getting video, and we're all going crazy—like, "They're up, let's go up!" Obviously, we couldn't because you'd get in trouble, you'd violate the rules. I remember sending anchors out, sending more people out the door, one after another for the story. It's probably one of the more bizarre stories I've ever covered in my life because you saw this train coming down the track, and you knew you were going to watch a train wreck. I just didn't want anybody to get hurt in the middle of this night. It was unbelievable. Some of us were in the newsroom for twenty-four hours.

Terry Ruggles, Reporter and Anchor, WCAU:
The first MOVE [confrontation, in 1978], which happened in Powelton Village, we had photographers up looking down on them. And we did the same thing the second time, not knowing what was going to happen, and we had made plans with people in the neighborhood, and Pete Kane was able to get into a closet, and when the cops came through, he stayed in the closet. And then when they left, it was his vocal reports more than his pictures that were giving us the importance of what was going on. We had the helicopter shots and the shots from a distance. One of the eerie things for me was the next day—we were trying to get in, of course, we were all kept out in a cordon around the area and couldn't get into it, and the only reason Channel 10 got the shots of the helicopter [with the bomb] was because we put a camera on top of the mast of the microwave, and that was our shot. The guy's name was Jim Barcher, who was a technician, and he said, "Why don't we hook this camera up on top of this microwave dish?" So we got it forty feet in the air, which is higher than the houses there. The next day, I got in, and I was friends with Jim White, who was the city's managing director, and I went in[to the area], and for some reason, the director let me in; he did not stop me. I went right up to the street, and you have got this street that has cinders and all of these steps going up to foundations where there is nothing there. The only thing I can think of—I'm not old enough to have been around for any of WWII, but this must have been what Dresden looked like when we dropped those bombs that created all the fires, because just as

far as the eye could see from my vantage point was all burned-down structures. Maybe one of the saddest times in this city's history.

Randy Covington, News Director, KYW:
I remember [the gas company] pumped mud into the natural gas lines so they wouldn't explode. We had sneaked a photographer into a house across the street from where the MOVE group lived. We had live crews stationed around the area.

Pete Kane, Photographer, WCAU:
I snuck into the back of a house. I went down the back alleyway and went into a house with Mr. and Mrs. Austin, their daughter, and kids in the house. I went up to the second floor and out the window, and I was looking down Osage Avenue. It was starting to get dark. They started to tow cars off the block. People were out, the gas company was out there, there were civil affairs officers on the corner, police around the corner, SWAT guys were out there. On the bullhorn, you could hear the MOVE members, Ramona and other members, saying things about the police department and stuff like that. The house I was in, the police came and said we had to leave. So [the Austins] said [to me], "You can stay here if you want," but the daughter said to negotiate a price or something like that. I called the assignment desk and said, "Look, I'm in this house, and these people are willing to let me stay here." She got Jay Newman on the phone, who was our news director then, and Jay said, "Pete, I don't want to put you in any danger." I told him I was going to be okay. We negotiated a price with the family, and that was it. They left the house. When I was in the house on the second floor, before they left, I put the window up a couple of inches, and I put the blinds up by eight inches and laid the microphone outside the window and closed the window. I left the blinds up, and the family left. They locked the front door, and everything was fine. All night long, I watched cars being towed, I watched the gas company come in and shut the gas down, I saw the electric company come in, and the whole time, you heard the bullhorn just going and going.

Steve Levy, Anchor and Reporter, WPVI, KYW, and WCAU:
We knew that it was going to happen. We were all in place at 5:00 A.M., and we went on the air at 5:30 A.M. Our police sources told us that this was going to happen, so we were all prepared—our camera crews, our

reporters were all on the scene, and of course, they were the heroes. I was in the studio anchoring it. We went on the air at 5:30 A.M., and I think the thing the people gave me the most credit for was not going to the bathroom for all of those hours. We were in place at like 4:00 or 4:30 [A.M.], and I did not come off the air until noon, and I did not go to the bathroom, and I was drinking coffee the whole time. The thing that stands out in my mind—besides the fact that my hometown was tearing itself apart—the thing that still hurts me is that we had a reporter named Harvey Clark on the scene, and Harvey and I were pals. He was doing the live report after some of the gunfire had quieted down, and we had a big monitor behind me on the set, so I would turn around from the anchor desk to talk to Harvey, and you would see both of us on the screen. Harvey and I were talking live on television, and some shots rang out, and Harvey dropped. Now, I didn't know if one of my best pals had been shot, but I had to turn back to the camera and take care of the viewers. I knew they didn't know what had happened any more than I did. I was talking to the viewers and trying to keep them calm and inform them with whatever information I had, and there wasn't much. I was worried the whole time that my friend was just shot. That's a moment that whenever I relive it, it's awful.

Robin Mackintosh, Reporter, KYW:
It wasn't really a bombing—it was a satchel charge. The idea was that [the police] were going to blow that bunker off the roof of the thing, and they had no idea that [MOVE] had barrels of oil in there, and when they dropped the satchel charge, it ignited all these barrels of oil, and it just spread like wildfire, and [the police] figured, "They are still shooting at us, why don't we see if we can smoke them out?" Unfortunately, it got ahead of them, and they couldn't control it.

Mike Strug, Reporter, WPVI, KYW, and WCAU:
I just remember very specifically watching that helicopter come across, something drops out, and the next thing you hear is a boom. I ended up doing stories because I was out there all night as the block caught fire, and it became a tourist attraction. People at three, four, five in the morning were driving by just to see this block on fire. I ended up doing a feature aspect on this thing. It was burned into your memory. You don't forget something like that.

Bob Kravitz, Photographer, WPVI:
I heard the helicopter above me and Chris [Wagner]. I pointed the camera up, and as I was pointing the camera up, the satchel with the bomb in it dropped, and I got that coming down right on the roof. And boom. It shook.

Michael Archer, Executive Producer, WCAU:
We did the best job of any station in Philadelphia and probably the best job of any station in the country that could have been done. Some of the early reporting that we did, primarily Harvey Clark. We had been working on the MOVE story for months in advance as that thing continued to boil up.

Dick Standish, Reporter, KYW:
I was over there during the shootout, assigned along Cobbs Creek Parkway. The only thing I remember there—it was the damnedest thing—you couldn't always tell where the shots were being fired. Everybody was getting crouched down behind a line of police and civilian cars.

Randy Covington, News Director, KYW:
I had Jack Jones and Walt Hunter crouched down behind a van as bullets were flying. I don't think it was aimed at them. I don't think anybody was wounded or anything, but as a news director, it was like, "Oh my gosh—get behind that van and stay safe."

Tim Furlong, Reporter, WCAU:
One of the things that made me actually want to be a reporter: I remember seeing Jack Jones from Channel 3 hiding behind a car, the late Jack Jones. I just remember thinking, "This dude is a hero. This guy is keeping his calm. He's telling us what's happening, and he is putting everything in context." I remember as a kid thinking, "This guy has guts." He made me want to keep watching. He was a great storyteller. I never got to meet him, but that's sort of one of the things that got in my head to do this.

Pat Ciarrocchi, Anchor and Reporter, KYW:
I was solo anchoring, and I had the greatest group of people out on the street. Walt Hunter was there, Jack Jones, Robin Mackintosh, Dick

Sheeran. Every great veteran reporter in the world seemed to be working for Channel 3 at that time.

Tom Kranz, Executive Producer, WCAU:
I would have to say that when we first heard the gunshots start to break out—and they just didn't break out one at a time—it was a tidal wave of sounds. I got scared because the bullets sounded like they were closer than they really were. We really were ducking down behind cars. Harvey Clark told me over and over again that because I was his field producer, he kept his eye on me the entire time. He knew that if I looked scared, he could see it in my eyes, it was time for him to move. He kept his eye on me, and I pretty much looked over his shoulder the entire time; as long as I didn't see anybody running our way, he kept going, and I stayed there.

Terri Merryman, Anchor and Reporter, KYW:
They had told us that this was brewing. Jack [Jones] and I were anchoring the news one weekend, and they said, "Look, this is about to come to a head." They told us all about the MOVE organization and "We may be asking you guys after the newscast to go out there and sit it out, pull an all-nighter." We were ready. After the newscast, they put us in a live van at 11:30, quarter of twelve, and they transported us out to the scene. It was rather quiet. Nothing much was going on. A lot of card games going on, and a lot of talking in the truck. Just waiting, a hurry-up-and-wait kind of thing. Lots of unmarked police cars and lots of people sitting around. A lot of news vehicles sitting around. Everything was really quiet. It escapes me when the big stuff started, but at daylight, more and more people started to show up. We figured that things might be escalating. They sent some producers to the scene, some field producers to help us out. They were quite helpful. They were gonna start various shows. The morning show was gonna have a hit, the noon show was gonna have a hit. I just remember that when it was my turn—and I don't remember what time of day it was, but when it was my turn to go live, you would be standing there with your microphone waiting to go, and they would have to find the perfect time to do a cut-in—it was my turn to go live, and I was just standing there with a microphone, and all of a sudden I heard something that sounded like firecrackers. I didn't flinch. I said, "Oh, it's just firecrackers." Duh—of course it was gunshots. The

next thing I know, there's this police officer, and he tackles me and sends me to the ground. It all happened so fast. He tackled me. He wanted everyone to get down. The gunshots were ringing out. The next memory I have is that I was in the truck, and it was Jack's turn to do a cut-in, and as he was standing and waiting to go live, then gunshots rang out again. He crouched down and was doing this live shot crouched down, discussing what was going on from his standpoint. It was something else. We worked out there and didn't leave for two days. No change of clothes or anything.

Pete Kane, Photographer, WCAU:
At some point at like 3:00, 3:30 [A.M.], I hear Ramona [Africa] saying [that MOVE would] talk and negotiate things. But [MOVE] wanted reporters out there, like Harvey Clark, Barbara Grant, Vernon Odom; they mentioned these reporters by name. . . . So around ten [minutes before] six, it started to get light. That's when the fire started. Small gunfire. It was small-caliber gunfire going on. I was looking out the window. When the gunfire started, someone in front of the house I was in, they turned around and looked up. I thought they saw me, so I immediately hid in the closet. I heard all of this noise and everything, but what happened was they went to the house next door. An AP [Associated Press] photographer was in there, and a cameraman from Channel 3 was inside the house next door. So, they went in there. I found this out two days later, when I got out of the house. [The police] went in there and locked them up because of the fact that they stuck their cameras out the window, and that's why they got caught. I didn't do that. When all of that settled down, I went back to the window and started to videotape the tear gas, the gunfire. They went through like ten thousand rounds of bullets from the time they started until it ended the next day. I could hear them whistling by, the whole bit. It was ugly.

I don't know when I started, but I was on the phone talking, giving live reports to Steve Levy. Back then, when they cut the power, the phone still worked, so I used the phone in the house to talk to my station throughout the time I was there. It was live reports throughout the morning, and the police department kept calling our station to find out the house I was in. I never gave my station the house I was in. I feared for my own safety also. They never knew what house I was in. I did that throughout the day. Larry Kane came in, and I talked to him on the air and explained to him seeing the whole bit. After 5:00 P.M., I got done with a live report on the phone with Larry. I went downstairs to the refrigerator to get something to eat. [The homeowners] told me they had food in the refrigerator. I got some cold pork chops and a Coca-Cola. I was down in the refrigerator, and all of a sudden, the house shock. I ran back upstairs and called our assignment desk and said, "What the hell just happened?" [Producer Karen Fox] said, "Pete, you need to go on the air as soon as you can. They just dropped a device from a helicopter," and that was the bomb that shook the area.

When I was first on the phone with Larry and looking out the window, I first started seeing black smoke. Then, all of a sudden, I started to see flames coming from the MOVE house. The fire started to spread, and I said to Larry on the phone, "Look, the MOVE house is burning. The homes on either side of the MOVE house are now in flames." They asked me if they were putting water on it, and I said, "No, they are not putting anything on it at all." As I recall, water didn't start hitting that house until thirty or forty minutes after the fire started.

Our microwaves had antennas that could go sixty feet in the air. So what we did was that day we had a loaner camera that Sony had loaned us to test out. We tied, wrapped, and taped that camera to our truck. Ran the cable to that camera down into that truck. On the monitor in that truck, we could see and pan the camera and see their bunkers.

When the fire started getting intense and being on each side, I heard yelling from the SWAT guys right in front of me [as they] started going in the door [of the MOVE house] and breaking the door down. I hear yelling and screaming: "They are coming out the back! They are coming out the back!" I started to hear semiautomatic gunfire. Finally, they told me to get out of the house three hours after the bomb was dropped. I exited the back of the house in total darkness. As I exited the back of the house, I was going down an alley in total darkness. When I was on the phone, [the station] told me where Harvey Clark and the crew were, two blocks away. I made it down the dark neighborhood, and I looked back, and all I saw was an inferno.

I ran three blocks with my camera gear—hadn't had a bathroom in a day and a half—and I made it to Harvey Clark and his crew and did a live report on the air with Harvey as I exited the house. I figured any minute going down that alley, I was gonna have a bullet in the back of my head. That was horrible.

My video next cut out until I left the house. I went into that house with two videotapes and two batteries. I told the station I needed some more batteries and more tapes. One guy from the station snuck down in the middle of the night and dropped off one battery and one tape in the back of the house I was in. Instead of bringing me a bunch of tapes, he brought me *one* tape and *one* battery. So, when I was in the house for twenty-four hours, I only had one hour of video. Each one of those tapes was twenty minutes. I had to be careful of what I shot throughout the day. Otherwise, I would have been out of video. When I left that house twenty-four hours later, I literally had thirty seconds of video left on that last tape I had.

Harvey Clark, Reporter, WCAU:
Neighbors were walking by, asking me, "Harvey, how long are we gonna be out of our homes?" "Harvey" this and "Harvey" that because they knew me, and I knew them. There was an old man named Watkins who was featured on television a lot because he was a jazz buff and had a huge jazz collection, and he said, "Harvey, I'm getting ready to fly to California tomorrow to see my daughter," I think it was. "The bags are packed and in the house." The cops told them they could be out of their house for twenty-four hours. I said to him, "If that's what they told you, then twenty-four hours is the number you will probably be back in your house by—twenty-four hours." They left all of their stuff in the house and left and stayed with somebody. Well, that morning, all hell broke loose. We had set up on the corner of 66th and Pine Street, right behind it. I had talked to some of the cops I knew who were stationed there right on the corner. I was so pissed off—personally—just pissed off at how everything just lost control in a matter of minutes. All of a sudden, there was machine-gun fire and all of this stuff. We were being told that this gunfire was going back and forth, and we believed that MOVE might have been shooting back and that kind of stuff. That was the early reports. It went on and on, and then it stopped in the afternoon. Everybody assumed it was over. There was a camerawoman that was watching this helicopter flying around. Nobody knew what the hell it was doing in the air. It would fly around and then dive down on the MOVE house and then pull up and take off. It did this two or three times. We were trying to figure out what was about to happen here. So, the next time it came around, this time, there's a guy in the doorway with his feet

hanging out of the helicopter, and he's got a satchel on his lap. I said to the cameraman, "Listen, this son of bitch is getting ready to drop some kind of explosive thing on the roof of that house." He laughed and thought I was kidding. So, the last time around, that's exactly what happened. This package comes out the door. Lands on top of the house. We had a camera that we put on the antenna of the truck. Nobody knew how we got all of the exclusive pictures. We gaffer-taped this damn thing to the antenna on the truck. So, when it went up 40 feet, we could see the antenna on the roof, see the bunker on the house, and see the water cannons and all of that stuff on there. Then, this package. Two or three seconds go by, and then boom—explosion. I said, "I'll be a son of bitch. I don't believe this is happening." There was a little bitty fire that started. MOVE had this little bunker thing on top of the house, and they had generators up there with gas cans around. Those gas cans caught on fire, and there was a little bit of smoke. Everybody thought [the firefighters] would put out the fire 'cause they were pumping the water for three hours on the house. What happened when they pumped all of that water on the house? They lowered the water pressure on the neighborhood so they couldn't pump water to stop that fire. So, the fire turned into a little fire, then a bigger fire, and then a bigger fire. It was confined to the MOVE house and the house next door. The thing was starting to spread, and nobody was shooting any water on it. All the reporters were going, "What the fuck is going on here?" The police commissioner, who I felt was an idiot, told the fire commissioner to let the fire burn: "They will come out of the goddamn house. Let the fire burn." And the fire commissioner let the fire burn. What really pissed me off—and I've never said this, and I thought I would never say this about Wilson Goode—but what really pissed me off as a black reporter: Here you have the first black mayor of a city, and this shit is going down, and he is sitting on his ass in his office, watching me on TV. He's not out there, and he's not directing anybody. In my opinion, he gives up his authority to the police commission and fire commission, and they are out there making decisions on the seat of their pants, and they burn the whole goddamn neighborhood down. I forgot the number, but it killed homes and women and children. They would later find out not one shot was fired out of the MOVE house.

They tried to run us away from our spot when the shooting started. You could hear the bullets going by—whoosh, whoosh, whoosh. You could hear them, and we're in danger. Cops said, "You have to move, Harvey. You have to go down the block." What happened was—it kind of saved us. There was a lieutenant riding a big white horse, and he tried to get the horse to knock over the cameras. Then, he looked into the truck and looked at one of the monitors in the truck, which had a picture of the MOVE roof. [The police] didn't even have a view of the roof. The highest mark they had was across the street on the second floor, and MOVE was on the third floor, on the roof. When they saw the monitor, they wanted to know how we were getting those pictures. I said to them, "That's not your business." We made sort of a deal with them that they didn't make us move the truck and let us leave a technician in that truck. We would leave, but the truck and technician stayed. They cut the deal on the spot, and a technician stayed in the truck to change the tapes and batteries and stuff. They got to look in the truck and see the MOVE roof.

Every hour, I was a little bit more pissed off than the hour before. If you recall, after the burn down, and the deaths, and Ramona [Africa] and Birdie [Africa] were the only ones to get their escapes from the flames, then [the city] turned around and put a MOVE commission together of normal people who were on the Watergate commission and all. This was supposed to investigate the incident, and I covered that. It was the WHYY auditorium, where the hearings were. The conclusion of that commission was that a federal grand jury should be impaneled to look into this, because there were many, many crimes committed. When I really lost hope in the system—with that recommendation, it just kind of disappeared. It went out as a recommendation, and you didn't hear much more after that. That was the single most aggravating, angry thing I've ever done in the news business. It carried on for days after that. I started drinking, and like a lot of people there, I was totally exhausted. I never got more than two hours of sleep for a week or so. When I did go to sleep, all I would be thinking about was something that pissed me off. It went on and on.

Pat Ciarrocchi, Anchor and Reporter, KYW:
I remember leaving the set after the MOVE incident, and coming back up, and the news director saying, "Really excellent work." I was so concentrated on the work I was doing, I wasn't thinking I would be getting some kind of celebratory response. It was the first time I ever came off the set and came into the newsroom and people applauded me. It wasn't

just me. I was the captain in that ship at that moment in pulling everyone else who really just did a great job of telling the story.

Terri Merryman, Anchor and Reporter, KYW:
The news media did an excellent job with what they were asked to do. They kept the public informed. The public certainly had every right to know what was going on, especially all the people in the neighborhood that needed to know how much danger they were in. If not for the media and getting that information out, I don't think a lot of people would have taken that seriously. They might have all thought it was just some troublemakers and it would go away, police will take care of it. I don't think people realized just how serious it was until the news media started doing the live shot and actually took them to the scene and let them know how serious of a situation it was.

LIVE AID

On July 13, 1985, musicians Bob Geldof and Midge Ure organized a worldwide rock concert called Live Aid to raise money for famine relief in Africa. The concert event was held in two locations: Wembley Stadium, in London, U.K.; and JFK Stadium, in Philadelphia, Pennsylvania. The event was a sixteen-hour televised concert that reached more than a billion viewers in more than 110 nations. Live Aid raised more than $125 million in 1985.

Around seventy-two thousand people attended the concert in London, and close to one hundred thousand people attended the concert in Philadelphia. Artists appearing in Philadelphia included Mick Jagger; Eric Clapton; Tina Turner; Hall & Oates; Bob Dylan; Phil Collins; and Crosby, Stills, Nash & Young. In the U.K., performers included Elton John, Queen, Madonna, Sting, David Bowie, Neil Young, U2, The Who, and Tom Petty. The concert was carried in the daytime, from 7 A.M. to 6 P.M. Eastern, by an independent network to more than a hundred U.S. television stations. JFK Stadium hosted twenty-six television and radio production vans, sound-mixing trucks, and satellite-dish antennae.

Fox 29 aired Live Aid from 7 A.M. to 6 P.M., gathering a 12.8 rating and a 39 share. From 7 P.M. to 8 P.M., WPVI aired a special show called Live Aid: The Philadelphia Story, *hosted by Gary Papa and Vernon Odom. The show won its time slot against other local stations, with a 16.2 rating and a 39 share. (WPVI sent reporters Harry Martin and Cathy Gandolfo and crew to Wembley Stadium in London for live broadcasts.) Channels 10 and 3 continued with regular programming that night and had ratings of 3.6 with a 9 share and 2.6 with a 6 share, respectively. At 8 P.M., ABC aired a three-hour special hosted by Dick Clark that featured highlights of the daytime performances in Philadelphia and London. That show did a 20.9 rating with a 40 share, the highest rating in the United States. Channels 3 and 10 continued with their regular programming and fell way behind, with a 7.8 rating and 15 share and a 3.5 rating and 7 share, respectively. All four local stations reported on the concert event in their regular news broadcasts.*

Ray Murray, ***Evening Magazine*** **Cohost and Producer, KYW:**
It was truly on the world's stage. One of the things that was amazing about the experience was that very early on, around 1980, we did a profile on Bob Geldof. Bob Geldof had come to Philadelphia, and he was really not known internationally at the time, and I don't remember the name of his band, but we did a story on him. We profiled him and did a piece for *Evening Magazine*, and he never forgot that. When Live Aid came around, he was the primary driving force behind it. He only gave one interview. He only gave one private interview on that entire experience, and that was to us. I think we did the interview at his hotel so [we could] really sit down and chat with Bob about Live Aid, and what were the motivations behind that experience from some of the roadblocks he faced, and what it was like to organize that. Truly extraordinary—I mean, he was really on the world stage in that moment, so it was an amazing experience. Most of our time was backstage. There was an energy that I think the city had not seen up until that point.

Bob Feldman, Producer and Assistant News Director, WPVI:
We had lines and crews at JFK, and we also made a determination that we'd better cover London. So, we sent a crew to London; I was with them. I took Harry Martin and Cathy Gandolfo, [and] two photographers. We were live in Wembley Stadium and covered the events in London while the event was going on in Philadelphia. We were able to cut back and forth.

Harry Martin, Weather Anchor, WPVI:
That was a moment when I kind of went, "Oh my God. I can't believe I am actually doing this, sitting in the London bureau doing a live shot."

We knew it was a big worldwide event. I don't think any of us realized how huge it actually was. In fact, I didn't realize how huge it was until I looked at the documentary drama on Queen to see what an amazing day it was with some of the backstory that led up to it.

Chris Wagner, Anchor, WPVI:
I was up in the press box, and the stadium was rockin' and rollin'. We were getting the feeds from Europe; we were getting the live performances in Philadelphia. The crowds on both sides of the ocean were just so into it. I remember standing with my assignment editor, who was an old-school rocker from way back, and we just grinned at each other. It was really, really fun. I hated to have to go get my story together to go on the air because I wanted to stay there and watch the whole thing.

Robin Mackintosh, Reporter, KYW:
I was at Atlantic Aviation. In those days—before 9/11 and all the tough security—you could walk out on the tarmac, and if a plane pulled up, whether you didn't walk in front of it, you could wait until the steps came down and talk to people. The first one was Mick Jagger, and we interviewed him and Hall & Oates. We interviewed them, and this was the day before Live Aid happened. Then, this beautiful white Learjet came in. The steps come down, we look inside, and it is all red leather, red velvet, and this great set of legs steps out the door. It was Tina Turner. I interviewed some high-end folks by the time I left there.

Vernon Odom, Reporter, WPVI:
I remember seeing a woman dancing around naked outside. They had to arrest her. She was determined she had to see Mick Jagger. It was nuts, man. It was very hot that day. The health commissioner of the City of Philadelphia called the fire department in and said to hose down the crowd. They were burning up out here. They opened up the fire hoses and just poured it on the crowd. Nobody objected. It was hot as hell down there. That evening, Gary Papa and I were cohosting. He had a show on called *Prime Time*, and I had a show called *Visions* at 7:30. We had me and him up in the booth, cohosting the first half hour mostly. It was scripted, and we showed highlights from the day. He did the first half hour, and I did mostly the second half hour.

Andy Doane, Photographer, WPVI:
Some people were passed out because it was so hot. Especially at JFK, everyone was crowded in there. People were passing out, and people were put on stretchers to cool off.

Liz Matt, Reporter, WPVI and WTXF:
It was really hot, and originally we were reporting outside the venue because we did not have a press badge to get backstage. We were there to just capture whatever we could see. Eventually, I believe the producers of Live Aid realized Channel 6 was outside and was going to stay all day. After a couple of hours, Larry Magid, who was the producer for Electric Factory, got us inside, and now I'm backstage under the tent.

Steve Schwaid, News Director, WCAU and WTXF:
I don't think we had any clue of what it was going to become. That's when JFK Stadium was still up. I think I was a nighttime executive producer, but I was a producer on scene, so I was down there. We had Judy Barton, and Trudy Haynes was there. We had photographers, we had network photographers there, and I just remember it was a really hot day. We're in JFK Stadium, there were no facilities to use. There were no bathrooms we had access to where we were as the press. We were literally on the rooftop. That's where they stuck us. We're watching this event, we can't believe we're all watching, we're trying to get interviews, and then we had Trudy Haynes. I'm trying to remember who all the acts were in Philadelphia, but every time you turned around, we had an interview with them.

Liz Matt, Reporter, WPVI and WTXF:
I became aware that Phil Collins was flying in on an SSP [airship] because he opened the show at Wembley Stadium, I believe, and then finished the show in Philadelphia. My focus was trying to get as many interviews with as many famous people as humanly possible. We were not a famous national crew. We were a local ABC station with all the national reporters there who had prime access for these performers.

Harry Martin, Weather Anchor, WPVI:
When you go overseas and there is a time difference, you end up working virtually around the clock. You work the day in London from nine

in the morning until six at night, and then because of the six-hour difference, now you are starting to do the American day. So, now you are working two days in one. It's pretty exhausting. We would get up at seven o'clock in the morning and not get to bed until eleven o'clock at night. You would go straight through because they would want us to do packages and that sort of thing.

Greg Meyer, Photographer, KYW:
We interviewed Bob Geldof sitting in the queen's box. He was the moving force behind it. That was very emotional. I remember that very, very well. He told the story of a sixteen- or eighteen-year-old girl who was working for the English Red Cross at a camp in Africa. They were starting to run out of food. This poor girl had to make a decision on who was gonna get the food that was left. At that point in time, I was very, very emotional. As soon as the interview was over, I said, "Bob here's everything in my pockets. I'm giving this to you. Make sure it goes to the right place." That interview really affected me with him.

THE SUICIDE OF R. BUDD DWYER

On January 22, 1987, Pennsylvania State Treasurer R. Budd Dwyer shot and killed himself at a news conference in his office in Harrisburg, Pennsylvania.

Dwyer drew a .357 Magnum revolver from a manila envelope during his public press conference, at which invited media had expected him to announce his resignation from office. Several reporters and other attendees in the room ducked for cover, and others tried to convince him to put the gun down. Dwyer pulled the barrel out of the envelope, put the revolver in his mouth, and pulled the trigger. He had been reading a nineteen-page statement in which he said, "It's too late for me" and "As my political career draws to a close. . . ."

Near the end of his speech, prior to shooting himself, he told the media in attendance at the news conference, "You don't want to take down your equipment yet." Dwyer then handed out three different envelopes, in which some thought were his letters of resignation, to his aides in the room, calling each recipient up to the podium. The contents were his final statement: "I am going to die in office in an effort to . . . see if the shameful facts, spread out in all their shame, will not burn through our civic shamelessness and set fire to American pride."

Weeks before the shooting, Dwyer and former state Republican chairman Robert B. Asher were found guilty of eleven federal charges stemming from the Pennsylvania Treasury Department's 1984 decision to award a $4.6 million contract to a California computer concern with-

out taking competing bids. Two of the company's officials testified that they had won the contract by offering a $300,000 payoff to Dwyer. One testified that Asher had found out about the offer and ordered that the money be diverted to the Republican State Committee.

Dwyer's suicide was not televised live—the press conference was at 10:30 A.M.—leaving TV news organizations to make and reevaluate their judgment calls throughout the day regarding what footage to show during their afternoon and evening newscasts. Every news organization, locally and nationally, had access to pictures and video of the event. Philadelphia TV news directors faced instant and difficult ethical dilemmas: How much do you show? And how do you justify the decision to show graphic images to viewers?

WPVI was the only station in the Philadelphia viewing area whose noon newscast showed Dwyer pulling the trigger. Viewers heard the gunshot and then saw his head jolt back and his body drop out of the camera frame. WCAU faded to black after showing Dwyer with the gun to his mouth.

"The decision is always first that you are appropriately conveying the content and context to the viewer," WCAU news director Jay Newman told the Intelligencer Journal. *"We felt we could convey the content and context of the story without being overly gruesome."*

KYW cut the video even sooner, stopping the video as Dwyer pointed the gun at the ceiling. By later newscasts, Channels 6 and 10 had trimmed the footage to a similar length to that of KYW. All Philadelphia stations gave strong warnings to viewers before showing their versions of the tape of the incident. Fox 29 devoted a segment of its Ten O'Clock News *broadcast to a survey of how stations had used the footage and a discussion of the news ethics involved.*

Channel 6abc received more than three hundred phone calls after their noon show playing the Dwyer video, most complaining about their decision, but a handful of callers asked when the video would be on again so they could record it. KYW 3 said that it also received a total of two hundred calls, with all but one applauding its decision not to air the entire tape. Channel 10 estimated that the two hundred phone calls it received were mostly supportive comments.

At the time, the Mental Health Association of Southern Pennsylvania urged television stations that planned to run footage of the suicide to first run a warning to viewers about the graphic images. The group feared that the incident would influence others who might be contemplating suicide.

WPXI-TV in Pittsburgh ran the full sequence of the suicide on its noon newscast, and WHTM-TV in Harrisburg ran footage in a cut-in that day. WHTM revised its position in later newscasts by freezing the image before the gunshot and letting the audio tell the story of what happened.

By the 6:00 P.M. newscast on WPXI that day, the film stopped with Dwyer holding the gun, the shot was heard, and the film then showed reporters scurrying in the room. WGAL was the only station in the Harrisburg TV market that ran the videotape edited, cutting to a picture of a nearby Dwyer staff member at the post when the treasurer put the gun to his mouth. The audio, however, continued to roll.

"It's an historic event," By Williams, WPXI station news operations manager, told the Intelligencer Journal *in Lancaster in 1987. "We've seen JFK shot to death 200 times. We've seen Bobby Kennedy shot to death. So, it's a reflection of a very important man in Pennsylvania society and what he did."*

Williams said that he made the decision not to show the gunshot a second time after a production meeting with WPXI staff.

Nationally, the networks approached the story with trepidation. CBS, NBC, and ABC had hours to decide what to show during their network newscasts. NBC Nightly News *showed Dwyer reading his statement and waving his gun, cutting to footage of the body being removed without showing the most graphic pictures. Neither ABC nor CBS used film of Dwyer's press conference on their evening news broadcasts. Both networks displayed a still photo of Dwyer in the background as anchormen gave brief accounts of the suicide. The picture used by ABC showed Dwyer holding a gun, while CBS's photo did not.*

CNN decided to stop the sound and picture before Dwyer put the gun in his mouth.

The day of Dwyer's death was also the day of a blustery snowstorm throughout Pennsylvania. Schools were closed, and parents were home, providing childcare. The unexpected snowstorm and the public suicide of the Pennsylvania treasurer boosted the newscast ratings for all news stations in Philadelphia. At noon, when the first Dwyer footage was shown, Channel 6 had a 15.8 Nielsen rating and a 38 percent audience share.

Channel 10 had a 10.5 rating and a 25 percent share, and Channel 3 had a 4.7 rating and an 11 percent share.

During its 5:00 P.M. newscast, WPVI had a whopping 33.6/50. At 5:30 P.M., WPVI had a 29.8/42, WCAU had a 13.1/18, and KYW did a 11.9/17. At 6:00 P.M., WPVI had a 32.7/44, followed by WCAU with a 12.4/17 and KYW with a 9.8/13; Fox 29's Ten O'Clock News *had a 6.3/8 rating. At 11:00 P.M., WPVI had a 23.8/40, KYW had a 14.5/24, and WCAU did a 11.4/19.*

Ned Warwick, Assignment Editor and News Director, WPVI:
That one was on me. We had made the decision that "Budd Dwyer's scheduled a news conference in Harrisburg" was an important story, and we needed to be there. Back then, in order to go live or immediate, we bought a line from Harrisburg to Philadelphia. We decided we would have something we would turn around, whatever happened in this mid-morning news conference for the noon show. That day was a snowy day. A big snowstorm came through that region. We had a crew there. We had a line. We were ahead of the competition by taking those steps. We were in a position to have the best coverage certainly out of Philadelphia on this story. Low and behold, what happened unfolded as a horror show before us. He shot himself minutes before our noon newscasts. We had to make a very fast decision about how much of that scene we were going to put on television. It was finally up to me to make the call and how far to take the video. I probably took it one frame too far. He pulls the trigger, but you don't see him at that point because he sags down the wall and onto the floor. It was one frame too far, especially given it was a snowy day and kids were home watching television significantly more than you would have for a noon newscast in the middle of the week. There was tremendous uproar. Radio stations from as far away as Hong Kong were calling for a comment. "How could you have done that? What prompted you to take such license with the sensibilities of your viewers?" It was really a tough position to be in. There was lots of criticism and lots of editorials.

Chris Wagner, Anchor, WPVI:
We were watching the live feed come in, and we saw it happen. Watching someone get shot in the head is not as pretty and painless and blood-

less as it looks on TV. It was a big, bloody, horrifying mess. Before [Dwyer] shot himself, he was waving that gun around, and the crews were scared for their lives. The reporters that were there were terrified because he was a madman. He was pointing the gun all over the place and—bam—he shot himself. The whole back of his head came off against the wall, and he slid down the wall. It was awful. For some unknown reason, our news director decided to run it on the noon news. The outcry from the public was instantaneous and really loud and vociferous. They were so horrified that we would show someone taking his own life, and we did not run it again at five, six, and eleven [o'clock].

Eliott Rodriguez, Reporter, WPVI:
Unfortunately, we were the only station, I believe, that showed the actual gunshot. It was in that noon show. That was unfortunate.

Marc Howard, Anchor, WPVI and KYW:
At five o'clock, everyone knew we had video. They thought we were gonna show it [again]. It also was a snowstorm day. The five o'clock newscast that day had the largest rating of any five o'clock hour in the history of the station. I was working that day.

Lisa Thomas-Laury, Anchor, WPVI:
The decision had to be made: Do we show [Dwyer] putting the gun to his head? Do we blur that out? Do we show any of it? Freeze the frame? There were a lot of decisions to be made about what we [thought] our viewers should and should not see.

Robin Mackintosh, Reporter, KYW:
That's probably one of the top-five worst things that Channel 6 has ever done. Our news director, when he saw it on Channel 6—because I think they broke into programming out of the noon show—he called in and said, "That does not go on the air unedited." Fortunately, we were able to avoid the problem.

Terry Ruggles, Reporter and Anchor, WCAU:
We had a huge snowstorm—I'm talking about eleven to thirteen inches of snow. We had a crew over there, and there was all of this controversy with Dwyer holding this press conference. I was on snow watch at the

station because of how you ramp up for snow. No one realized Dwyer was gonna do this. People were concerned about the snow, and they were watching for that, and all of a sudden this Dwyer thing comes on. I saw what we did. We did not broadcast him actually pulling the trigger or show it.

Liz Matt, Reporter, WPVI and WTXF:
I offered to go into the control room to see what had just happened, but I didn't go look. I just couldn't stand the idea of watching a person die. Lots of people around me watched in the newsroom, but I did not go look at the tape. It was too tragic for me.

Steve Levy, Anchor and Reporter, WPVI, KYW, and WCAU:
I was anchoring the noon news that day. This happened at about 11:00 A.M., the news conference. We knew it happened, we knew that we would have to talk about it, we knew they were going to feed video down the line. I didn't trust the news director we had at the time, I didn't trust his judgment—I thought he was a doofus. I walked up to him before the show and—because I didn't trust him, I knew that they were going to be feeding this stuff down the line—and I said to him, "Listen, I want you in the control room, I want you to take a look at this video, and understand something: This is my show, these are my viewers. I don't want my viewers to see anything they shouldn't see. You make sure you cut off that video at the proper point," because with cameras rolling, he put that gun in his mouth. He blew his head off right in front of TV cameras. I said, "I don't want my viewers to see this, do you understand?" And he assured me he did. Two things about that, what they said to me in my ear: "We've got it." I still said to the viewers, "We have just gotten this video, and I have not seen it. I don't know what we are about to air, and you may not want to watch this." The news director did the right thing—as Dwyer lifted the gun to his mouth, we froze the video. *Action News* made a mistake, and they rarely made mistakes. They aired that on a snow day when kids were home. I didn't trust my news director, so I still gave a very strong disclaimer to the viewers.

Jim Sinkovitz, Anchor and Reporter, WPHL:
At some point, [Dwyer's] press secretary, Duke Horshock, reached in because he didn't hand out the final page of his press release. "I'll pass

that out later," he said. [Dwyer] started calling employees up and giving them envelopes, and as we would later find out, it was a donor card. They were basically instructions for his funeral and his family's afterlife. He pulled his .357 Magnum out, and it looked like a cannon. He held it up, and we were pinned against the table, and four of us were TV reporters, and our cameras were behind us. We weren't going anywhere, and he pulls out this cannon, and he says, "Everybody step back, I don't want to hurt anybody," but I thought at the moment he was just going to shoot us. Having already been shot once in my life in Vietnam as a Marine, the air just went out of me. It became clear that he wanted to harm himself, and some of us said, "Don't do it," and he put the gun in his mouth, and he killed himself. He shot himself, disappeared, and at about that time, I got up and walked through the back and found a phone and called my desk, and they didn't believe me at first. The hardest part about that was I had to cover that story where the Associated Press sent in reporters to replace us reporters who had witnessed it. Most of us in local TV had to go back, and we had to do the story, and we had to sit there and look at the video. We decided not to run the video of him actually placing the gun in his mouth and pulling the trigger. We stopped it with him holding the gun up in the air. I remember when [station management] said we could go to the county for psychiatric help or counseling or we could pick our own people, and I chose a friend of mine who was a counselor, and I talked to him about it one day. I had the next day off, and it had snowed really bad, and there were drifts on Front Street in Harrisburg. I just took this five-mile walk down to the capitol and back through snowdrifts just to get it out of my system.

Ned Warwick, Assignment Editor and News Director, WPVI:
It was my fault that I called for the video to run up to a certain point, and I needed to cut back by a second or two, which we did for the five o'clock show. I made the call, so I take responsibility for what happened.

Don Polec, Features Reporter, WPVI:
Everyone gathered around the monitor, watching the video come in, and there's Budd Dwyer coming into the room, and we were all looking at each other, like, "I'm not sure I wanna watch this" because we all knew what was about to happen. It was like a car wreck. You couldn't take your eyes off the screen, knowing what was coming. You're sort of, "Ah,

geez, I don't want to." I remember watching it all the way through once, and that's the only time I ever saw it. I think they just faded to black and kept the sound, you know what I mean, to hear the gunshot. The cameraman in our Harrisburg bureau, he kept the shot steady, the whole thing, and got it all and then said, "Okay, I'm going out to get drunk tonight."

Roger LaMay, General Manager and News Director, WTXF:
I can remember the intense debate about what we would put on the air. I think that was a debate that happened across newsrooms. That's one of those times when you are the news director, and you get people's input, but it's your job to make that call. Our conclusion was to show [Dwyer] raising the gun but to stop at that point. I think people made different decisions that day. You try to envision different scenarios, but that's not one that you anticipate—at least not in 1987.

Harry Martin, Weather Anchor, WPVI:
We decided to air the tape without going to black when he actually fired the weapon. As I remember, there was a lot of debate on whether we do it or whether we don't. I think the news director at the time decided it was such a catastrophic event that we should air it. We got such an incredible amount of blowback from it that we later decided that was probably not in the best interests of the public. We would then go to black when [Dwyer] fired the gun, but even that was gruesome. It was so bone-chillingly gruesome.

Paul Moriarty, Producer and Reporter, WCAU and KYW:
Our photographer actually got all of the shot. Then, he had a presence of mind to keep rolling and put the camera on the floor, and he did get underneath the desk. You could see [Dwyer] under the floor, and you could see his head. He kept rolling.

Michael Archer, Executive Producer, WCAU:
I remember being in an edit room with the news director at the time, Jay Newman, looking at it. Obviously, it was very graphic. We discussed how much of it we could use and what was appropriate. We decided actually seeing [Dwyer] pull the trigger was too graphic to put on television, whether it was during the time when kids were watching or even

during the evening newscasts. What we decided to do was take it right up to the point where he raises the gun, and we cut it there. We did not show him shooting himself, but we did show what led to that, and him talking and him sweating profusely. You could hear the reporters yelling when he pulled the gun out not to do it.

Dick Standish, Reporter, KYW:
Channel 6 decided instead that it was important or newsworthy to run the tape on their noon news. By way of background, in those days, the saying was just because you *can* show something doesn't mean you *have* to show something. I think that's long since been forgotten.

Ned Warwick, Assignment Editor and News Director, WPVI:
There were people in the newsroom that would have done exactly the right thing. We shouldn't apologize for it or change it for the early-evening newscasts. But I was convinced otherwise. There was not a question in my mind that we needed to trim what we put on the air. We proceeded to do that, but there were others who said it was the right call. It was ugly. It's about the ugliest story I've ever been involved with.

Vernon Odom, Reporter, WPVI:
I was in the room when the decision was made. It was talked about before we went on the noon news. In retrospect, I'm still not sure what I think about it. [Dwyer] was a major public official of Pennsylvania. This was no stranger to the public. I was in the room when they made the decision. Somebody said, "Why don't we go out and freeze it when he puts the gun to his mouth, and you hear the shot and hear people screaming?"

People were very angry, and they called into the station complaining. I actually had friends of mine, and I won't go into any names, complaining about it. They said, "We missed it at noon," and they said, "It's a disgrace they put that on. My daughter was scared." And then the same people said, "Can we come down to the station and see the tape ourselves?" They were condemning us on the air and then wanted to come in for a private showing.

Randy Covington, News Director, KYW:
I was in the office, and I had a group of people watching the feed coming in. One thing was quite obvious, and that is I wasn't going to put

any raw tape on television. I wasn't going to run the risk of running the raw tape and somebody forgetting to push a button. We had to make an editorial decision on what we were going to show. It had to be edited in the next fifteen minutes, roughly. I remember having a group of folks, news managers, producers. I remember our number-one anchor at the time, Steve Bell, happened to be in the newsroom. There was a debate in the newsroom. We were certainly going to edit the tape. There was no question about whether or not to put it on the noon news. It was a major story. Philadelphia is a competitive news town. What were we going to show? There was one producer that said, "PVI was going to use the shooting, you gotta use it," PVI being the long-time dominant station in Philly. Another person argued for stopping the gun when the gun went into Dwyer's mouth and freezing the picture at that point. That's what the *Philadelphia Inquirer* shows on the next day's front page. A decision had to be made. In that era, I had positioned KYW as less tabloid than PVI. PVI would show the body bag and the pool of blood on the sidewalk, and we made a conscious effort not to show those shots. There was no question in my mind there was no way that we were going to show Dwyer pulling the trigger. If PVI wanted to show it, they could. I wasn't going to. The argument for putting the gun in the mouth—I understood it intellectually, but the image is a horribly grotesque image. I remember thinking I had two young sons at the time, and it was a snow day in Philly. Kids were at home. I remember thinking to myself, "I don't want children to see that image." I made the decision that we would show a little of the news conference. We would allow him to pull the gun out of the envelope and to start the motion of bringing the gun out up to his face, but that we would stop it before he put the gun in his mouth. I let the audio, though, continue so viewers could hear the gunshot and could hear people screaming. If you look at the three stations on that noon newscasts the day it happened, PVI let him pull the trigger.

Larry Kane, Anchor, WPVI, WCAU, and KYW:
The interesting thing was it was more horrifying on the radio than it was on the television because on the radio, you heard [Dwyer] speak, and then you heard the shots. It was really something else. He gave this long speech, and people were yelling, "Budd, Budd, don't do it!" A series of events happened that day that caused a lot of problems for Philadelphia

television. Number one: It was a horrible snowstorm, so kids were home. Channel 6, I believe, showed the whole thing live 'cause no one knew what he was going to do. They quickly went off of that, but you have to check with them. This was 1987. I had just come back from Harrisburg because Governor [Bob] Casey was sworn in, and I covered it two days after that, when he shot himself. It was a horrible thing. A lot of people had to make hard choices.

It was really a case of what do you do in a situation like that? It's very few [events] that really happen in American television. There were a lot of arguments about it. We all covered it as well as we could. To me, going on the air and just hearing the sound was more frightening than anything else. Very frightening story.

Randy Covington, News Director, KYW:
We had to offer psychiatric counseling to the photographer and reporter. It was horrific for people who were in that room. I remember in the overnights that PVI had an extremely large audience that night at 11:00 P.M. My sense was, number one, it was a big news day, so people would gravitate toward the news leader, but also there is an element of the viewing population where there were probably some people who were disappointed that PVI did not show the actual shooting, but that element, I would argue, is a much smaller portion of the audience. The overwhelming reaction of the audience was negative. It's pretty unusual for a television station to take calls in largest numbers protesting something that another TV station has done.

Paul Gluck, Executive Producer and News Director, WCAU and KYW:
I was the eleven o'clock producer. What complicated matters in a hundred ways was we were in the middle of a snowstorm. I was the late-news producer for Channel 10, and I knew my opportunity to get in was through the kindness of weatherman Herb Clarke. Herb picked two or three of us up who lived along his route to the Channel 10 studio in Haverford. I lived in Ardmore. We had some colleagues who lived in Narberth. In the meantime, we got there mid-morning, and the Budd Dwyer shooting had happened in Harrisburg. What I knew about it, I only knew from KYW Newsradio. We got there, Tom Kranz, among others, Michael Archer, and Jay [Newman]. Jay called a bunch of us in his office and said, "The challenge here is this is on videotape. Do we

show it or not?" The consensus was we don't necessarily want to show the worst of it, but we've got to find a way to tell the story. Tom, who had come from radio—Tom and I went to Temple together—was news director at WRTI. Worked at WCAU radio when it was all news. Tom has this great sense of cutting sound from his radio training and natural talents with radio, so he crafted a piece where the video would go to black when the shooting happened. You heard it all. You experience it like you experience a radio show. We made sure all the video was set up in that moment. You heard the worst of it, but you didn't see it, and we moved on from there. The consensus was we need to show and tell the story somehow, and it was complicated because in Wilmington, we also need to talk about a snowstorm.

Tom Kranz, Executive Producer, WCAU:
I had to watch the video of [Dwyer] blowing himself up maybe thirty times that day, over and over again, because there was a day-long debate on how much of that moment to show. I think I ended up cutting it a number of different ways for every tease and every piece. I was the person who was cutting that video. It turns out after the fact we were actually using Channel 6's video the whole time. We actually didn't have our own video, or we didn't get it until later. We thought we had our own video, but it was actually their video we used the whole time. They didn't care at the end of the day. I think Jay Newman talked to their news director. It was one of those "the event was bigger than who got the video first." It was shocking to me, number one, that the guy was disturbed enough to actually orchestrate to do it in front of cameras, and then having to watch it over and over again really stayed with me for a couple of weeks after that. I saw the shot, and there was a tremendous amount of blood. I didn't show that moment. We chose to cut away the second he put the barrel of the gun in his mouth.

Eric Schoenfeld, Executive Producer, WPVI:
I was sitting there, writing the story, waiting for the decision. I left a spot for the video: "Okay, here is the video" with all kinds of warnings. For my worst memory of it is that I saw the video that we never saw on the air. The video that was never shown on the air, I can never get out of my head. I saw what happened after [Dwyer] put the gun in his mouth and after he pulled the trigger. It was horrifying. I'm just happy that no one

ever had to see those pictures. It was simply horrifying. That stays with me to this day.

Ed Schimmel, Executive Producer, WPVI:
Still to this day, I still think that was the proper way to handle it. We got incredible flack for this in the press and around town. I think it was undeserved. If you looked at the *Inquirer* the next morning, there was a front-page picture of [Dwyer] with the gun in his mouth. You could look at that all day if you wanted to and still could. Whereas we for a fraction of a second had no video of it and just the audio. I don't know why everyone was giving Channel 6 a hard time for that because I thought we handled it [appropriately]. If I had to do it again, I don't know if I would have the final say, but I would have made the exact same decision.

Randy Covington, News Director, KYW:
Of the three stations, we were a little more conservative. There was an enormous backlash against PVI. I don't know how many calls KYW received protesting WPVI's decision to allow [Dwyer] to pull the trigger. I would say probably KYW received one hundred calls: Many of them I took, but there were many others that were at the switchboard. People were outraged at PVI's decision to allow the image of Dwyer pulling the trigger on television.

AND FINALLY, TONIGHT

Behind-the-Scenes Stories from the Era

On Christmas Eve in 1978, two guards and a social worker were held at knifepoint for five hours by four inmates protesting for better food, medical care, court procedures, and sanitary conditions at Broadmeadows Prison in Delaware County. WCAU anchor Terry Ruggles had just completed anchoring the 11:00 P.M. newscast when a Broadmeadows Prison official called, asking for his presence in Delaware. The prisoners wanted Ruggles to serve as the peacemaker and debater to ease the tensions at the prison. Ruggles and a cameraman traveled to Broadmeadows Prison quickly after the newscast to help out. He met with the prisoners as armed police provided backup. After an exchange with Ruggles lasting about three hours, the prisoners stood down. Ruggles would receive a Pennsylvania Meritorious Citizenship Award later that year.[1]

In March 1979, then–WCAU anchor Larry Kane was on assignment in Israel, covering people's reactions to the Camp David Accords, a pair of political agreements signed by Egyptian president Anwar Sadat and Israeli prime minister Menachem Begin following negotiations that started in 1978. Kane was dispatched to gauge the reaction of Philadelphia Jews who were living in Israel at the time. During their five-day assignment overseas, Kane, producer Andrew Fisher, and cameraman Tom Watson

1. Bob Warner, "3 Hostages Freed by Delco Inmates," *Philadelphia Daily News*, December 26, 1978.

were eating at a restaurant in East Jerusalem called the Dolphin. During their meal, terrorists threw two hand grenades outside the restaurant on the sidewalk, shattering windows and damaging the building. Kane and his team were not seriously injured in the attack and later safely returned to Philadelphia.[2]

In July 1979, two members of the KYW-TV camera crew were killed when a helicopter they were riding in crashed and sank into the Schuylkill River near the Spring Garden Street Bridge in Philadelphia. Video technician Bill Loomer and KYW cameraman Daniel Preuhs were killed on their way to film the American Cancer Society Jog-a-Thon along the Schuylkill River. Larry Belhumeur, the pilot of the chartered craft, escaped from the wreckage and was rescued by police, firefighters, and spectators. Several people jumped into the river to help keep Belhumeur afloat until rope could be lowered for safety. He was then taken to Jefferson Hospital for multiple spinal fractures. Loomer's and Preuh's bodies were recovered three hours after the chartered copter sank into thirty feet of muddy river water. The helicopter was flying from Eakins Oval to the finish line of the race on West River Drive. Investigators from the National Transportation Safety Board and the Federal Aviation Administration examined the wreckage to determine what had caused the motor to stop running while operating.[3] Authorities later determined that a power failure was the cause of the crash.[4]

In November 1980, three employees of WPHL-TV resigned over allegations they scalped Philadelphia Phillies World Series tickets. The tickets were sold to WPHL, which was a television partner at the time with the Phillies, at face value for the three home games in the World Series against the Kansas City Royals. Philadelphia Phillies executive vice president Bill Giles said that the WPHL contract to broadcast Phillies games contained a clause granting the station the option to purchase seven hundred tickets for every home game, including the three World Series games, for a

2. Mike Freeman, "Terror Blasts Peril TV Newman," *Philadelphia Daily News*, March 26, 1979.

3. Philp Weiss, "KYW Copter Tragedy: Dead Technician Always Watched Out for Others," *Philadelphia Daily News*, July 16, 1979.

4. Tom Schmidt, "Heroine Routed 3 Muggers," *Philadelphia Daily News*, August 23, 1979.

total of 2,100 tickets. It was not known how many tickets were scalped or for what price.[5]

Also occurring in November 1980 was one of Philadelphia television's most infamous on-camera moments. Former Philadelphia mayor Frank Rizzo had retired to his home in Chestnut Hill, Pennsylvania, where he was involved in two separate incidents with KYW: one in which he damaged KYW photographer Greg Meyer's camera equipment and another in which he challenged KYW reporter Stan Bohrman to a fistfight. KYW reporters in a private, unmarked vehicle with tinted windows were investigating the sizable amount of personal security Rizzo had retained since leaving public office. The investigation was an exclusive story reported by KYW's "I-Team."

Rizzo, accompanied by several police officers, approached Meyer and asked him to identify himself. Even though he was not the mayor of Philadelphia anymore, Rizzo still used the Philadelphia Police Department as home security. After looking at Meyer's press card, Rizzo said, "Take that thing out. Unhook it, or I'll throw it in the middle of the goddamn street. You turn that off."

Rizzo was seen on camera hitting the equipment, scuffling was heard, and KYW's footage went to black as the camera was destroyed. A week later, a second incident occurred when KYW reporter Bohrman approached Rizzo for an on-the-spot interview as the former mayor was walking his dog outside his home.

"I'm busy," Rizzo replied. "I wouldn't talk to you under any condition." He then asked Bohrman to get away from him as the conversation got heated.

Rizzo continued to get physical and grabbed the microphone from Bohrman's hand. Rizzo then said he would get physical with everyone who was with the KYW news team that day.

"I want to fight ya. You're a crumb, a creap, lush, coward. You are a lush. I can tell by looking at ya. I was a cop all my life, and I know a lush when I see one, and you are a lush. You are gonna have a hell of a story on that one. Play every word of it, crumb," Rizzo stated.

KYW reported that Rizzo used night police officers as security at his home for nine months, at a cost to the city of $250,000. After the inci-

5. "3 Alleged Scalpers Quit TV-17," *Philadelphia Daily News*, November 13, 1980.

dents, the police officers were pulled from Rizzo's house. KYW aired the entire confrontation on its newscast in an investigative feature lasting seven minutes and thirty seconds.[6]

In March 1982, Philadelphia mayor William Green III sued CBS and five employees of WCAU-TV for a total of $5.1 million after the station reported that Green was the target of a federal probe into what some described as a kickback scheme. WCAU said in a news story that Green had received $50,000 in kickbacks for awarding a $7 million sewage-removal contract in May 1980 to Modern Earthline Companies of Philadelphia. WCAU also reported that the same firm had received a city contract totaling $24.7 million. Green's five-count suit alleged that WCAU aired that news story on its *Live at 5* newscast and repeated the story four times before retracting it. The station issued a formal retraction and an apology after the FBI and the U.S. attorney's office said that Green was not the subject of an investigation. The defendants named in the suit were anchor Larry Kane, reporters Francis X. Geary and Bill Baldini, news director Thomas Dolan, and general manager Jay Feldman. Mayor Green demanded a jury trial, seeking $20,000 in compensatory damages and $1 million in punitive damages from the defendants for each of the five counts arising from the broadcasts of the story. Green said that the repeated report was "utterly false" and "defamatory" to his honesty and integrity.

In response to the suit, WCAU said publicly, "Although we appreciate Mayor Green's strong feelings regarding our mistaken report, we regret his decision to pursue this matter through litigation." Station management also pointed out that they believed the report to be true when broadcast. WCAU admitted that the station had mistakenly cited Green but added that its reporters stood by the portion of the story that said there was a probe of a sludge-removal contract with the City of Philadelphia.[7]

---

6. Frederick Cusick, "Incident at Rizzo Home Spurs KYW Complaint," *Philadelphia Inquirer*, November 19, 1980; "Rizzo Causes Row over TV Coverage," *Tyrone Daily Herald*, November 20, 1980; Ken Lockerby, "Rizzo, TV Crew Go Eye-to-I," *Philadelphia Daily News*, November 19, 1980; Greg Walter, "Baiting the Bear Proved One Point," *Philadelphia Daily News*, November 21, 1980.

7. Roger Cohn and George Anastasia, "Channel 10 Retracts Its Report, but Green Says He Isn't Satisfied," *Philadelphia Inquirer*, March 27, 1982; Mark Manoff, "Green Files $5M Libel Suit against CBS," *Philadelphia Daily News*, March 31, 1982; Kit Konolige and Kathy

In May 1982, Rob Luck, KYW-TV sports director, was suspended for two weeks pending the outcome of investigations by federal authorities and the station into allegations of a payola scheme involving Atlantic City hotel casinos. The *Philadelphia Inquirer* reported that Luck was receiving bribes from Atlantic City hotel casinos in exchange for plugs on the news about upcoming events. Luck would later submit his resignation letter to KYW station vice president and general manager Pat Polillo.

"I have never sought or received anything of value in return for television coverage and I am confident that I have always acted within the confines of the laws which regulate me and the station," the *Philadelphia Inquirer* reprinted from Luck's resignation letter.

Luck worked at KYW for a few months in late 1974 and early 1975. In a letter to Polillo, he stated that "the allegations that I have broken the law are untrue." A federal investigation produced no charges. Luck found new life in 1984 at WCPX-TV in Orlando, Florida.[8]

In October 1983, KYW reporter and anchor Jessica Savitch drowned when a car she was riding in plunged into the Delaware Canal in New Hope, Bucks County. Savitch was driving with Martin Fischbein, vice president and assistant general manager of the *New York Post*. According to the *Philadelphia Inquirer*, the two were dating and were on a weekend outing away from their homes in New York. Their car was discovered upside down and partly submerged in a lock of the canal.

"She was a hometown girl. Philadelphia's own daughter. This is quite a great loss," Pat Polillo, vice president and general manager of KYW, told the *Lancaster New Era* in 1983.

According to authorities, the front windshield was broken, and the rear window was rolled down, signs of the two struggling to break out of the vehicle. Savitch was just thirty-five years old.

In 1972, Savitch had joined KYW-TV as a general assignment reporter and weekend anchor. Savitch grew up in rural Kennett Square, Chester County. Savitch would stay in Philadelphia for five years as her

---

Sheehan, "Outraged Green: 'False, Malicious,'" *Philadelphia Daily News*, March 26, 1982; Gary Ronbery and W. Speers, "At Channel 10, Retraction, Short-Lived Party," *Philadelphia Inquirer*, March 27, 1982.

8. Bill Collins, "Channel 3's Rod Luck Resigns with Letter Denying Wrongdoing," *Philadelphia Inquirer*, May 29, 1982; "KYW Suspends Sportscaster Pending Probe," *Philadelphia Inquirer*, May 18, 1982.

popularity grew; she was perhaps Philadelphia's most popular female anchor before she joined NBC's national network broadcast in 1977. At NBC, Savitch delivered the one-minute prime-time news updates during the week and was featured on Saturday's edition of *NBC Nightly News*.

On October 3, 1983, during a live NBC news update, Savitch became incoherent on the air, slurring her speech and ad-libbing her reports. While some in the media speculated that she was using drugs prior to the newscast, Savitch would later blame her mishap on troubles with the teleprompter.[9]

---

9. Tom Jory, "Jessica Savitch Killed in Accident," *York Daily Record*, October 25, 1983; Associated Press, "Savitch, Man Trapped by River's Mud," *Intelligencer Journal*, October 25, 1983; "Jessica Savitch, Rough Seas on Voyage to Become an Anchor," *Philadelphia Daily News*, October 26, 1983; Associated Press, "TV's Jessica Savitch, Friend Drown in Bucks Canal," *Lancaster New Era*, October 24, 1983; Paul Horcitz, John Hilferty, and Matthew Purdy, "Jessica Savitch Drowns in Canal," *Philadelphia Inquirer*, October 25, 1983.

PART II

Rise of the Mass-Media Era

FIRE AT ONE MERIDIAN PLAZA

On February 23, 1991, a twelve-alarm fire struck One Meridian Plaza, a thirty-eight-story high-rise office building located across the street from city hall in the Center City neighborhood of Philadelphia. The fire blazed from the twenty-second to the twenty-ninth floor, resulting in the deaths of three Philadelphia firefighters from Engine No. 11 in South Philadelphia. Captain David Holcombe, fifty-one, who had been a firefighter for twenty-eight years; Phyllis McAllister, forty-three, a ten-year vet; and James Chappell, twenty-nine, who had been married just two months before the fire and whose wife was expecting their first child, all perished. The fire also sent more than ten other firefighters to the hospital for related injuries. The building burned for nineteen hours, starting on Saturday at 8:30 P.M. *and ending at 3:00* P.M. *the following day. Philadelphia Fire Department officials reported that the building's fire-prevention systems failed to function, including the building's emergency electrical system, backup emergency electrical systems, emergency lights, backup emergency lights, internal fire pumps, and internal water pressure. Officials stated at the time that if those prevention systems had worked properly, the fire could have been put out. The building would remain vacant for years following the blaze, as structural engineers declared it unsafe due to fears that all eight floors that had burned would collapse. The building was demolished in 1999.*

That same night of February 23, 1991, U.S. troops and coalition forces moved into occupied Kuwait, beginning the ground portion of the Gulf War.

Jim Gardner, Anchor, WPVI:
It was like, "What do we do here? We've got two extraordinary stories happening at the same time." Someone had to make the decision which was number one and which was number two. We are a local television station, and we were losing firefighters across the street from city hall. That became number one, but it was one of those nights that I remember pretty vividly, that the energy was just extraordinary, and work was extraordinary, and we did a good job. I don't know if there has been another situation during my time where two enormous stories were synched up like that and broke at exactly the same time. You had to make choices, and you also were spread pretty thin.

Robin Mackintosh, Reporter, KYW:
I turned on the TV, and I am watching this fire. I am saying to myself, "What am I doing standing here? I need to get to work." I wasn't scheduled to go to work, but I drove into town and stood there and watched the thing burning. They had just lost two of the guys. [The station] ended up sending me over to the firehouse where these guys were out of, and I interviewed some of [the firefighters] who were hanging black bunting over the doors of the firehouse.

Harvey Clark, Reporter, WCAU:
I shot up there, and we got across the street at the municipal building over there. When I got there, it looked like fire was coming out of one office. Way up out of this one set of windows, smoke was billowing out.

Lu Ann Cahn, Investigative Reporter and Anchor, WCAU:
I remember I found my way up into one of the buildings next to the clothespin [sculpture]. I got into one of those buildings as the fire was raging. I got up into an elevator, and I got up into the offices, and I looked straight out across from that building to the fire. I was at the same level. It was a terrifying night. It's hard to believe that it was a

building right across from city hall that could go like that and change the landscape of that area. I remember I stayed out there all night and into the morning.

Rich Noonan, Anchor and Reporter, WTXF:

I was coming down the expressway late, maybe eleven o'clock or whenever the fire was burning. I saw the fire and went right to the scene. I forget if someone called me or not. I don't even know if I had a cell phone in those days. That fire was just incredible. People may not realize how incredibly devastating that fire was. I had covered literally hundreds of fires. Even at that young time in my life, I had covered lots of fires. When you are small-market television, you cover lots of fires. Just seeing that fire burning in a high-rise like that and just watching the firefighters do anything they could to try and get to it was just incredible.

John Mussoni, Executive Producer and News Director, WCAU and WTXF:

We considered ourselves very much "The Little Engine That Could" of these operations. We were scrappy. People respected what we did. I think on some level, we weren't always taken as seriously as the other operations because we hadn't been around for that long, in addition to the fact that we were able to mobilize. Practically everybody on staff was called in. Photography was to go to different staging areas and try to get the best angles for shots. It also became a technical logistical nightmare because as you're setting up a new operation, you don't always have all the bells and whistles that [Channels] 3, 6, and 10 did, and one of the things that we did not have was the ability to do a live shot from city hall. We had a microwave truck, and everybody could get their signal to the transmitter at Roxborough, but stations who wanted to do that remote from Center City had to have another antenna in Center City. It became one of those things where we had a portable microwave—and this is how bizarre but how clever we could be in terms of getting on the air—we had a portable microwave that one of the engineers had to hold out the window of our newsroom at 4th and Market so the truck could transmit back to the transmitter. You know how microwaves work in a line of sight? You had to hit it right on the nose, but that gave us the technical ability to broadcast from the scene.

David Henry, Reporter, WPVI:
You stand on that plaza outside of city hall, looking at the building—it was a such a prominent landmark. You see nothing but black windows surrounded by fire equipment, wondering if the city will ever recover from something like that. For many years afterward, that building remained boarded up. It was an incredible eyesore before they finally tore it down and replaced it. Standing there, you are always struck by the loss of life and wondering how, in this modern day and age, a building of that size would not be equipped with standpipes and wondering what kind of a city would allow something like that to be built as unsafe as it was. Of course, over the controversy with the standpipes and everything else that followed long after, it led to most of the buildings in downtown Philadelphia being retrofitted with sprinkler systems and standpipes and everything else. It was amazing that it was a fairly modern skyscraper inadequately equipped to handle a high-rise fire. I think that negligence directly cost the lives of those three firefighters. It was a tough blow for the city and I think something that we learned a lot from.

Terry Ruggles, Reporter and Anchor, WCAU:
Because of my connection with the [Fireman's Hall Museum], I have always had an in with fire commissioners, and Roger Ulshafer was the commissioner at that time. We got to go up into the fire scene afterward, and that had to be shared as a [press] pool, but we got to go up and see. The theory on [the fire] was that it started with linseed oil or some flammable materials that combusted. I actually tried to do that as a show-and-tell, and sure enough, my stuff in the heat and sunshine did combust. You use a piece of cotton and put that linseed oil on it, and it starts.

Lu Ann Cahn, Investigative Reporter and Anchor, WCAU:
Many things changed in terms of high-rises, building high-rises as a result of that fire and safety regulations. I also think in terms of the way firemen approached it as well. It was tragic and a terrible night.

Rich Noonan, Anchor and Reporter, WTXF:
We got a high-rise burning to the ground, firemen being killed, and we are going to war. That night was an all-night affair, of course. It was just live on the air the whole night. It was just incredible. It was one heck of a news night.

CHANNELS 3 AND 10 SWITCH NETWORKS

In September 1995, KYW 3 and WCAU 10 switched networks, with KYW joining CBS and WCAU joining NBC. Until that point, WCAU had been affiliated with CBS since 1948, and KYW had been affiliated with NBC since its inception in 1949.

The WCAU and KYW swap came to fruition from a deal in July 1994, when the Westinghouse Broadcasting Company, which owned KYW, agreed that its five stations across the country would become affiliated with CBS. The four other Westinghouse Broadcasting Company stations were in Baltimore, Pittsburgh, San Francisco, and Boston.

At 1:00 A.M. on September 10, 1995, KYW-TV and WCAU-TV officially swapped network affiliations.

WCAU produced a special-edition late show featuring anchors Ken Matz and Renée Chenault-Fattah.

"We are proud as a peacock that you tuned us in," Matz said on the air.

NBC10's Siani Lee was outside the studio, kicking off a historical moment for the station, unveiling the new signage of NBC10 WCAU outside its City Avenue studios in Bala Cynwyd, Pennsylvania. Longtime WCAU reporter Herb Denenberg and another employee helped raise the new NBC10 flag live on the air. The live report also featured SEPTA buses wrapped in Friends *and* Seinfeld *promotions, displaying the new time slots for the hottest shows on television. The show continued to push promotions, stating that "News 10 Is Everywhere." Hours later, NBC10 kicked off its morning show with the announcement of the "big switch" and even showcased a graphic that read "Change is good."*

WCAU introduced a new morning show from 5:30 to 7:00 A.M. with Steve Levy and Connie Colla. Channel 10 also expanded its noon newscasts by a half hour, featuring Siani Lee and Tim Lake.

Channel 3 launched new programming at 5:30 A.M. with News 3 This Morning *with Pat Ciarrocchi and Brandon Brooks,* KYW News 3 at Noon, *6:00 P.M. newscast* KYW News 3 *with Stephanie Stahl and Don Cannon, and an 11 P.M. newscast with Larry Kane. On KYW, a promo aired with Larry Kane, David Letterman, and Candice Bergen. Another promo followed, with the announcer saying, "KYW 3 is now your CBS station."*

Two thousand people called KYW's toll-free phone line with concerns about where to watch their favorite soap operas.

"I put Channel 10 on today," a viewer told the Philadelphia Inquirer *in 1995. "I knew the U.S. Open tennis final was on. Yesterday, it was on 10, so maybe today it is on 3? But yesterday it was on 10."*

WCAU opened its phone lines on September 5, 1995, and got more than eight thousand phone calls in just four days. The two numbers for viewers to call about the change were 800-KYW-IS-CBS and 800-WCAU-TEN. The Associated Press reported that KYW spent $1.5 million on its new phone-calling system campaign, hiring more than one hundred operators to talk to current and new station watchers. WCAU's toll-free line also included a taped message from then–late night host Jay Leno.

Popular shows Another World, Days of Our Lives, Today, *and* Dateline NBC *moved to Channel 10, while* As the World Turns, The Price Is Right, *the* CBS Tuesday Movie, *and* The Late Show with David Letterman *moved to Channel 3.*

"I'm on Channel 3, and I'm not wearing pants," Letterman said in the KYW promo. In a separate promo, he told viewers, "Spell Ciarrocchi *and win a KYW tote bag."*

Although many local observers speculated that WCAU initiated the move strategically to broadcast NBC's primetime lineup, it was the natural result of KYW parent Westinghouse's new CBS affiliation, leaving WCAU available for a new affiliation. Even with the new powerhouse primetime lineup now being featured on WCAU, Channel 10 took only a baby step forward in the 11 P.M. news race, and KYW stayed about even in the ratings. WPVI continued its ratings dominance before and after the affiliate switch.

Amy Caples, Anchor and Reporter, KYW:
The last show was *Saturday Night Live* when we were still NBC. When we went on the air that Sunday morning, all of a sudden we were CBS. The context of this was [NBC's primetime lineup,] "Must-See TV." NBC had all of the shows. CBS evening programming was terrible. We were building all of this momentum and then—boom—you pull the rug out. If your eleven o'clock is not popping, nothing else is popping. This is back in the day; if you went to bed watching Channel 3, that's the channel that you turned on in the morning. Habits were so different then. They had Thursday Night TV. NBC was unbeatable in the mid-nineties. We show up that Sunday morning, and Channel 10 at that time had started a new morning show and—my god, the promos. They had planned ahead to win because they knew that they were getting NBC's programming. It was like a party at NBC. For us, we did a phone call saying, "Hey, I think we have CBS coffee mugs—can you put them on the set?" That was literally all we did. CBS had nothing at the time.

Larry Kane, Anchor, WPVI, WCAU, and KYW:
It was kind of strange. I began anchoring there [at KYW] in early 1994. I was doing *The Bulletin Show*, which was a great *60 Minutes* type of show we did over at Channel 3. It was upsetting to me because [before the switch,] NBC had allowed us to go into primetime. We weren't an NBC-owned station; we were owned by Westinghouse. As a result, they had to make an affiliate switch. When the station switched over to CBS, then Channel 10 became the beneficiary of all of that great NBC programing. It didn't change my life, except I was back with CBS management again.

Marcellus Alexander, Vice President and General Manager, KYW:
Any time you have an affiliation change after a number of years being associated along with one network, it's difficult for viewers to make that transition. That difficulty is enhanced when you consider that sometimes, there is obviously network programming that goes with a network, but then there is syndicated programming that varies across sta-

tions and some markets. It's not a complete transition of all CBS from NBC programming that viewers are accustomed to. They see parts of it, but not all of it. Some syndicated. Some network. Some local news, of course, is all a part of that chain. It's really confusing for viewers to know to make those kinds of changes. At the end of the day, it is the local news that really does help to define what a station's presence is in a market. That local news is what we focused on, as did the other stations.

Ukee Washington, Anchor, KYW:
My main concern, and it lasted for years, was how the viewing audience would respond to the change. To this day, when I run into some of the "veteran" viewers, they still think we are NBC. It took a while, but "all is good in the neighborhood" now, as the old saying goes!

Tom Lamaine, Sports and Weather Anchor, KYW:
Total confusion with the viewer. The viewers didn't know one way or the other. They thought, "Aren't you CBS? How did you become CBS?" "No, we were NBC." "Wait a minute—how did you become CBS?" "Well, we bought the company." It was Westinghouse at the time, and Westinghouse purchased CBS, so obviously Channel 3 had to become CBS, so that left Channel 10, which had been CBS, without a network. Channel 10 picked up NBC. To this day, people still say, "Aren't you still with NBC?"

Paul Moriarty, Producer and Reporter, WCAU and KYW:
It's not something that people get over in a month or two. People were very confused, no matter how much you tried to explain it to them; they didn't know what was going on. It's hard to get people out of patterns. Internally for me, it didn't mean anything.

Dawn Stensland-Mendte, Anchor and Reporter, KYW and WTXF:
I remember viewers would say, "What? Why would they do that?" I would say, "I have no idea. It was a business decision."

Pat Ciarrocchi, Anchor and Reporter, KYW:
I think it was a big deal, probably more for advertising than it was for us on air. People would say to me, "Did you guys move to City Avenue?" I said no. I said to people, "Imagine it's just like this. There is a gigantic plug that says 'CBS' and a giant plug that says 'NBC.' You unplug it out

of each one of the receptacles, and you plug it into the opposite receptacle." That's what it was really like for us.

John Bolaris, Meteorologist, WCAU and WTXF:
Back then, I tell you, everyone was scared shitless. I wasn't because I kind of felt okay, and it didn't matter to me. It really didn't. I felt fine and secure, but everyone else who had been around a long time were wondering what was gonna go on. People were really nervous and beside themselves. I don't blame them. It's their careers and jobs. There was gonna be a complete changeover during a certain time of a certain day. Then, all of a sudden, CAU becomes NBC. You gotta remember: All of the signage was waiting. Let's put it this way. As soon as the change was made, it was nuts.

Cherie Bank, Health Reporter and Anchor, WCAU:
We didn't know who would buy us, if anybody, or if we would have any job. We didn't have any job security. You could have a contract with a company, but if the company is no longer there, you are out. We were really upset because we thought if anyone, it would be Fox [that would have purchased us]. [Fox] was not our first choice. We were all upset about it. WCAU had to start taking the CBS logo off of everything, so they can only have, like, cups and T-shirts and things that said "CAU." You couldn't say "CBS." It was sad.

Bill Henley, Meteorologist, WCAU:
[Viewers] were confused because, you know, Dan Rather started showing up on Channel 3, and Tom Brokow started working at Channel 10. It took people a long time to get somewhat comfortable with it. If you talk to some older people, they probably still are a little bit confused by it. For the people working at the station, we knew that we no longer were going to be CBS, but we didn't know who was going to pick us up. We could have gone to Fox, and the other possibility was NBC. For a long time, we didn't know. People were hopeful it would be NBC, to be honest, because Fox at that time was still unknown as a network. It was kind of in its infancy. Nobody knew how it was going to turn out.

Vai Sikahema, Sports Reporter and Anchor, WCAU:
In the interim, the year or year and a half that we were waiting for the approvals from the various governmental agencies, we sorta shifted

and we downplayed our CBS credentials, but we couldn't say that we were about to become NBC. So, there's a year of time when our mic flags—I don't think it had either the CBS eye or—we just became a generic brand. The brand was News Center 10—sort of a "man without a country" kind of thing. It was strange to all of us. Nobody had gone through anything like this. We were excited because, while we were leaving the Tiffany Network, which had a lot of gravitas, we were also assuming the NBC brand, which dominated at the time with *Seinfeld*, *ER*, *Friends*. The Thursday-night lineup created the "Must-See TV" jargon. It became a part of the TV lexicon, but our Thursday-night lineup was such a powerhouse. We were excited for that. We were excited that they were spending money on us and sending us on trips.

Larry Mendte, Anchor, WCAU and KYW:
We branded ourselves really well. The programming was so good. If you remember that, you had "Must-See TV" on NBC. People easily found it, and they were searching for it. It's not like it hurt us in the least, and people quickly figured out that we were NBC more than anything else because of the programming. We had *Friends*, *ER*, *Seinfeld*—it never really affected us, and we never felt it.

Lu Ann Cahn, Investigative Reporter and Anchor, WCAU:
People were going to watch us again, was the way we felt. Remember, this was before the Internet and everything. Our lead-ins to our newscasts, especially at night at eleven, were so incredibly important to people staying and watching us. Before, we had nothing. CBS was giving us nothing, and we felt we were dead in the water. Then, NBC is coming in, and we were like, "Yay: life, money, and resources!"

Kathy Gerrow, Producer, Writer, and Assistant News Director, KYW and WCAU:
In my mind, that's when the race between NBC10 and *Action News* really began. Before then, neither 3 nor 10 had much of a chance against *Action News*. I remember during that time, there were plenty of ratings books when you could add the ratings of Channels 3 and 10 together and you wouldn't top Channel 6.

Paul Perrello, Host, the Comcast Network and WPHL:
We're talking about the people that grew up in the era, you know, the baby boomers, they grew up with television. They were indoctrinated to know [Channels] 3, 6, and 10. They knew the people on 3, 6, and 10. And all of a sudden, they started rearranging the deck chairs, and the only consistency was Channel 6.

Dann Cuellar, Reporter, WPVI:
We thought, "Wow, that's going to confuse a lot of people," because they are going to be looking for their shows, and they are not going to find them on the channel they were accustomed to. They are going to have to figure out what happened, and maybe not everyone is keeping up with the news. That's going to cause chaos in the market, and wow, did it ever. I remember one time, it was during our five o'clock broadcast, that we lost our signal or something happened in the studio. The only thing we had was color bars on air. Color bars beat the ratings of [Channels] 3 and 10 combined. There were more people watching color bars on our station than watching 3 or 10. That just blew us away. Let that speak for itself.

Connie Colla, Anchor and Reporter,
WCAU and the Comcast Network:
I think it's always exciting when there is change. WPVI, you could run color bars, and they would still get a 40 share. It was time for a little bit of a shake-up in the market. For there to be competition and a little more opportunity for better content from all of the other stations combined, I thought it was exciting and fun.

Carl Cherkin, Sports Director, WTXF:
It was confusing. Forget it as a competitor. You see the uncertainty and people not understanding what was going on. As a viewer, I never knew what to tune into for, what, for a couple of years. Maybe I'm not the brightest bulb in the chandelier either.

I'm an outlier when it comes to this. I love change. I believe change is good. If you embrace change, you get to a whole other place as a result. Most people don't like it. Most people don't like change at all.

Rich Noonan, Anchor and Reporter, WTXF:
I thought it would help the stability of the ten o'clock news. Any of that confusion was good for us because everyone knew that there was only one station on at ten o'clock, and that was us. We chuckled at it, laughed, and hoped that viewers were really confused because we looked at them as competitors, even though they really weren't at the time slot.

THE BLIZZARD OF 1996

On January 7–8, 1996, Philadelphia was hit with more than thirty inches of snow during a severe nor'easter that would later be named the "Blizzard of 1996." The official observation station at the Philadelphia International Airport recorded 30.7 inches of snowfall, which was a record-breaking storm in the area. Within twenty-four hours, 26.6 inches of snow fell, which is a city record to this day. The School District of Philadelphia was closed for about a week as city workers attempted to move huge amounts of snow off the street. The high amount of snow in the city forced officials to dump it into the Delaware and Schuylkill Rivers. Philadelphia was not the only city with huge snow totals on the East Coast, as New York City, Baltimore, and Washington, D.C., were also hit.

During the blizzard, all Philadelphia television stations offered coverage. WPVI offered nonstop coverage the day leading up to the storm from 6:30 A.M. until 7:00 P.M., with a rating of 27.5 and a 37 share. WPVI's 6:00 P.M. news scored a rating of 31.7 and a 40 share. The day of the storm, WPVI also offered continuous coverage from 5:00 A.M. until 1:00 P.M. On Channel 6's broadcast, a man who identified himself as a Pennsylvania Department of Transportation spokesman announced that one of the region's main highways had been closed; the "spokesman" caller was actually a Howard Stern fan on a prank phone call. WCAU's coverage was continuous from 6:00 A.M. until 11:00 A.M., with afternoon cut-ins every half hour and a special report during the Eagles-Cowboys game in Dallas, Texas. WCAU averaged a rating of 19.9 and a 25 share. The following day, the station began coverage from 5:00 A.M. until 2:00 P.M. WCAU was referring to the blizzard as the "Storm of the Century," a term that it would notoriously recycle for a different storm in 2001.

KYW was continuously on air from 6:30 A.M. until noon on the Sunday the storm hit, and then 5:00 A.M. to 11:00 A.M. the following day. WTXF aired the Eagles-Cowboys game on Sunday, accounting for the majority of its ratings and time. The station added a special at 6:30 P.M., and its 10:00 P.M. newscast went on for seventy-five minutes to cover the storm.

Elliot Abrams, Senior Vice President, AccuWeather:
The European model had predicted [the storm] very well many days in advance. Everything was right for it. It was extremely cold going into it. We had a large storm that came up the coast and gathered lots of moisture. The snow was thick and heavy. It had car-capturing, bus-blocking, SUV-stalling drifts.

Cecily Tynan, Meteorologist, WPVI:
Every day we got closer to the event, it looked bigger, and the [projected] snow totals went up. We always play things a little bit conservative because you hate to forecast a foot of snow and then get two inches. I remember the day before, I think we just went one to two feet, which was very unusual for our weather map.

Amy Caples, Anchor and Reporter, KYW:
I said goodbye to my husband and my kids. My work said, "Get in whenever you can." I left my house with clothes for days. You just stay at a hotel and work and work and work. We were on for seven and a half hours that day with Brandon Brooks and I. We went on at whatever time, and it wasn't until Pat Ciarrocchi came on for the noon [broadcast] that we went off the air.

Rob Guarino, Chief Meteorologist, WTXF:
I decided to go back to Delaware to visit my parents in Wilmington. I got on the plane in [Indianapolis], and it was connecting to Detroit. In Detroit on that connection, I ran into the Fox Sports [WTXF] people. I

didn't know them personally, but it was the weekend sports crew. They were delayed three days getting back because of the Blizzard of 1996. They had been covering the Eagles-Dallas game in Dallas. So because they were delayed three days for the blizzard, they happened to be at the airport where I was at the same time. The story is, I went over to the photographer and said, "I'm from Philly. I watch you guys all of the time. I grew up in Philly." One of the members of the crew said, "Listen, I heard internally that there is a weekend weather position opening up in Philly," and it wasn't announced yet. It was small talk about it opening up. Well, the next day, I called the news director in Philly, John Mussoni, and said, "Hey, I'm from Philly. I'm in town, and I have one out on my contract." Out of the whole country, to give me one city was Philadelphia [meaning that the only city he could work for under his contract at the time was Philadelphia, so if Philly offered him a gig, he could take it and not have to pay out his contract].

Just as I was getting married, and I heard I got the job in Philadelphia on my honeymoon in Hawaii when they called me. Long story is, if the blizzard doesn't hit, I never meet [that crew,] and I would have never known about that weather opening.

Steve Doerr, Executive Producer and News Director, WCAU:
Covering a blizzard in the nineties in Philadelphia was sort of a big deal and required a lot of resources, and it was expensive. CBS, back in those days, was sort of tight with a nickel, but NBC came in and threw down. They said, "Go all out! Do what you need to do." About halfway through the second day of coverage, we couldn't move. I had four-wheel drive, and I lived in Lower Merion, so I could get back and forth to the station. We had people sleeping on the floor, we had people sleeping at the Adams Mark Hotel. The second day, we saw an SUV pull into the parking lot, and it was our new general manager and our new creative services director. They brought food, and it was like Santa Claus arriving. People hadn't eaten in a couple of days.

John Bolaris, Meteorologist, WCAU and WTXF:
I'm on the beach [in Mexico]. I get a call from my news director, Steve Doerr. I'm looking at some of the stuff, and I'm always checking things or getting hints of what is going on. I wasn't paying attention because, finally, I'm away. He goes, "What are you doing right now?" I said,

"Well, Steve, I'm drinking a Corona on the beach." He goes, "How quickly can you get back here?" I told him, "I will start packing now." I turn to my friend, and he goes, "What, are you out of your mind? Why are you going back? There's other people to do it." I said, "I can't miss this storm."

I'm pulling up, and Steve Doerr was waiting for me and sees me and says, "What took ya!" They had a suit and tie for me and a suit-jacket top I always had at the station. I sat down, and I never left that seat for thirty-six hours.

Glenn Schwartz, Meteorologist, WCAU:

Since it was just the two of us—it was me for the morning shows and Herb Clarke for the late afternoon and evening—I volunteered to overlap some. I would come in at four in the morning to get ready and do the morning broadcast and then stay up until 6:00 or 6:30 sometimes so that I could be on with Herb and help him out since he was not a meteorologist and just used the National Weather Service forecasts. That was a long, long week, but for meteorologists, that's the Super Bowl, if you see it coming. It's easy to work sixteen or eighteen hours in a day when you have something like that coming.

Mike Strug, Reporter, WPVI, KYW, and WCAU:

You could take off any other day of the year, but if it snowed, you damn well better get to work.

Bill Baldini, Reporter, WCAU:

I always hated doing weather. When the weather is bad, the weather people who get paid to do the weather are always inside. The reporters are always outside. They are not weather people. I used to say in the office all of the time, "Why aren't the weather people out there?" Which would really piss them all off. I did what I had to do. It always amazes me—we have incredible ratings during weather when we are telling people what they know by looking out the window. Do I really have to tell you that it's snowing out there?

Kristen Sze, Reporter, WPVI:

Live shots were twelve hours straight in the cold, but then remembering all the cool people that watched *Action News* and would see me out in a certain location, and they'd bring hot chocolate, bring pasta or pizza, because they saw that we were out there freezing our butts off and reporting on what was happening.

David Murphy, Meteorologist, WPVI:
In the middle of reports, here comes a guy who is in a private vehicle. He's not supposed to be there, as I could tell. So, I'm live on the air and saying, "They are really telling people to stay off the roads." I turn around, and here's a guy who necessarily shouldn't be here, and he's having trouble driving though here. The guy stops, and he gets out of the car with about six pizzas, and it turns out he's a local delivery guy from a pizza shop down the road who saw us on the air and said, "Those guys look hungry." So, I got pizza delivered to me live on the air.

Susan Buehler, Reporter, WTXF:
There was literally nothing open. I remember there was a family that lived in Plymouth Meeting that felt so sorry for us after a while because we were outside in the freezing cold, and there was literally not even a Wawa or gas station open. They brought us spaghetti and meatballs after an early-evening live shot, which was incredible. So, we did get some warm food in the live truck, but it was an incredible storm. It was such a storm that the *Inquirer* and the *Daily News* weren't even able to deliver the newspapers, so I ended up somehow getting a copy somewhere and showing the headlines and showing the coverage that most people never even saw in the newspaper.

Janet Zappala, Anchor and Reporter, WCAU and WTXF:
I think I was in Wayne, and I had a four-wheel drive, and I could not get out, so the Police Department had to come and get me and take me to the station. I'll never forget, I saw Tim Lake, so Tim and I were anchoring that morning, and he comes running out of the station, like, "You gotta get inside now! No script! Just get on the anchor desk! We gotta start!" So, luckily I got there in time, and we just went on the air live and started covering it from there.

Flora Posteraro, Reporter, WPVI:
I remember getting on the [Pennsylvania] Turnpike and thinking to myself, "I am probably going to die tonight," because they literally had one

small lane plowed on the turnpike. The snow was piled up on both sides, and it was higher than the news van. I was never so terrified in my life. That should have been maybe a two-hour drive to get back to Harrisburg, but it took me four to five hours because I was driving so slowly, and it was dark. It was like driving through a tunnel of snow. That was just unbelievable. When I finally got back to Harrisburg, I couldn't even get back to my house because they did not plow my neighborhood.

Rich Noonan, Anchor and Reporter, WTXF:
I lived in Pier 3 at Penn's Landing. I was single at the time, and I could walk to work. I was a young, aggressive guy trying to make my name. I got up really early, and I walked up the steps from Pier 3 on Market Street. Walked to the station, went into the station, and was the only guy in the station. Nobody was there. Got a camera and called a couple of camera guys and said, "How do you turn this thing on?" Went down to Market Street, shot some video. Went down to Independence Mall to shoot some video. Nobody was at work for a couple of hours, at least. I had a couple of stories done before anyone got there.

John Mussoni, Executive Producer and News Director, WCAU and WTXF:
We weren't in the business of doing wall-to-wall snow coverage for the sake of wall-to-wall snow coverage. It kind of became important to us to strategically decide what we were going to do on the air and how we're going to do it.

Lou Tilley, Sports Reporter and Host, KYW and the Comcast Network:
I was staying at the local Holiday Inn down by 5th and Market, which turned into just forty-eight hours of the biggest drinking party I've been a part of since I was in college. In between, we would stomp around in the snow around Independence Hall with our yardsticks, measuring the depth of the snow. We'd get together at night, have a few beers, and laugh about what a joke our weather coverage was.

Frank Cariello, Meteorologist, WTXF:
The entire crew was at the Holiday Inn on 5th Street. It sort of became home base for a long time. I remember coming into the news meeting,

talking about the potential for snow. A lot of news managers listen, and then there are the producers who think every[one] is crying wolf when it comes to weather. We decided to beef up coverage and bring some extra people in for two or three days down the line when the snow was supposed to start. It started just as it was supposed to. We actually got more snow than we were supposed to.

Cecily Tynan, Meteorologist, WPVI:
I stayed at, I think, the Crowne Plaza hotel. A bunch of us tried to navigate through the snow from the station at midnight. I remember getting on the shoulders of Dan McKenna, one of our assignment editors, and falling into the snow. It was a big pillow, and you could just hear the snow falling. Since we were all working crazy hours, we had to party for a few more hours to blow off steam. I still remember John Morris—he was our morning producer. I remember going to our hotel room and the doors for the elevators opening up, and he was going in for the morning show, and the night people were just going to bed after partying. The look on his face was "What are you guys doing?" Then, I realized I had been up twenty-four hours straight. It was one of those things where you were fueled by adrenaline.

Rich Scott, News Director, WPHL:
I figured out a way to keep things going. We had to find a way to feed our staff, had to find places for our staff to stay the night. [The storm] was perhaps when it was still *Inquirer News Tonight*; it was probably the biggest event that *Inquirer News Tonight* had covered since it was on. It was a crazy time. We basically lived in the newsroom for a couple of days.

David Henry, Reporter, WPVI:
The state had shut down all of the highways, so there was no civilian traffic allowed. You would be stopped by a police offer and be arrested if you tried to drive your own car out there. We pretty much had the roads to ourselves. I remember doing one live shot standing in the middle of the Schuylkill Expressway, in one of the buzziest sections, just completely deserted. One lane had been plowed. Standing there in this kind of otherworldly environment that had completely transformed and the city completely shut down.

Bruce Gordon, Reporter, WPHL and WTXF:
It was really a surreal experience, like it was like a neutron bomb went off, and all of the people were gone, and the buildings were still there, and the snow was still there, but there were no people in sight.

Larry Kane, Anchor, WPVI, WCAU, and KYW:
It was not only a bad blizzard but the aftermath was this gorgeous crystallization of the trees. So everybody had this ice all over the place. The ice was on the ground for three or four days.

Jim Sinkovitz, Anchor and Reporter, WPHL:
We got three feet of snow, and it shut everything down, especially South Philadelphia. They couldn't get trucks through the narrow streets because cars were parked on one side, and South Philadelphia, for all practical purposes, was just shut down for three weeks, and it was every single night going down there and dealing with angry residents who couldn't understand why they couldn't get their streets plowed.

Larry Cosgrove, Meteorologist, WPHL:
Not only did it snow and paralyze the city; but you had another kickback from it when it all melted and it rained on top of it. That part of the system was equally forecasted as well. I knew when I was on the air on Monday; I made a graphic saying "Blizzard of '96" and then afterward "Flood of '96." All of those things happened. It was like a dream come true for me. Again, I know it was an imposition on people that lived there and it was dangerous, but if you are a meteorologist looking for stuff like that, it's like an amazing system to behold.

Nora Muchanic, Reporter, WPVI:
I used to have a T-shirt, but I think I threw it out, and it said, "I survived the Blizzard of '96" that Channel 6 had made for everyone who worked on that.

THE START OF *GOOD DAY PHILADELPHIA*

On April 1, 1996, Fox 29 entered Philadelphia's weekday morning news programming with the launch of Good Day Philadelphia.

The two-and-a-half hour show debuted at 7:00 A.M. *with anchors Donya Archer, Don Tollefson, and Tracey Matisak; meteorologist Jim Castillo; features reporter Grover Silcox; movie reviewer Bill Wine (appearing three times a week); and two general assignment news reporters, Cathy Matusiak and Steve Keeley. The show was produced by Mary Fay, with an ensemble crew of more than thirty people. The* Philadelphia Inquirer *reported in 1996 that WTXF's parent company, Fox, pitched in $4 million to help with staffing and equipment for the first year of the show's launch, doubling the size of the station's newsroom by ten thousand square feet. Fox 29 planned to send out six to eight news crews, including three live trucks, for every show during the week.*

For two hours, the show covered various topics, including hard news, sports, traffic, and weather reports, and a wide variety of local feature stories from Philadelphia, Southern New Jersey, Delaware, Allentown, and the Jersey Shore. Good Day Philadelphia *has competed locally with nationally established network franchises in ABC's* Good Morning America, *NBC's* Today Show, *and* CBS This Morning.

In its first few weeks on air, Good Day Philadelphia *featured Philadelphia mayor Ed Rendell, Councilwoman Augusta Clark, Phillies owner Bill Giles, Flyers owner Ed Snider, district attorney Lynne Abraham, and then-Senator Joe Biden.*

"It takes an Ice Age for Philadelphians to change their viewing habits," the Philadelphia Inquirer *wrote in April 1996. "But the new show already has a lot to recommend it. With some modifications, it would become a potent alternative to the network morning shows."*

In 1999, Mike Jerrick became the new cohost of Good Day Philadelphia *alongside Archer. In 2002, Jerrick left Philadelphia to become the weekend host of Fox News's* Fox and Friends. *Fox 29 then brought in new cohosts, George Mallet and Kerri-Lee Halkett (Mayland). Anchor Sheinelle Jones joined Fox 29 in 2005 as a general assignment reporter and became the cohost of* Good Day Philadelphia *in 2009. Also in 2009, Jerrick returned to Fox 29 after his national show on Fox News,* The Morning Show with Mike and Juliet, *was canceled.*

After nine years at the station, Jones left Fox 29 in 2014 and later became an anchor with NBC's Today Show. *In June 2014, Alex Holley was named the new cohost of* Good Day Philadelphia *alongside Jerrick. Prior to arriving in Philadelphia, Holley had worked at WMBF-TV in South Carolina. In 2014, WTXF launched weekend programming with* #Fox29Weekend, *which later carried the same title as the weekday program,* Good Day Philadelphia.

As of this writing, Good Day Philadelphia *consistently is the highest-rated morning show in the Philadelphia area and airs seven days a week, from 4:00 A.M. to 10:00 A.M.*

Richard Manieri, Reporter and Anchor, WTXF:
It was exciting because it was something new. We hadn't done anything like that before. It was a sign that [WTXF] was getting bigger. It was a really exciting time. Doing new things, developing, and growing were not really foreign to us. We just kind of dove in and did the best we could. I did think it worked, and there was a place for it, an all-local TV news show in the morning.

Steve Keeley, Reporter, WTXF:
Our first show is supposed to be [the Phillies] opening day at [Veterans Stadium], April 1, 1996, and it got rained out. They know it's going to pour the day before. We had to scramble, and we had a lot of these feature stories ready. We had all of these live guests ready. We had to scramble. How are we going to put a show together? They call a senator, lo-

cally, named Joe Biden, and they say, "Hey, we are going to rent a satellite truck from WHYY, drive it as close to your house as we can—can you just go outside your house and talk to Steve live?" There wasn't even a topic. There was a [microphone] in my ear, and it was throwing me off interviewing Joe Biden. I wasn't pouring on any tough questions. I was probably asking, "Hey, you've been a senator this many years, blah blah. . . ." Who would have thought: Our first show, and the first guy I interview is now the president of the United States.

Tracey Matisak, Anchor and Reporter, WTXF:
It was so exciting. I felt like this was the job that I had been sort of looking forward to my whole career. When they started talking about creating a morning show, I was all in. I wanted to be part of that show, and I wanted to be the host of that show. I really set my sights on that from the very beginning. It was incredibly exciting because we were bringing in some new people. A lot of our exciting people were now being taken off the ten o'clock [newscast] to work on it. I had to audition for it, just like everybody else. It wasn't like, "Hey, you are going to do *Good Day Philadelphia.*" I had to go through a round of auditions and all of that. By no means was it a lock that I was going to get that job, but really, that was something I so looked forward to, just the idea of building something from scratch. They created new sets, new theme music: That was just so exciting to be in on the ground floor of something like that. When Tolly [Don Tollefson] and I were chosen to do that job, we did this round of promotional things where we were on billboards and on the side of SEPTA buses. We had a publicist who was promoting us. That was a whole new world, for me at least. We had a series of rehearsals that we would go through when we were trying to see what our show would be like if we had our reporters out doing live shots at different places and try to do it in real time. Rehearse as best you can for a live show that you have no idea what's going to happen. That was probably one of the most exciting times of my career.

Carl Cherkin, Sports Director, WTXF:
I saw [*Good Day*] as a drain on our resources for the ten o'clock news. I understood the company opted to do it, and then obviously the success of that entity today would probably underscore the reasons they wanted to do it back then. It was not as well conceived or supported as it might

have been. I'm sure the anchors were the right anchors. It was more confusion and a drain on the resources than anything else.

Rich Noonan, Anchor and Reporter, WTXF:
I remember all of a sudden we had all of these new people. I remember feeling immature territorialness about it, if that's a word. I thought, "Who are these people? A bunch of out-of-towners. They don't know anything about my hometown." I remember thinking that. And then I remember that they kind of changed the way I felt about TV news in a good way because they really did lighten up things.

Rob Guarino, Chief Meteorologist, WTXF:
I was the main weather guy when it launched, and Jim Castillo was the morning guy. When it first got launched, it was interesting because it was so different than the typical morning show of [Channels] 3, 6, and 10: very news-based, very structured, and time, temperatures, here's the weather, and back to the *Today Show* or *CBS This Morning*. Where Fox didn't have that "back to the national news"—it was just all local. The first thing I always thought with that show was that you had to always fill it with a lot of things. There also was a lot of ad-lib because you were kind of flying through this [show] where it didn't have "back to the *Today Show*," which covered most of those mornings or cut-ins with local [broadcasts for other stations].

Andrea Lacca Bille, Traffic Reporter, WTXF:
It was something that was new, so we all pulled together. We did a lot of social events together that sort of made it so that, hopefully, it transferred on air, for the chemistry between everyone.

Grover Silcox, Reporter, WTXF:
I was a little nervous because I was among seasoned journalists. That really wasn't my focus up until this point because I was a writer. I was a little nervous rising to the occasion. I wasn't sure exactly what they wanted because they brought me on because I had some credibility, being a comedian, [doing] radio and some specials on local television. I was kind of the odd person out, really. I was welcomed very warmly by my colleagues. It was very exciting because it really was a whole new

format. It was information, but it was also entertainment as well. They wanted it to be light and loose and fun. I think, at least in my experience, for those first formative years, they really had a "let's try things" attitude.

John Mussoni, Executive Producer and News Director, WCAU and WTXF:
The philosophy was that we are a local show, and we're going to give you all the information you need. You know what? If we need to pivot at the last minute, we're going to do it. It's not a news show, per se, because you do want all the news that needs to be out there. You gotta know that there's a point where it's, like, people's saturation points have maxed out and the ability to pivot on a dime.

Tracey Matisak, Anchor and Reporter, WTXF:
They have found the right mix of information and entertainment. Morning is a special time slot because people are just waking up, just getting themselves oriented, they want to know what happened during the night but also don't need any added stress to start their day. Channel 29 has managed to find the right combination and entertainment, and also I think there have been some personalities who have been there from the beginning.

HughE Dillon, Photographer and Blogger, *Philly ChitChat*:
It's the most personable station. They really interact. They think like we think. They are covering subjects we want to cover. It's not always gonna make the news or general news. Sometimes, they cover something, and then it does make the news. The other stations are interested in it. Their personalities and what they bring—it's like a radio station on TV.

Lucy Noland, Anchor, WTXF:
If you do it well and they do it well, you can become must-see TV in the morning because you are all about the neighborhood. You are all about the events. You are all about whatever people are worried about within the city. It's completely city-centric. The great thing about Philadelphia is that Philadelphia wraps its arms around those who open their arms to the city. That's what I think *Good Day* does.

George Mallet, Reporter and Anchor, WTXF:
The main thing about *Good Day* is that it's entirely local. It's competing with the *Today Show* program and *Good Morning America*, and they are all focused on big national events and national celebrities. We were just going all in on [racehorse] Smarty Jones or the Philadelphia Flyers when they were in the playoffs, the Phillies—whatever the town was talking about, we were all in on it.

Dawn Stensland-Mendte, Anchor and Reporter, KYW and WTXF:
At the time, we were all really involved in the community, all of those nonprofits. And part of the connection and part of the success at that time and for *Good Day* right now is that we weren't just people on the news. We were in the community and genuine about it. It was an authentic love of the community. Like, "Hey, we are here, we love Philadelphia, and we care." We weren't just showing up for breaking bad news—we were part of the good news too.

Roger LaMay, General Manager and News Director, WTXF:
It feels like it's got that Philly view of the world. They want rough edges. They don't want this homogenized court-viewing thing. *Good Day Philadelphia* has always had that sort of rough-and-tumble, we-will-do-anything kind of feel to it that a lot of the audience appreciates.

Liz Matt, Reporter, WPVI and WTXF:
The newsroom was under a lot of pressure to get live shots and cover breaking news while a chirpy, happy-go-lucky show was going on, so you go from a cooking segment to someone out live at a prior murder scene. It was a long show.

Alex Holley, Anchor, WTXF:
It's a difficult dance. It's a dance we have to do every day. I think what motivates me and the reason why it's so important is that there is so much heavy news going on. If you ask a lot of local people about local news, the number-one thing I always hear is that the news is so negative. That's constantly what we hear. What drives us is, yes, we have to tell you what's going on and what you need to know, and some of the stuff is sad or scary, but we are also going to make you laugh and put a smile on your face.

Sometimes, you have to be that real. Sometimes Mike will even say, "Wow, I know the past five minutes have been tough with serious stories. Let's lighten it up a little bit," or "Let's pivot, and here's something else we might talk about to help us out." It's just being real with people.

Jennaphr Frederick, Reporter, WTXF:
It's a natural human conversation—that you go to a funeral, you walk in, you're so sad for the family, and then you are like, "Are there snacks?" I think that's what *Good Day* is. For us, that doesn't seem false. It seems actually more real than most of the other news products you will see. It's a combination of we are living in an ADHD, cell phone–distracted world at this point and, at the same point, remember, the show is on from 4:00 A.M. to 10:00 [A.M.]. The 4:00 A.M. [hour of the] show looks way different than the 9:00 A.M. hour of the show. Steve Keeley, you are going to see more in the 4:00 A.M. hour because you really need more of the nuts and bolts, if you will. At the 9:00 A.M. hour, we get your kids on the bus, you have some time, but if there is a bus accident, you're gonna hear from Steve Keeley. I always say that the people that watch our show are dipping in and out. They are getting in the shower, they come back, and we are still on TV. They go to Starbucks? They come back, and we are on TV. They are not always seeing it from me to Steve Keeley. I think it is a normal flow of how we live our lives.

Robin Taylor, Reporter, KYW and WTXF:
I don't think people would watch things if it was a serious news show. It wouldn't be appealing, and you don't have the same kind of guests or the things that the other network shows have, but you have something different, and it's local. People grew really attached to the personalities. And then over the years, the personalities have changed, but the format has really made it work, so you can have different personalities come in and out as well as they're having fun with the show.

Tracey Matisak, Anchor and Reporter, WTXF:
There was always pressure to hit the ground running. We knew on the one hand that this is new and it's going to take time for people to (a) know that we are here, (b) start watching, and (c) start watching on a regular basis and then start to figure out what's the secret sauce in terms of the news, features, and interviews, funny stuff, what is sort of the

right formula for that. Because really, we were creating this thing from scratch. There was a pressure, and we knew we had to get it right.

Rob Guarino, Chief Meteorologist, WTXF:
What they did with me was they would occasionally have me do feature reporting—like, give someone twenty bucks around Christmas time or best cheesesteaks in Philly. They would throw me around to do not just weather but fun feature small things once in a while to help add content to the show. It also gave us visibility that the night weather guy, which was me, the chief meteorologist, was on the morning show. So, people who might not watch the ten o'clock would say, "Oh, that's the weather guy!" We would cross-promote the two shows because you still had two different audiences, in a way.

Alex Holley, Anchor, WTXF:
I don't think anyone can understand *Good Day Philadelphia* unless they have been watching it for a long time or they have actually gotten time to experience it here in the area. I will admit, when I was a reporter, you know, you get breaks because I only had certain live hits. In between commercial breaks, I would sit in the live truck and watch the show from Myrtle Beach. I thought it was fascinating to see people's morning news like I hadn't seen before. The fact that they were so open and they just seemed to be so real. They would do things off the cuff, and I just thought it was must-see TV, and it was something I hadn't seen before when it came to morning television. It fascinated me.

"What are they doing now?" That's kind of how you have to watch this show. "What are they gonna do next? What are they doing now?" Because every time you think you know where it is going, you think, "Oh, they wouldn't do that," and they do that on *Good Day.*

Clayton Morris, Reporter, WTXF:
You have a real buy-in to the product. If you are at a Phillies game, and you see someone talking, and this person can eat a cheesesteak in three seconds next to their friend, and they are having a cheesesteak-eating contest, and you are over seeing that, that's an opportunity for you to say, "Hey, guys, why don't you guys come on *Good Day*, and we are gonna have a cheesesteak-eating contest." You are a producer. The con-

tent is yours just as much as the actual producers'. I loved that about the show.

Chris Murphy, Reporter, WTXF:

I went to the Bruce Springsteen show in September of 2016 at Citizens Bank Park. There's a guy who Bruce called up on the stage. I was there with one of the producers—he and I went to the show together. [Springsteen] played "No Surrender," and he was a college student, evidently. He then went back into the crowd, and Ryan [a WTXF producer] went over to him and got his cell number. He said, "I'm a producer of our morning show—would you come on tomorrow morning?" The guy said he was happy to. He was actually from Texas and flew to Philly with his Dad to see Springsteen because that was the closest show they were gonna see. Instead of flying back, he had some time to go on our show. We even showed video from the show and even asked people in the crowd, "Hey, can we get your cell phone video to show the guy?" You are always producing the show. Even when you are at a rock concert, you are thinking about the next day's show. It takes that kind of thinking.

Steve Schwaid, News Director, WCAU and WTXF:

I can take two anchors from any other station in that market and drop them in there, and the show would fail—not because the support staff weakens the people who are working the show. The anchors have their shit together. They know what they're talking about. They're on top of the news, so when you have a big day, the next day you bring the police commissioner in, they don't need an hour of prep time to say, "What are we bringing him here to talk about?" They know.

Tracey Matisak, Anchor and Reporter, WTXF:

Even though there have been a number of different hosts, and personnel has changed over the years, there have been people who have remained a constant. I think in a marketing line in Philadelphia, there is something really comforting about seeing the same faces. I mean, Jim Gardner is proof of that, right? I think there's a certain comfort in seeing those same faces over the years, especially when some of these news stories have broken locally or nationally. There is a comfort in getting that news from the same people.

Sue Serio, Meteorologist, WTXF:
Here I am, watching *Good Day Philadelphia* while I'm feeding my baby, and all I could think of was that I wanted to be on that show. I wanted to be on that show. I had some contacts of my own at Fox 29. The next thing I knew, I was freelancing at Fox 29, and then the weather guy left. Suddenly, I was the weather anchor of *Good Day Philadelphia*. It didn't happen that magically, but you look back at it, and I went from sitting in a rocking chair, watching *Good Day*, saying, "That's that kind of show I want to be on" because it was personal. It was almost like every other job I had before that was kind of leading to this. When I was able to actually make that come true, I was like, "Oh, man!" Sometimes, you can make up your mind to do something, and it actually does happen.

Dave Warren, Meteorologist, WCAU and WTXF:
I think what really works is Mike Jerrick: He's different in how he can tell you the news and be serious but also make you laugh and not look like he is forcing it. Some people look like they are trying to force their personality. He didn't have to force it.

Mike Jerrick, Anchor, WTXF:
The Philadelphia TV market saved my TV career. I was floating around because of a family issue I had to deal with for two years. I had to move back to Lawrence, Kansas, and got out of the business, basically, to take care of this family situation. It got rectified in two years, and now I'm ready to get back into the business. I was like, "Oh my God!" One thing they teach you is "Don't ever get out." It was hard enough getting in. Don't get out because it will be even harder to get back in. That was my dilemma. I got a call from a woman by the name of Lisa Kridos, and she was the executive producer of *Good Day LA*. So, she had heard that they had let a host go here [in Philadelphia], and I think it was an immediate termination in 1999. Like, one day he was here, and the next day he was gone, so now they needed to find somebody. So, she suggested to the powers-that-be here—a guy named Roger LaMay, general manager, and news director John Mussoni—that they look at me. They flew me in. I remember the day, August 16, because it was Elvis's death and Sue Serio's birthday. They fly me in, and I do an audition after *Good Day* ends. I was with Donya [Archer] and Sue [Serio]. They put me on the anchor desk, and we ad-libbed for ten to fifteen minutes or so. When it

was over, Roger LaMay said, "Let's walk over to Buddakan and have some lunch." We sat down, and he went, "Listen, do you want the job?" I said, "Hell yeah! I want the job."

Oh my God, I'm back in the business, and I'm doing a show like *Good Day,* like *Good Day LA* and *New York*, and this is in Philadelphia. Okay, I don't know much about Philly, but I'll do it. It's the perfect show for me. I love doing morning television. It's exactly what I wanted to do when I started in this business. I wanted to do something that was halfway between the *Tonight Show* and the *Today Show.* Serious, but you can also be funny. It was tailor-made for me. It all worked out. Two weeks later, I was here. Thank God the city of Philadelphia and the viewers really accepted me immediately. I'm truly grateful it happened because it truly did reconstruct my career. The show was very successful.

Steve Schwaid, News Director, WCAU and WTXF:
They got Mike Jerrick. I was fortunate to work with him. He is really smart, really clever, opportunistic. There may be times he kind of crosses the line, but it's all with good intentions, it's never malicious intentions involved. He is just very strong, and that makes the show strong.

Kerri-Lee Mayland, Anchor, WTXF:
I remember coming from Boston, being a serious journalist. I just got off fresh extended coverage of 9/11, and then I was paired with Mike Jerrick, who really taught me what it's like to totally push the envelope. I remember my news director saying, "Kerri-Lee, I want you to go off on the ledge and then go just a little bit further." *Good Day* was exhilarating. It was freeing. I think I learned some incredible skills in the very short time I worked with Mike.

Kerry Barrett, Reporter, WTXF:
I started before Mike Jerrick. I think he and Sue Serio are the longest-tenured people on that show. There is something about both of them that they have very different personalities, but they always push you to be your best in very different ways. I remember when I first started on that show when I was working with Mike. I told him this before, but I would literally go home and cry because I would wonder why he was so mean. He wasn't mean, but I was being pushed in new directions, and I was

really breaking boundaries of what TV was in this *Good Day* format. I always wondered, "Why can't he just dial it down a little bit until I get comfortable with everything?" But that's the beauty of his genius. He doesn't dial it down. He is who he is, and it pushes everyone to be better, even if the way he does it is somewhat unconventional. I can never thank him enough for the learning that I did while I was there and working with him. He taught me what compelling TV was and is along with everyone else there. He specifically was just so unique and is a genius when it comes to TV. He thinks way out of the box, which is great because that whole team is constantly flexing their creative muscles, and I think that's what made it such a special place to be.

Mike Jerrick, Anchor, WTXF:
I wanted to be different than anybody else. I was like that in my personal life. I was the fifth of six kids. I think that's how I ended up on television. I never wanted to be, like, this regular anchorperson in any market. The key was to be myself. I learned that in Topeka, Kansas. I said, "Okay, this will be different, and the way to be different is be yourself." What a shocker. I was watching a lot of people on TV and knew them personally, and they became a different person when they went on TV. It wasn't a conscious thing, it was a [feeling of] "I just need to be myself," and I always have been. If you're just yourself, you can pivot from silliness to tragedy in five seconds because if you and I get cocktails or whatever and we are talking, we can change subjects on a dime. Do it in a decent, natural away. You just pause for a second or two and then just change your tone, like you would if you need to be sympathetic, if someone you are talking to is across the table. That comes from being yourself.

Jennaphr Frederick, Reporter, WTXF:
Have you ever hung out with a toddler? I say that with the biggest compliment. Think about a toddler—they want what they want, and they want it now. When they don't like it, they don't like it. That speaks to how we are in this world. The Mike [Jerrick] that you see sitting on the desk, where you see him get frustrated when they are not bringing up the graphic, or the Mike that you see that gets so happy 'cause Kansas is in the stupid March Madness, that's the Mike Jerrick we all get behind the scenes. He's the quarterback, and the quarterback knows what

he wants, this and that. He will literally say something, like someone will be unveiling something at noon, and he will be like, "Well, if they want to be on *Good Day*, they need to do it at 9:45." I'm always like, "This is never going to work out," and sure enough, it does work out. His expectations for the respect our show should get daily manifests itself. He thinks and knows our show is the biggest thing going on in Philadelphia. Because of that, he wants all of the good stuff, and he wants it now. I will get a text at ten o'clock at night [asking] whether or not I have a shirt with a hamburger on it, and if I don't respond at ten o'clock at night, he will respond to ask if I'm paying attention.

Lucy Noland, Anchor, WTXF:
Mike Jerrick is a beast as far as a journalist goes. He's phenomenal. He's as Philly as all get out, but when stuff hits the fan and you need a great journalist to walk you through what's going on, he is the man to do that. He is really, really good. I worked with him in New York City. I did *Good Day* in New York, and we worked together here and there. I loved him then, and I love him here. He is phenomenal. You've got people like Sue Serio, who is as sweet in person as she is on air. What you see is what you get. Philadelphians can see through all of the stuff, ya know? If you are not the real deal, they see right through that, and that's why I love this city so much. Sue Serio is "what you see is what you get." I think one of the greatest causes for the station was Bob Kelly. You know, they got Bob Kelly from CBS 3 and scored Kathy Orr back then, and both are incredibly beloved people and just lovely people.

Bob Kelly, Traffic Reporter, KYW and WTXF:
I thought to myself, "They are always having fun over there. It must be a great place to work and a great show to be on." I always thought about that. It was loose, fun, and it wasn't so much the hard news. Yeah, we do the hard news, you have the top two stories, but it always got more fun. Fifteen [minutes] after the hour, that block became fun, and it became more fun as the morning went on. I recognized that. I said, "You know what, that is me." I always felt to myself that I would be a great fit at Fox. Others said that as well. That's why I'd spoken a number of times to the folks at Fox about an opportunity. For various reasons, it wasn't right along the way, but it eventually became the right time. It's fun to go from watching the show, knowing how much

fun it could be, and now being a part of that fun and taking it to the next level.

Dan Gross, TV Columnist:
[Mike] Jerrick is great, and most of the people he has been partnered with the last number of years have been amusing too. To me, he's the thing that makes it funny and ties it all together. It's fun, it's a different vibe, if you want to watch them in the morning. That isn't just straight news. I think they do a good job of that.

Alex Holley, Anchor, WTXF:
From the moment [Mike Jerrick and I] met, we kind of connected. To my understanding, he was obviously involved with the selection process. When I came, we had a chemistry test. Within minutes of meeting him, we went on camera, and they said, "Let's do a whole news block and see how that works." From what I remember, when Mike and I talked about it, it wasn't until the chemistry test went fine, but it was when we went to lunch afterward at Buddakan. It was just around the block. We were sitting there having lunch, and he always makes fun of me to this day because I ordered a lemonade to drink, and he had something a little stronger. We were sitting there, and he started singing Teddy Pendergrass, and I finished the lyrics for him, and we both started singing together. That's when we were like, "Oh, okay. We have something here," and we connected through music. We both love a lot of Philadelphians and the music that we have here. That was a special moment. Since then, we were going to events together, and he wanted to help me know the area and get to know Philly. He was really big on one point—he said to just be yourself: "I'm not gonna tell you how to do this, I'm not gonna tell you to do it this way or that way because Philly would love for you to be you." I don't get a lot of instruction, much to my confusion, and it was a little concerning to me at first because everyone kept telling me, from my bosses to Mike, "Just be yourself; we don't want to tell you anything" and "Go out there, and whatever you think you should do, that's what we want you to do." They are so into not having a mold about how a newsperson should be. Just be you. That's what makes the show what it is. Everyone is being themselves. We just happen to be on TV.

Billy Vargus, Sports Reporter and Anchor, WTXF:
I think it's the personalities on the show, first of all, that make it. It's special and even moreso nowadays, when you can find online most whatever information you want. It's already there. You can get it instantly before a news show or a morning show even comes on the air. People are tuning in because they would rather hear it from the person they trust and admire, who can make it interesting.

Roger LaMay, General Manager and News Director, WTXF:
Chemistry is king in those kinds of situations. At night, you wanted sort of a trusted source or whatever. You wanted a greater comfort level in the morning. People get up, and they don't want to be preached at. A lot of the audience wants somebody who they are comfortable with and they feel like they could talk to. They want to see people get along. You are not gonna feel like part of an extended family if the folks on the screen and in the studio aren't coming across as being a family. It doesn't mean families don't have their moments. Chemistry in the morning is arguably more important than any other time of the day. As you start your day, you want to feel comfortable.

THE BIRTH OF COMCAST SPORTSNET AND NBC SPORTS PHILADELPHIA

Entrepreneur and philanthropist Ed Snider emerged on the Philadelphia sports landscape in 1964 as the Philadelphia Eagles vice president. Two years later, Snider helped bring a National Hockey League franchise to the city, establishing the Philadelphia Flyers. Snider brought the 76ers franchise out of bankruptcy in 1972 and later sold the team to billionaire Josh Harris in 2011. In 1973, Snider created Spectacor, a management company that would oversee the Flyers and the Spectrum arena's business endeavors. In 1976, Snider's vision turned to broadcasting as he created PRISM (Philadelphia Regional In-home Sports and Movies), a twenty-four-hour regional sports and entertainment network that operated from 1976 to 1997, serving the Philadelphia television viewing market with a mix of sports programming, movies, concerts, and other forms of visual entertainment. In 1996, Snider sold a 63 percent stake in Spectacor to Comcast, but he remained president of the rechristened Comcast Spectacor and held a 24 percent stake in the company until his death in 2016.

On April 25, 1996, Comcast Spectacor formally announced plans to create a new all-sports network in Philadelphia. The new network, Comcast SportsNet, introduced a seven-days-a-week, 12-months-a-year schedule of television sports coverage of the 76ers, Flyers, Eagles, and Phillies. Comcast SportsNet debuted on October 1, 1997; in its first year, the network aired forty-seven Philadelphia Flyers regular-season games, sixty 76ers regular-season games, and sixty-five Phillies games. In addi-

tion, Comcast SportsNet televised thirteen Philadelphia Phantoms American Hockey League games, a dozen Philadelphia KiXX National Professional Indoor Soccer League games, select Temple University Southeastern Conference football games, and about fifty college basketball games and boxing matches.

The debut of Comcast SportsNet in 1996 had to overcome some on-air problems. Cable viewers in South Jersey and surrounding Philadelphia counties were greeted by a variety of sound and audio glitches in the first hours after Comcast SportsNet's 5:00 P.M. debut. The majority of the problems affected the audio of the channel's first two programs: The Making of Comcast SportsNet *and* Daily News Live.

Comcast SportsNet broadcast a morning show called SportsRise, *anchored by Ron Burke, and a late-night postgame show that featured Michael Barkann. The prime-time show* SportsNite *was anchored by Neil Hartman and Leslie Gudel, a show that featured local sports highlights, news, and interviews.*

When Comcast acquired NBCUniversal in 2011, Comcast SportsNet incorporated NBC Sports branding into its productions and branding. In January 2014, as part of a huge twenty-five-year broadcasting contract with the team, the Philadelphia Phillies acquired a 25 percent equity stake in Comcast SportsNet Philadelphia.

In April 2015, Comcast SportsNet launched Breakfast on Broad, *a morning sports talk show that ran from 7:00 A.M. to 9:00 A.M. on its sister station, the Comcast Network, and replayed on Comcast* SportsNet *at 11:00 A.M. The show was hosted by Rob Ellis, Jillian Mele, Sarah Baicker, and Barrett Brooks. After two years of up-and-down ratings, Comcast SportsNet canceled* Breakfast on Broad *in February 2017. (The* Philly Voice *reported in 2017 that* Breakfast on Broad*'s ratings during its first few months were as low as 0.2.)*

In October 2017, Comcast SportsNet officially changed its name to NBC Sports Philadelphia, joining Chicago, Washington, and Boston in the rebranding of other Comcast SportsNet networks.

In February 2019, NBC Sports Philadelphia canceled Philly Sports Talk *(named* Daily News Live *prior to April 2013) after a twenty-one-year run with the network. Notable guests on the show included Charles Barkley, Billie Jean King, Kareem Abdul-Jabbar, Bill Walton, Jim Cramer, John McEnroe, Jon Bon Jovi, and others. Taking over the time slot was a television version of* The Mike Missanelli Show *from sports talk radio station 97.5 The Fanatic. To this day, 97.5 The Fanatic airs their radio show on NBC Sports Philadelphia.*

Jack Williams, President and CEO, PRISM, Comcast Spectacor, and Comcast SportsNet:
You only get one chance to make a first impression. We wanted to hit the ground and be professional from day one. We rehearsed. There were probably rehearsals for over a month before anything ever went on air, with the full staff there working on it and getting it down. The day we went on, I think, really changed the way sports was reported in Philadelphia.

Stephanie Lafair Smith, Director of Marketing and President, Comcast SportsNet:
We all held our breath. It was like a countdown. We went live at 5:00 [P.M.], and it was literally like a moon launch, with a countdown of 10, 9, 8. I remember I was actually with Jack Williams and Ed Snider, and we were all holding our breath, saying, "Please . . ." as the countdown went to 5, ". . . let there be something that shows up on the screen." We put this together fairly quickly from the standpoint of creating the newsroom and the engineering aspect.

Pete Christy, Anchor and Reporter, Comcast SportsNet:
If it was easy, everybody would do it. What they were trying to do with this SportsNet wasn't easy. We were kind of the guinea pigs going through the hardships. The best part is that they had the glass there [in the stadium], so when people were at game, they would be able to look at us doing the show.

Jack Williams, President and CEO, PRISM, Comcast Spectacor, and Comcast SportsNet:
We had a very firm idea of what we wanted to do and what we wanted to accomplish. It was basically getting facilities built. We had to build an addition to the CoreStates Center [now the Wells Fargo Center] at the time to give us office space and a studio and then put a staff together.

Maureen Quilter, Senior Director of Communications, Comcast SportsNet:
The arena was the first arena to have a network located in the facility. That was pretty wild and something we could help promote.

Neil Hartman, Sports Reporter and Anchor, WPHL, KYW, and Comcast SportsNet/NBC Sports Philadelphia:
The first few months when we were on the air, we actually had temporary trailers in the parking lot. You would walk through mud to get into the only operating part of our offices, which was our studio. The studio had this big window, which you could look out into the concourse of the stadium. So, in the beginning years, people would hang by the window; they would look at what you were doing.

Derrick Gunn, Reporter, Comcast SportsNet/NBC Sports Philadelphia:
We were walking across wooden pieces and boards, trying to get into the studio. It still wasn't quite finished. We had a target date to launch October 1, and we had to hit the ground running. When we went into this thing, we wanted to be able to tell extended stories that the other stations couldn't tell for time restraints, whereas we had ample amounts of time to tell in-depth stories. I think that was the biggest hook for a lot of us. Number one: We would be a part of Philadelphia TV history. Number two: We would have platforms to be able to tell stories the way we wanted to tell them, with very little limitations on time in terms of how we were going to put the stories together and what we could incorporate. I think from day one, we were able to establish that.

Stephanie Lafair Smith, Director of Marketing and President, Comcast SportsNet:
I went from a fancy office at 18th and Market, where I looked out on city hall. I had this plush gorgeous office, and then I walked into a trailer that was not a John Madden trailer, by any means. This was what would have been thrown away in a trailer park. It barely had running water. Every time I had to use the facilities, I had to run to the Spectrum to use the bathroom.

What it did was make us all really—and it sounds corny—a family early on. You were working in one big common space. What Jack [Williams] did was hire people who were very good in their respective disciplines and let them do their job.

Tom Stathakes, Senior Vice President of Programming, Comcast SportsNet:
The biggest challenge for me and for us was we had a very short timeline. We basically were all hired in May, and we had to be on the air in October. There was a lot of fanfare to it. We were not shy to go outside Philadelphia and hire people. We hired a lot of people in Philly, but we also hired a lot of people from ESPN. We hired people from all different places.

Ron Burke, Anchor and Reporter, WCAU and Comcast SportsNet/NBC Sports Philadelphia:
I had worked at Channel 10 for eight years prior to that, so I had a pretty lengthy Philadelphia experience before that. I left Channel 10 and went to New York to work at a startup, and it didn't last long. It lasted five months. So, here I was, at this point in another startup situation, but in a comfortable environment because I was familiar with Philadelphia.

Ray Didinger, Football Historian and Author:
I thought it was a can't-miss. You have a great sports town with passionate fans. You have all major sports represented here, and your studio sat right in the middle of all of it. To me, it was a can't-miss. It was one of those things when it started—why didn't this happen years ago? It was so obvious. The aptitude in this town and the interest was such that it would absolutely support its own television network. I thought it was a slam dunk right from the start.

Rob Ellis, Senior Producer and Host, Comcast SportsNet/NBC Sports Philadelphia and KYW:
Nobody was mailing it in. Oftentimes in any workplace, you are going to have some people going through the motions. That really wasn't the case at our place. I knew pretty early on. There was a lot of buzz in the city leading up to it. Once we started going with programming—this was pre–social media—I would hear from people, my friends or other people on the street, that would say to me, "Oh my God—how about what you guys did the other night?" or "How about this or that dis-

agreement on *Daily News Live*?" or "That was pretty cool you guys did that for our high school team," or whatever.

Lance Crawford, Anchor and Reporter, Comcast SportsNet:
Those people there at Comcast, I felt, elevated my game. I was a better broadcaster for working with people there than I had been in these smaller markets.

Michael Barkann, Anchor and Host,
KYW and Comcast SportsNet/NBC Sports Philadelphia:
There's an old line, "You can never go home again," and for me, even though I didn't grow up here in Philadelphia, Philadelphia is my home. My wife is from here, my daughter at the time was about to turn one. My son hadn't been born yet. We were going back and forth on whether to stay in Boston. We loved it, but do we come back? So, we came back. There was nervousness too. Those first couple of weeks, there was a [feeling of] "Did I make the right decision?" and I was very trepidatious about it. I had a lot of trepidations.

The moment I saw we weren't doing it with two cups and a string, I was like, "This is going to be awesome," and it has been.

Leslie Gudel, Anchor and Reporter,
Comcast SportsNet/NBC Sports Philadelphia:
Neil Hartman and I were arguing about whether or not we got scripts for our highlights. You are talking about a time when the Internet was not what it is today. Everything was barebones.

I remember when we first went on the air, I remember [pitcher] Curt Schilling had to walk across the rubble to get into the studio for the first show of *Spotlight* that [Michael] Barkann launched with. He's going across the construction zone to get into the studio. We built something. There was a lot of pride that we built something. The other part is—and this changed when it became more corporate—is that we grew it, and we had input. We got to make decisions. This was not where somebody at the top was telling us what to do every day. This was a bunch of people with creativity and drive and ambition and desire to create something that was ours. We all had a say. From producers, production assistants, to directors, to everybody. While we had a shell of what we were doing, Tom [Stathakes] and Jim [Cuddihy] were very open-minded in allowing people to provide input and direction for what we should be doing. There was a real ability to feel like you contributed. If you had a story idea that you wanted to do, no one told you you couldn't. You arranged for a camera and went out and did it.

Dei Lynam, Reporter, Comcast SportsNet:
There were some people who told me, "It's a startup. Are you sure you wanna do that?" Some of it is exciting to do, and some of it—well, what if it doesn't work? As it turned out, it was great, and it was very successful. It was successful because we had great leadership and we had great people who worked. There were some really good creative ideas that came out of it. I think it's an entirely different product today.

Tom Stathakes, Senior Vice President of Programming, Comcast SportsNet
We hired really well, and we hired a lot of good people that got it, wanted to be there, and we didn't have many prima donnas. We just didn't have it. Jack [Williams] wouldn't tolerate it. I think it goes back to management. There are times, especially upper management, all they are worried about are themselves. They are not really invested in their employees. Jack was invested massively into the employees. Everyone kind of felt it. He could be tough, and he could be demanding, but he was a great listener. He legitimately cared about the people that were around him. We respected him as the boss, and we were also, like, "He's also a good guy, and he has our back." There is nothing more important.

Jack Williams, President and CEO, PRISM, Comcast Spectacor, and Comcast SportsNet:
We wanted to have something that anybody could tune in anytime day or night and have something that would be interesting to see. There was no morning sports show at all. We did try to do it live in the beginning, and it was very difficult to make everything work that early in the morning. What we did was we would wait until all of the West Coast games were over, then we could do the show and have the scores, results, and highlights from all of the games in whatever season it was and have the complete story. We felt you really needed something all of the time. We did the morning show and then repeated it several times. Then, we did the noon show, and then *Daily News Live*, local news at six [o'clock],

and then going into the games. We wanted to have that channel be something that people would turn to to see what was there.

Rob Ellis, Senior Producer and Host,
Comcast SportsNet/NBC Sports Philadelphia and KYW:
Being from here, I didn't want to be associated or be a part of something that wasn't going to be up to Philadelphia sports fans' standards. Our standards are very high. There's an accountability level, I think, that people can see through when you are not doing legitimately good work and representing your team. As best as I could, I wanted to represent the city. It was a unique situation because we really didn't have that. There was PRISM, which wasn't fully committed to sports; it was movies, entertainment, and that kind of stuff. There was a sports channel that kind of was sports, but wasn't on a full-time basis. The beauty of what it was then—it's not that way now—was live, local, we are gonna give you everything. Everything from the Sixers, Phillies, Flyers, Eagles, college hoops, college football, the high schools—you name it, it was Philadelphia-centric. At that time, in 1997, you didn't have that where it was going to be 24/7 dedicated to one region's Philadelphia sports. We were the birth of all of the other regions that came out of that. There were definitely challenges.

Derrick Gunn, Reporter,
Comcast SportsNet/NBC Sports Philadelphia:
We were the new kids on the block, and obviously we tried to compete with the likes of the established stations, like Channels 3, 6, 10, and Fox 29. Of course, when we were trying to make in-roads with PR departments and things like that, they would look at us a little sideways, like, "Who are you guys?"

Michael Barkann, Anchor and Host,
KYW and Comcast SportsNet/NBC Sports Philadelphia:
The teams all came to Jack [Williams] and said, "What are you going to say on this new network? What are you going to do?" He told us this at the first meeting of the announcers on September 15, 1997. We were in a conference room at the Wells Fargo Center. He said, "Teams want to know what we are gonna say about them." Jack's an Oklahoman; he said, "I told them, you play good? We will say so. You play bad? We will say so." We weren't there to take cheap shots or be there to have some

fun, don't get me wrong. It was really to convey to the Philadelphia sports fan what was happening on an hourly basis, if not a minute-by-minute basis, at some points.

Pat Boyle, Reporter and Anchor, Comcast SportsNet:
I think a lot of people thought we were just going to be a mouthpiece for the team and weren't going to cover stories and get you behind-the-scenes access that local sports just didn't have the time to give. I think we surprised a lot of people in Philly.

Tom Stathakes, Senior Vice President of Programming, Comcast SportsNet:
Ed Snider would get pissed off at something we said. The Phillies would get pissed off at something we said, but we stuck to our guns. It was really a big credit to Jack [Williams] and Sam [Schroeder] that they would say, don't make it personal, but if they stink, you need to say they stink. And we did.

Bruce Casella, Anchor and Reporter, Comcast SportsNet, the Comcast Network, and KYW:
They respected what we did from the very beginning: All of the athletes did. They knew that we were there to help them market the sports. They knew that we were no longer going to be two to three minutes. Some of the smarter athletes, like Curt Schilling and those guys, knew that we were gonna be there, and their stock would go up because they were gonna get more airtime and more in-depth coverage.

Scott Hanson, Reporter, Comcast SportsNet:
Prior to that, everybody got their sports news on television on six o'clock and eleven o'clock news in little two-and-a-half[-minute] snippets. We were all sports, all day. Where else could it work at its highest level except for Philadelphia?

Neal Slotkin, Producer, Comcast SportsNet/NBC Sports Philadelphia:
I know me personally, I never questioned whether the model would work. I only questioned the first couple of months: how we are going to put out enough content on the air and come out strong because you want to gain the viewers from day one and really kind of make an impact and

really put your footprint in the market. I was always, "This is going to work, I know it," but the technical questions and how are we going to pull this off is always a question.

Jack Williams, **President and CEO, PRISM,**
Comcast Spectacor, and Comcast SportsNet:
We had to be able to perform from day one. We had to be accepted. We had to be legitimate. Our goal from the beginning was to become *the* sports source in the Philadelphia marketplace. Looking for people, we wanted to hire a diverse staff. Some that had lots of experience, others that were newcomers that were talented, and we figured we could bring people in and stay a couple of years or so and probably move on. As it turned out, a lot of them stayed a long time.

Brian Monihan, **President and General Manager, Comcast**
Spectacor and Comcast SportsNet/NBC Sports Philadelphia:
PRISM did some news and other things, but this was going to be 24/7, and you had to get it right. You had to make sure even though you were partially owned by the Phillies and partially owned by Comcast that you were not going to be a complete homer. You were going to report the news and the sports news in a way that was going to be authentic and be able to allow people to see both sides of a coin.

Lance Crawford, **Anchor and Reporter, Comcast SportsNet:**
I only was in town a couple of weeks. I went up to Lehigh for training camp. I'm brand-new, and I don't expect anyone to know me. And sure enough, there is some guy that said, "Hey, Lance." It was another guy on the other side of the barrier. I said, "How do you know me?" He said he watched [Comcast SportsNet]. It was just an example of just how closely sports fans did follow their teams. I bet I had only been on the air for ten days, maximum, and the guy knew me. That didn't happen in any other place I have ever worked. Some places you can go to for years, and people still barely know who you are.

Derrick Gunn, **Reporter,**
Comcast SportsNet/NBC Sports Philadelphia:
Even as the network continued to grow, the one thing I will always be happy about is that we sat there and caught up in the newsroom. We

argued sports, we debated topics, we exchanged barbs with each other. Nobody got offended, and there was no animosity. When you bring in a group of people who don't really know each other like that, you always wonder how much tension there could be in a newsroom. Even the producers, the assignment editors, things of that nature. We assembled a group of people that knew when you walked in that door, you left the ego outside if you had an ego. We had to be worried about the common good of the overall product—not just the first day, but every day.

One of Comcast SportsNet's biggest success stories was its launch and growth of Eagles Postgame Live, *a program featuring live in-studio guests with a roundtable discussion about the just-completed Philadelphia Eagles game, including interviews with players and coaches. The show debuted in 1997.*

Jack Williams, **President and CEO, PRISM, Comcast Spectacor, and Comcast SportsNet:**
We had the rights to televise the Flyers, Sixers, and Phillies. The one team we didn't have was the Eagles. The way the NFL is set up, you would never get those rights during the regular season. We wanted an association with the Eagles, and the postgame show, we felt, was the best way to do that. We worked with the Eagles organization and put together a plan on how to do it. We couldn't use footage. We had the people that would come in: Ray Didinger, the governor [Ed Rendell]. It was a good show. The people were quality people.

Tom Stathakes, **Senior Vice President of Programming, Comcast SportsNet:**
I was adamant, I was absolutely adamant, that we were going to start *Postgame* as soon as the gun sounds. It was the only way we were going to train [viewers] to come over there [to *Postgame Live* after the game ended]. That took a while. We didn't do any numbers, early. It took about a year. We would be in the middle of a volleyball match, and the [football] game would end. At times, the producers would be in there, ready to do *Postgame*, and they would let the volleyball match finish, or let the horse race or let a golf match finish. I would be like, "Guys, this is nothing more than filler bullshit. The second the game ends, I'm

talking when the clock goes to zero, I don't care if the announcers are still talking—you have to roll the open and go." It took a little while, and it was a lot of aggravation and a lot of teamwork. Then, we started getting it.

Brian Monihan, President and General Manager, Comcast Spectacor and Comcast SportsNet/NBC Sports Philadelphia:
When you look at it from even outside of TV, when you look at a show that runs on a different channel after a game and manages to get everyone to change the channel, that's really impressive. That's so hard to do. That's a real accomplishment, when you get a real committed audience like that, and when you come into running a program that's highlighting something that is not even on your network, that's a big deal.

Ray Didinger, Football Historian and Author:
Two things: Number one, I said I would do it, but number two, this doesn't have a chance in the world of succeeding. I said, "There is no chance anybody is going to watch this show." My thinking was, you are going to have a panel show. By the rules of the league, you weren't allowed to use highlights on that show. You weren't going to be able to show any footage or highlights. The show was just going to be three or four guys sitting at a desk, talking. I said to Tom [Stathakes], "Nobody is going to watch that." I said, "It's like watching CSPAN" and chances are, a lot of Sundays, if the Eagles play at one o'clock and we come on at four o'clock, there are going to be live games going on on other networks. It's going to be unlike the Phillies postgame, Flyers and Sixers postgame, where the game was on Comcast and the game runs right into the postgame show. I said, "The Eagles game is going to be on another network, so somebody is going to have to pick up the remote and switch over to our show to watch four guys at a desk?"

Rob Ellis, Senior Producer and Host, Comcast SportsNet/NBC Sports Philadelphia and KYW:
We were all in the mindset that any kind of postgame show has to be breaking film down and breaking the highlights down. We thought, "Man, are we really going to get through?" I don't remember what it was originally, an hour and a half or two hours or whatever, without any

kind of film, with people just talking about it. Once you kind of got an idea of the opinions and then the ability to go outside the locker room and talk to folks, you started to think, "Okay, this can work."

Derrick Gunn, Reporter,
Comcast SportsNet/NBC Sports Philadelphia:
I knew going in I had to build relationships with [Philadelphia Eagles] players to trust me. Even before we would go on live, we would talk about certain things. A player would tell me, "I would talk about that [one thing], but I don't want to talk about that [other thing]." Things that weren't talked about in a locker room. Obviously, players are a little hesitant, especially when you are a large media market like Philadelphia or warming up to media people, 'cause they are always thinking somebody is gonna burn them along the way. I always knew because of my history of covering teams like the Chargers, Packers, and Steelers, if I stayed true to who I was, that I could win over more players than not. Once players, coaches, team officials, front office, and trainers know you can be trusted, they open up to you, and they are more comfortable with you. For me, I knew for what I was going to have to be in terms of input of that show, I just couldn't get one or two players. We needed multiple voices.

Neal Slotkin, Producer,
Comcast SportsNet/NBC Sports Philadelphia:
You were eagerly waiting for those guys to come out and talk to him. Even if it was a loss or a win, it didn't matter. Derrick [Gunn] got those guys to open up. I know I'm biased because I was there, but to me as a sports viewer, sometimes the talking-heads part gets a little cumbersome and a little over the top. I want to know what the players are thinking. There's nobody that I ever worked with that was better at getting guys to, like, open up and talk than Derrick was.

Derrick Gunn, Reporter,
Comcast SportsNet/NBC Sports Philadelphia:
When *Postgame Live* really got going, the Eagles had a group of not just great players but characters in that locker room. Jon Runyan, Hugh Douglas, Ike Reese, Chad Lewis, Hollis Thomas, Jamaal Jackson: guys like that who were personalities as well. In a lot of cases, they would

come out, especially after wins, and take the mic from me, and I would stand back, and it was a show in itself. I had to be the ringleader out there, but they were passionate. Brian Dawkins: my goodness, Lito Sheppard, Sheldon Brown: It goes on and on. What really helped was once these guys got comfortable with that platform. A lot of times, these guys, after spending twenty to thirty minutes talking to fifty to sixty media people in the locker room, didn't want to talk. As I got to know them and they trusted me, we became more than just a reporter and interviewee. There was a friendship and a bond there. A lot of them did it for me. When they left the team, they would pass the baton and tell other people "Hey, you can trust this guy. He's gonna ask you the tough questions, but you can trust him." It kept going from there. That's why my input in [the show] became so popular, because of the personalities I was able to get. Some of the things I was able to draw out of them that people in the locker room weren't able to get out of them. That became a cult following itself. That's one of my proudest moments in terms of the twenty-three years I contributed to that show.

Neal Slotkin, Producer,
Comcast SportsNet/NBC Sports Philadelphia:
I am the biggest Ray Didinger fan in the world. To me, knowing that guy is amazing. He is an encyclopedia of Eagles knowledge. He is like that grandfatherly expert on any topic, but he has a calm demeanor. After a game, you would see so many of the guys, a late loss, they would be distraught, and there's Ray with the calm Xs and Os: This is why they lost.

Ray Didinger, Football Historian and Author:
[Ed Rendell] was a politician, but he was the anti-politician in the sense that he is going to tell you exactly what's on your mind. He's the least political politician that I've ever known. He tells you exactly what he is thinking. He's got strong opinions, and he's not afraid to voice them. That was the great part of having him on the show. You think about having a mayor or a governor on a sports show, you think he is going to be a fence-straddler. That's what politicians tend to be. He was not. He told you exactly what you were thinking, and he was clearly an Eagles fan. He was rooting for them like crazy, but if they played poorly, he had no trouble calling them out. That's why it worked. That's the only reason why it worked.

Ed Rendell, Former Philadelphia Mayor and Pennsylvania Governor:
I would call in twice a week to Angelo Cataldi's morning show. It became known I was a big Eagles fan, and I had a strong opinion about the team and how it was being run, etcetera. When Comcast decided to do the show, I think it was the second city they went into to do their own postgame show. They asked me, and I was surprised.

I remember the first game. I'm sitting there, and I look at my watch, and it's been an hour and fifteen minutes, which passed by as if it was twenty minutes, so fast. I said to myself, "Do people actually get paid for this? A bunch of guys sitting around talking about a football game they just watched?" I said it was amazing. When I first started out, I didn't accept any salary. The other people were, and they were all paid. I didn't accept a salary because I did business with Comcast as mayor, and if they paid me, it might set up or look like an appearance of conflict of interest.

I thought Eagles fans were berserk enough that if we made this show entertaining, I thought we had a chance to succeed. When we did our first show, I thought we were doing great. I thought we had a perfect blend of some good football insights, some answers to the controversial plays or controversial calls, play calling, or defense. I thought we discussed those well. We did it in sort of a fun way. We always had fun with the show. That's what set it apart.

Amy Fadool, Anchor and Reporter,
Comcast SportsNet/NBC Sports Philadelphia:
When I first started and saw it, I said, "The governor of our state is on our show?" They said, "Yeah, he's been doing it since he's been there." I said, "Does anybody else think that's insane? That's crazy talk." So I met him, and he's there and comes in with Secret Service guys, and I said, "This is bananas. I'm in the green room, and here's the governor of our state."

Angelo Cataldi, Radio Host:
[Ed Rendell] did establish that he was a very good commentator on sports on my radio show. I'm positive about that. He was a very regular caller, and before that he just seemed like he was a fan. He became more than that on our show. He became more than that by great opinions. He knew what he was talking about, and we had a big incident—and he was a huge part of the incident—when we booed Donovan McNabb. His profile as sports

commentator was established then when we booed Donovan McNabb because he goaded us into it, and it was a fun thing at the time. He wanted Ricky Williams. We would go along with the mayor, and eventually *we* wanted Ricky Williams. When they named Donovan, we booed them, and then we all blamed the mayor. I think he kind of earned his reputation as a sports guy by the radio show. But what he did by the TV show was fantastic in itself. He really was a great voice of the fan. There's a reason why he was such a successful politician. He knew what the fans thought. He spoke for them so often, and so often he was saying on that show what the fans would be saying on my show the next morning after an Eagles game.

Another show that was added to the programming at Comcast SportsNet was Daily News Live, *a live evening program with host Michael Barkann that included* Philadelphia Daily News *columnists, coaches, players, and local celebrities.*

Rob Ellis, Senior Producer and Host,
Comcast SportsNet/NBC Sports Philadelphia and KYW:
[*Daily News Live*] was a pre-pre-contrived debate show. Like, now you can flip on any network, and you see one on-air host is told to have an opinion and the other one is told to have the opposing opinions, and then they have these faux arguments, and people are hot-taking and all of these other stuff. This was before any of that. Whether you agreed or not—and you could certainly disagree with any of the opinions—it was actually that person's opinion. People weren't afraid to step on toes.

We also got creative. I used to have Dick Jerardi get a makeover on the air. We had a newlywed game. We would go out of the box a little bit. We would take shows on the road. By the road, I would mean Citizens Bank Park or [Veterans Stadium] back then, outside for a tailgate for a Flyers game. We would do that kind of stuff and be out there with the people. I think it was just passionate people not being afraid to share opinions, and I also think it was a lot of ways—you have to understand the climate. It's pre–social media.

Neal Slotkin, Producer, Comcast SportsNet/NBC Sports Philadelphia:
It kind of was a mutual benefit. It gave us guests every day and gave us topics. It also gave them an outlet to really almost expand on their articles that they were covering or columns.

Tom Stathakes, Senior Vice President of Programming, Comcast SportsNet:

If you look at that time, you had Ray Didinger, Stan Hochman, Bill Conlin, Dick Jerardi, Mike Kern, Paul Domowitch. I mean it was ridiculous how many great journalists there were in town. Initially, not all of them wanted to do it, but when they started getting paid and started to realize when they walked into a Wawa that people started to realize who they were, they really started to like it.

Michael Barkann, Anchor and Host, KYW and Comcast SportsNet/NBC Sports Philadelphia:

To me, that show was the crux of it. That's what helped Philadelphia sports fans gain more insight into their teams, and it gave them a place to turn when the stuff hit the fan. Terrell Owens leaves camp and is doing sit-ups in his driveway, or the Phillies make a trade, someone is injured for the Sixers, there's an argument in the locker room, who is not getting along with who, things that can affect play, plus the live interviews with coaches and players. That had never been . . . before that, you could be sitting in your living room in Philadelphia and listen to Claude Giroux, Rick Tocchett, or Ron Hextall, or any of them. Take your pick. We got some pretty damn good guests.

Rob Ellis, Senior Producer and Host, Comcast SportsNet/NBC Sports Philadelphia and KYW:

Michael Barkann was the ultimate maestro. He was just phenomenal and was a great quarterback and great point guard at being able to inject his opinion but also keep it moving and get other people's opinions. [The show] was really ahead of its time in a lot of ways. If you look at what's on now, a lot of it I wouldn't say is stolen but borrowed from, or at least the blueprint was laid by, *Daily News Live*.

Dick Jerardi, Columnist, *Philadelphia Daily News*:

What was cool about the show was, whether it was an Eagles game or an upcoming event or some controversy you could talk about, the cool thing was we had so much time. I remember Stan Hochman and I did an entire show with Michael [Barkann] on Babe Ruth.

Rob Kuestner, Producer and Assistant News Director, Comcast SportsNet and WCAU:
The moment we changed as a news gathering organization, really, was Terrell Owens being booted out of training camp. We broke that story. Barkann got it from a source, and our ability to be there before everybody with the volume of resources we were able to put on it and then just literally take everything live. It was like nothing I don't think anyone had seen before.

Derrick Gunn, Reporter, Comcast SportsNet/NBC Sports Philadelphia:
The writers in particular—you saw their signatures on their articles, columns, and in the newspaper, but it gave the fans a perspective of visually being able to see these people on a daily basis to get a better feel for them and their personalities. We knew what kind of writers they were, but now you got to see the personalities behind the writer. The quick wit, the guy who was just a regular guy like the rest of us at home. They had a family. They had other things outside of being a sports columnist or just a coach or just a player.

Brian Monihan, President and General Manager, Comcast Spectacor and Comcast SportsNet/NBC Sports Philadelphia:
[*Daily News Live*] gave rise to personalities like Marcus Hayes, John Smallwood, and a lot of these other writers who people otherwise didn't get a chance to see behind the print.

Les Bowen, Columnist, *Philadelphia Daily News*:
I think one thing I didn't understand initially was how much it would raise our profile. I think when you write for a living, you want to think that people know you from that and are really reading what you write. What I found over the years is that when it came to being recognized in public, many, many more people watched me on Comcast [SportsNet] than actually read what I wrote. So, it became kind of a celebrity thing—obviously not to a great extent, but in the heyday, I would go to the grocery store, and twelve different people would ask me questions about the Flyers or Eagles when I started to cover them.

Mike Kern, Columnist, *Philadelphia Daily News*:
I used to joke with people all of the time. We would be down the shore for the summer, and my son would be laughing because he would say, "Dad, as we were walking off the boardwalk, ten people turned their heads and knew who you were." It's the truth. Once they see you, it's not a byline anymore. I guess my picture used to be in the paper, and I did my college football notes column, but it's different when you're on TV. I'd have people come up to me and say, "Are you going to spring training?" I would say, "I'm not the Phillies writer," and they wouldn't get it. They would be like, what do you mean? I said I had never been to spring training in my entire life. I was covering college basketball at that time. Because you went on *Daily News Live* and talked about everything. That was a big part of it. That gave me an identity.

As Eddie Barkowitz said, when we finally learned it was coming to an end, and then it lasted a couple more years of Philly sports talk, "We had a longer run than *M*A*S*H*!" When you think about it in terms of TV, I guess when you are on for fifteen or sixteen years, I'm not sure what it was, that's pretty good.

Bob Cooney, Columnist, *Philadelphia Daily News*:
It was a connection to the people that said, "Wow! I'm a sports fan; so are they. They just have access, and they are trying to provide me with the information." I think that came across much more on *Daily News Live* than it could just by writing a column with our name at the top of it.

Through the years as *Daily News Live* progressed, when you talked to athletes after they would appear on it, they appreciated it. Athletes, coaches, visiting coaches, or writers, they just appreciate something like that, when you have a broadcast of "Oh my God—I'm not just a behind-the-scenes guy. I can actually show people what I'm thinking, and what we are thinking, and how day by day going about covering a team, a sport, whatever it may be, how it really happens."

Pat McLoone, Managing Editor, *Philadelphia Daily News*:
We expected Comcast SportsNet to be big. We expected the TV show to be big and be a big part of it, but the impact Comcast SportsNet had on Philadelphia and what *Daily News Live* meant for the profile of the *Daily News* sports staff and the *Daily News* in general—yes, it far, far exceeded that. You would like to think that as a writer, you can stand

on your byline and the body of your work, but guys who had been at it for ten, twenty, and thirty years were now getting stopped in Wawa and stuff because people instantly recognized them from *Daily News Live*.

The constant use of the logo and the branding and the very name itself, *Daily News Live*, that was branding that was critical to the *Daily News*, and we couldn't have asked for anything better.

HURRICANE FLOYD

On September 16, 1999, Hurricane Floyd hit the Delaware Valley. The hurricane formed off the coast of Africa and lasted September 7–19, hitting Florida, North Carolina, and cities along the mid-Atlantic. Philadelphia experienced a record rainfall of 6.8 inches in a single day that resulted in one thousand evictees and more than 3,500 homes flooded. Hurricane Floyd's total damage between the United States and the Bahamas was estimated at about $4.5 billion.

Rob Guarino, Chief Meteorologist, WTXF:
What really stuck out to me was when I looked at the first model that came in: The amount of rain was ridiculous. I almost thought it was an error. I was like, "Wow—this is going to be a really bad flood." Then, the next model came in, which was the European model, and they all kept matching up to be a really big rain event. Essentially, what the storm was was a railroad track that went right up the coast, and it squeezed all of the moisture out of the Atlantic and pushed into the Philly area and kept rotating, spiraling in with more and more rain. It wasn't the biggest hurricane as far as wind, but it was the wettest.

Glenn Schwartz, Meteorologist, WCAU:
I kind of remember the weather pattern for that. Even though it was tracking up the coast, I saw a front developing right over the I-95 area,

which would kind of focus the rainfall. So, we were not just focusing on the shore where the track of the storm was going and the highest winds were. That was the area that got the biggest rains and the biggest flooding, right where the front had developed. We brought in Doc John Niese from the Franklin Institute. We had an association with him, and we would go down there and give talks regularly. I got to know him, and we needed some extra bodies because we were going to go on and stay on. He was somebody that really had the history of Philadelphia weather pretty well in his head and was a great resource on and off the air to talk about the place in history of the particular storm. That was something rare that happened: to pull somebody in from outside to put them on TV.

John Bolaris, Meteorologist, WCAU and WTXF:
It was scary to forecast that because you knew it was going to be life-threatening, and it's going to be in your neighborhood. Like, I was thinking of Manayunk at the time. I didn't live there, but I knew it was going to be hit particularly hard from some of the data I was looking at. There is a sense when you are on the air that is to always remain calm and be focused without getting high-pitched or racing. You just have to take it one step at a time. I always felt that's when you really earn your money and that's where you want to make sure people understand and have a responsibility to make sure they are okay. Despite what everyone always says about hype, I did not hype. I always saw the way I read it, saw it, or analyzed it. I never hyped. I just gave the forecast as I saw it.

Carla Carpenter, News Director, WPVI:
Whenever we had a storm coming, we tried to be prepared to cover the storm from every neighborhood possible; that was a part of the Channel 6 mission, which was to cover everyone: Every neighborhood counted, every person and everything counted. I do remember during that storm or another one, looking at the screen at a live feed at one of our photographers and seeing Upper Darby suddenly under water, various strip malls under water, which were not even near water, just from the amount of rainfall. I had a home on the Delaware River. I could see my own home under water. We put Chopper 6 up because it was the safest and easiest way to cover significant storms and storm damage. It was interesting, to say the least, to see your own house underwater, but it's good

because it shows you how difficult it is for those people that live in homes that get regularly flooded.

Susan Buehler, Reporter, WTXF:
I actually won an award for Hurricane Floyd from the White Marsh Township Police Department. I won a Citizens' Award. We were crawling along the river in Blue Bell in Wissahickon, covering flooding, and came across a bus full of children, a school bus. The school bus driver thought that she was going to be able to cross the road and was completely swept away by the raging water. The kids were trapped in the bus, and the photographer and I rescued the kids out of the bus while we were calling 911 to get the rescue squad there. We pulled out the kids one by one and walked them to safety before the bus was swept away. It was kind of sitting along a fence, and we were afraid the fence was going to break and the bus would just wash away, so we ran over and called 911 and started pulling kids off the bus until the rescue squad got there. So, we ended up getting an award for that one.

Rich Scott, News Director, WPHL:
One of the interesting things about working in Philadelphia for a long time is when storms hit, you sort of know where to go, the usual places where flooding happens, but that was some of the worst flooding that I ever saw. Those pictures of water gushing down the streets in Montgomery County—it was incredible, and nobody expected it to be that bad. That was originally supposed to be a coastal storm, not an inland storm, and all of the stations, I recall, were positioned along the Jersey Shore, and then suddenly all the rainfall actually fell inland. It was a huge challenge. There was water everywhere, and I remember there were concerns about a dam breaking, and there was just flooding everywhere, and the reports came in so quick. Weather is always unpredictable, and you prepare for what you think is going to happen, and then something totally different happens, and you're out of position, and you have to scramble to get to places. Weather stories are perhaps the most challenging to cover because you never know what's really going to happen. You make all these plans, and then it's totally unexpected, some of the worst flooding, some of the most spectacular flooding videos that I've ever seen, spectacular in terms of so much water in places you wouldn't expect it to be.

Robin Taylor, Reporter, KYW and WTXF:
I get sent out to the Jersey Shore, and it's raining like you wouldn't believe. Wind is blowing, and we have to find somewhere that's sheltered enough so we can put the mast up because you can't put it up on the van and have it break or have the whole thing blow over because the wind was so strong. We got the mast up, and we got the signal in, but our equipment got so wet that we couldn't even feed our story back, and so we were just kind of like, "Oh my gosh—this isn't working." So, they sent us to another location, and we were farther out from the Jersey Shore, and the eye of the hurricane came through. You go from this tremendous rain everywhere and wind to all of a sudden being still and the sun coming out, and it was just so odd because it hit around five or six o'clock, and we were able to get a signal out from there because the equipment dried off enough. So, we're doing all this hurricane coverage, and the sun's out, and then we go off the air, and we have to come back again and make our way back to Philly, and we're no longer in the eye, and it's blowing wind and raining and everything, and we get back to Philly, and it turns out that they had been wrong with all of their predictions. The predictions were that it was really going to be bad on the coast, but it wasn't.

Amy Buckman, Reporter, WPVI:
We were in one of the smaller live vans, and we were parked in Sea Isle, sort of at the end of a street where we could hit the tower in Atlantic City without putting the mast up on the van too much because if you were to put it up, it would blow over. It kind of jutted out over the ocean a little bit, and we were able to hit the tower, which was on top of one of the casinos in Atlantic City. We were there for the duration, hopping in and out of the van and doing live shots. I did all the "windblown and barely being able to stand up" shots. I was even in rain gear, and I was soaked through. And there were people staying in their house on the block where we had parked, and they kind of came out and checked in on us from time to time. At one point, we went into the house, and I literally stripped down, and the woman let me borrow some of her clothes to put on under my rain gear, and she put all of my clothes in her dryer. It was a really long day. I remember they talked about "the calm before the storm" and "the calm after the storm." When it was over, I was just amazed because everything became completely calm, and there

were people walking out of their houses that had stayed through the storm and brought out their fishing rods. The ocean had been so turned up, there were fish that you could actually stand on the beach and cast your rod and go fishing. It was calm and beautiful afterward, which was bizarre.

Bill Henley, Meteorologist, WCAU:
I do remember the tail end of it, when it was quickly tailing out. I talked about on the air how quickly it was clearing out, and people didn't believe me, and then it did happen.

Jane King, Business Reporter, WPVI:
With that particular story, I did a lot of business coverage. There were kind of a lot of insurance stories, and we did a lot of the economic damage in Manayunk, and I remember going there and covering stories and talking to some of the restaurant owners and how were they going to come back after a hurricane.

PIER 34 COLLAPSES

On May 18, 2000, Pier 34 overlooking the Delaware River in Philadelphia collapsed under its own weight, sending the nightclub that had recently opened on the pier into the water. Three women who were in the nightclub drowned in the collapse: Jean Marie Ferraro, twenty-seven; Monica Kristina Rodriguez, twenty-one; and DeAnn White, twenty-five. Forty-three people were also injured the night of the accident, including eight rescue workers.

According to the Philadelphia Inquirer, *a study conducted in the 1970s by the Philadelphia Department of Commerce determined that Pier 34 had a load capacity of five hundred pounds per square foot and an estimated useful life until 1990. Years prior to the incident, the owners of the pier had been informed that more than $1.2 million in repairs were needed to fix the pier.*

Michael Asbell, owner and developer of Pier 34, and Eli Karetny, manager of the nightclub, were criminally charged with third-degree murder in connection with the deaths of the three women who were killed. They later went to trial, resulting in a hung jury. According to the Philadelphia Inquirer, *Karenty pleaded guilty in 2007 to involuntary manslaughter and reckless endangerment. Asbell pleaded no contest to involuntary manslaughter, reckless endangerment, conspiracy, and risking a catastrophe. Both men were sentenced to one thousand hours of community service and eleven to twenty-two months on house arrest.*

The night of the incident, WCAU used a split screen with details of the disaster running as text across the bottom of the screen. The station was airing heavily promoted season finales of Friends, Frasier, *and* ER. *During the breaks in the shows, a split screen aired reduced images from NBC's feed on one side and video from Pier 34 on the other. At the end of its primetime shows, WCAU expanded its 11:00 P.M. newscast to sixty-five minutes.*

WTXF was also in the midst of a complicated sweeps broadcast, airing the film True Lies, *starring Arnold Schwarzenegger, which originally bumped its 10:00 P.M. newscasts to 11:00 P.M. The station offered a five-minute insert at 10:00 P.M., urging viewers to continue watching after the movie for coverage of the event in the evening newscast.*

WPHL added four-and-a-half minutes to its newscast at 10:00 P.M., which delivered the station a 6.5 Nielsen rating, more than double its normal figure at the time. KYW's 11:00 P.M. newscast was expanded to fifty minutes.

WPVI had inserts for a total of eight minutes and at 10:00 P.M. trimmed four minutes from Behind the Scenes of *Who Wants to Be a Millionaire? WPVI's newscast went fifty-six minutes longer than normal.*

Pete Kane, Photographer, WCAU:
I had just finished my shift at five-something. I'm on my way home. I keep my scanner on all of the time. I hear on my scanner of a water rescue on Delaware Avenue. I punch up the fire frequency, and I hear them saying that the pier collapsed and people were in the water. They are calling marine units, and they are calling in everybody. I race down to there and go two piers over and go onto a private property that goes out as far as that pier went. I'm on a two-way [radio] with some other guys that are headed down there, and I tell the desk where I'm going. I look across, I see the pier that collapsed in the water. There are people that they are pulling out of the water.

Terry Ruggles, Reporter and Anchor, WCAU:
I was at a dinner recognizing the Burlington County Public Information that night, and I was with Nora Muchanic and someone from Channel 3, and our phones went off at the same time, and we all left to go [to the

scene]. I was sent to Camden to Wiggins Park because that was the vantage point [from which] you could look right over the piers.

Jim Sinkovitz, Anchor and Reporter, WPHL:
I was the first one there for our station. That was another tragic story, especially for one of the young girls, who had just started working at the aquarium. She was just starting work there, and the girl she was replacing was with her that night, and they were having a party. Apparently, too many people were on the pier, and it collapsed, and people careened into the water, and these girls got stuck under some tent material and drowned. When we got there, of course, we were kept back, but it was right next to the *Moshulu* [restaurant on a boat], and so I had seen it before. That was very tragic.

Rich Scott, News Director, WPHL:
I remember Jim [Sinkovitz] was live down there on the pier. He was nearby getting ready to do another story and got there late when that happened, and that was another one where this was unfolding. And I was like, "The pier collapsed? What?" Jim did an outstanding job interviewing people who witnessed the whole thing. He just rolled up on the scene, was in the right place at the right time.

We were lucky that we had somebody who was nearby and got there quickly, so we got there very early on the scene. It's all about logistics. It's all about being in the right place at the right time.

Dann Cuellar, Reporter, WPVI:
You see a chaotic scene. Ambulances everywhere, trucks and police cars everywhere. The confusion and chaos about what happened: Are people in the river, or they needed to be helped? People were looking, and there were helicopters flying in the sky. I think there was a search looking in the river for survivors. This was one of those stories where they want you on the air as soon as possible.

Bruce Gordon, Reporter, WPHL and WTXF:
The thing that stands out there was kind of a feeling of helplessness as I stood for what seemed like hours on end right at the river's edge there. You could see the police boats, the search crews out there, and you had

a sense of the urgency of what was going on but also the sense of helplessness. Whatever had happened, there wasn't much anyone could do about it. This was pretty quickly determined to be more of a recovery effort than a rescue effort, per se. There was just a sense of helplessness as you describe these things. As is often the case when there is a huge story, you are there live for long stretches of time. You are trying to process all of this in real time while you are live on the air. It was a challenge to bring people meaningful information when there was just this sense of "we are doing everything we can out here in the water, but this is not gonna end well."

Carla Carpenter, News Director, WPVI:
I'll never forget one piece of video, which was of a young woman who had passed on the gurney. Her one hand was set like you would think it was a thumbs-up. Her eyes were open, and she had a smile on her face, but she wasn't alive, but she looked like she was alive. That was another one of those: really traumatic for your photographers, reporters, crews on the scene. Then, the people back at the station have to look at the tape and make sure what tape can get on the air and what can't. In the early stages of something like that, we do feel—when something big happens—we do feel it's more important than any television show that's on at the time. That was a very big event.

Jesse Gary, Reporter, WCAU:
That was another one of those moments when you realize how fragile life is, how quickly it can go, and you don't even see it coming. There's no way those kids went out for a night with their friends on the Delaware River, as I have done many times myself, and thought, "I am going to wind up in the river, drowning to death." You think to yourself how lucky you are that this didn't happen to you, how painful and how sad it is for the parents who will never get over it. They will go to their graves carrying that with them.

Dawn Stensland-Mendte, Anchor and Reporter, KYW and WTXF:
It was surreal to imagine you had all of these people celebrating on this beautiful Philadelphia evening, and you heard the stories of many people. They were celebrating a new job, an engagement, a lot of people

were there for a celebration or just "hey, let's go out tonight" and whatever. To have that tragedy happen, cover it, and then do the follow-up and find out, tragically, it could have been avoided. It was a lack of inspection. My thing was some of the victims, when I continued to follow them over the years, and their pain and anguish. I know for some of the victims, their parents—for example, DeAnn White—left her room the same. The dog would still sleep in that bedroom. It was heart-wrenching.

Doug Shimell, Reporter, WCAU:
It's one of those things where you are fishing people out of the water, they are coming out with blankets, they are in their nice evening attire, and they have hypothermia, and they just lost their friend, and it was sort of other-worldly. I hadn't covered anything like that, and it was different from a plane crash, it's different from a hurricane victim. These were people out having a good time, and for no apparent reason, the pier collapsed. What we found out in the succeeding weeks and months and years was that there were known cracks in the cement, and they put QUIKRETE in them, they put rugs over the cracks, so it was a known entity, and there were a lot of claims and civil suits afterward. I think there was a general outrage on the part of the parents and relatives of the victims that there was not more punishment for the people that owned and managed the pier and the club.

Robin Taylor, Reporter, KYW and WTXF:
I was out there the next day covering it, and it was just cold, pouring, a miserable day, and there were all the news crews from New York and from the networks that were there, and it was just a big scramble to cover that tragedy and try to get all the relatives.

Susan Buehler, Reporter, WTXF:
The most interesting thing about that story is that it turns into a major investigation about whether or not they knew if there were significant issues with the club and with the deck before they even had the celebration, which in itself turns out to be a horrible ending. It was a really big story for its time, and I think it's changed the landscape of the clubs down there on Delaware Avenue ever since. There was no shortage of angles to cover on this story.

THE "STORM OF THE CENTURY"

On March 5, 2001, the infamous "Storm of the Century" brought scant snow accumulations to Philadelphia and the Delaware Valley. The potential storm had been hyped up to viewers by WCAU Channel 10—one newscast predicted potentially over a foot of snow—but in fact amounted to only one inch of coating. During its 10:00 P.M. primetime showing of Law & Order *on Wednesday, February 28, WCAU ran a crawl announcing that the storm of the decade would hit in the upcoming weekend: "The NBC10 Earthwatch team is now tracking the possibility of one of the biggest East Coast storms in the past decade. NBC10 will have the very latest following* Law & Order."

The announcement sent confusion throughout the newsrooms in Philadelphia and made viewers rush to get their last-minute snow and food items as well as prompting cancellations of schools and transportation. WCAU meteorologist John Bolaris took the lead during the subsequent 11:00 P.M. newscast in which he discussed the potentially hard-hitting storm. Bolaris warned viewers on the subsequent Sunday, March 4, 11:00 P.M. newscast that people should stay home from work and school the following day because the light rain and snow forecast could explode into a major blizzard by the late afternoon.

Longtime Philadelphia Daily News *columnist Stu Bykofsky issued a friendly wager with Bolaris for $100 that the storm would not happen. If Bykofsky was right, Bolaris would write a check to the Variety Club, a local charity for children with intellectual disabilities. If Bolaris was* *right, and Bykovsky's newspaper led the following day's paper with coverage of the big storm, Bykofsky would donate $100 to the Children's Hospital of Philadelphia.*

"My problem was not with his forecast—he's not making this stuff up (I'm pretty sure)—as with the crawl, which was calculated to keep viewers riveted to his station for the news. The crawl would make viewers think the storm was maybe in Pottstown ready to swoop down on a defenseless Delaware Valley like a peregrine falcon on a city pigeon," Bykofsky wrote in March 2001.

A day after the "storm" hit, the Philadelphia Daily News *front page read, "Snow Job: Now that the hysteria has outdone 'The Storm,' who overhyped it the most?" giving readers an option to call the paper's hotline number to vote which station overhyped the storm coverage the most. NBC10's John Bolaris received 4,827 votes, compared to 6abc's Dave Roberts (596), KYW's John Stehlin (176), and Fox 29's Rob Guarino (140).*

Over the next few days of the aftermath of the debunked forecast, Bolaris reportedly received more than a thousand emails and a few threats for his miscalling of the storm. Bolaris told the Philadelphia Inquirer *in 2001 that he received a voicemail that said, "If I owned a gun, there would be one less person I'd need to worry about." Bolaris also told the* Philadelphia Inquirer *at the time that the storm was the worst call of his career, bringing him local and national media attention.*

Popular speculation was that the "storm of the decade" was a ratings publicity stunt created by the higher-ups at WCAU, as the station was inching closer to beating WPVI in the 11:00 P.M. ratings. The hype of the storm worked in favor of WCAU, as it topped WPVI for the first time since May 1971 in the 11:00 P.M. newscast ratings. The 11:00 P.M. newscast anchored by Larry Mendte and Renée Chenault-Fattah averaged a 12.6 rating and 22 share during February sweeps, whereas WPVI had a 12.0 rating and a 21 share. (Each local ratings point was equal to 27,034 homes, per the Philadelphia Inquirer *in 2001.) The loss for WPVI was anchor Jim Gardner's first time not leading local news ratings since becoming the* Action News *anchor in 1977. The other time slots between WPVI and WCAU were distinctly different compared to the 11:00 P.M. newscast. WPVI continued to beat WCAU in the 5:00 A.M., noon, 5:00 P.M., and 6:00 P.M. newscasts, with the largest gap between the two stations being WPVI's 6:00 P.M. newscast, with a 15 rating and 26 per-*

cent audience share, compared to WCAU's 8 rating and 13 percent audience share. WCAU celebrated its achievement in high fashion, with news director Steve Schwaid hanging "number one" signs in his office; offering breakfast, cold-cut sandwiches, and evening dinner for staff; and even serving a celebratory cake for the big ratings wins.

In May 2001, WPVI reclaimed the 11:00 P.M. ratings title it had lost to WCAU, with a 11.7 Nielsen rating and a 22 percent audience share. Channel 10 had an 11.1 rating and a 20 percent audience share. KYW with Larry Kane continued to trail with a 5.8 rating and 11 percent audience share, down 15 percent from May 2000.

Rob Guarino, Chief Meteorologist, WTXF:
If it wasn't for the ratings book, it would have never happened. It was the end of the ratings [period], and it was a tie [between the stations]. That's why this happened. If this was December, a non-ratings book and Christmas, this storm wouldn't have been hyped up as much. It would have been talked about around the holiday, and no one would have remembered it today. Because it was at the end of the season, and it was a tie there, it was played up to be the biggest one of all time days out. That's what people remember. It went from forty inches to not even an inch. I mean, that's a really blown forecast. You go forty and then you get twelve, you still have a big storm, or maybe it wasn't that big. This was a total bust—probably still the biggest bust in Philly TV history, I believe, to this day.

Neal Zoren, TV Columnist:
In 2001, Channel 10 was always promoting themselves: "We are the first," "We are the best," "Channel 10 knows things you don't know." The hype of Channel 10 was extraordinary at the turn of the [twenty-first] century. Television always wants to keep you watching at home on television. They are always telling you not to go out and not to do that.

John Bolaris, Meteorologist, WCAU and WTXF:
This is what happened: We were in a ratings battle at the time. It was the last night of the [ratings] book, a Wednesday. We were battling neck to neck with PVI, who's never been toppled on the eleven o'clock news since 1975. My news director [Steve Schwaid] goes, "Anything going on?" I said, "Not tonight, but there is a potential for a storm—could be

significant to major—on Sunday or Monday, but it's early yet. This is some of the computer models that are suggesting we could be in for something pretty nasty come late in the weekend and/or Monday. I'm not certain yet." He said, "What are you going to do with it?" I said, "Well, I can tease it and say coming up, we have potential for a significant storm waiting in the wings, or if it's something major, I will give you the details on when and how." He goes, "Okay." You know what he does? He runs a crawl on *Law & Order* of that night: "potential of a storm of the century to be hitting Philadelphia and the surrounding suburbs." I was shocked when people said "Bolaris: Storm of the Century." What are you talking about? I never said "storm of the century." I went running into his office and said, "What the fuck is that?" "Well, can it be?" he asked. I said, "Steve, it could be a major storm, blizzard, a monster, or it can be nothing. I don't know yet. Where did you get 'storm of the century'?" This is the guy, you gotta remember, who named storms for The Weather Channel and also had a blue light special, which meant you had two minutes to get it together if those alarms went off inside the newsroom. Blue lights? I said, "Steve, that's crazy and insane."

I went on the air and said that night, "There is a potential for a major storm on Sunday into Monday, and it could be a major storm of six inches or more. We don't know yet, but it's something we will look at." We had a lot more to go to really nail this down. The potential was there. I would always say, "We will let you know when to panic—not yet."

Steve Schwaid, News Director, WCAU and WTXF:
It was probably about 9:30 at night, ten o'clock at night, it was the last night of the ratings period. My tradition was always to stick around in the station on the last night of the ratings period to be with the staff. I was in my office. [John] Bolaris walks into my office and talks about how we have this massive, massive, massive, massive storm coming this way. He used the term "storm of the century," and I sat down, and we wrote a crawl, and I was probably the one who typed it, but whatever I typed, it was Bolaris over my shoulder telling me what I should say. We ran that, and I remember the next day, you know, the "storm of the century," and I wake up, and there's nothing. I said, "John, what happened?" He tried to give me all these different excuses, and I was like, "John, we gotta figure out what we want to say on the air, and the best

thing to say is this is what we forecast, it didn't happen, this is a thing about storms like this and how quickly they change." It became an event in itself.

Larry Mendte, Anchor, WCAU and KYW:
I was in Steve [Schwaid]'s office when [John] Bolaris came in. Bolaris said, "We are tracking a storm that is so big, it could be the storm of the century." It was Schwaid that said, "You know what? We are gonna run a crawl that says it has the potential to be the storm of the century." All three of us were all for it. I know John was all for it. I know John has given different stories about it since then, but I was right there. He was all gung-ho for the crawl. I remember the ratings that night—I think it was *Law & Order*, it was a finale of *Law & Order*—but no one gets ratings like this anymore, by the way, because of streaming and cable, but it was a 17.1 rating—not a share. We held it because of that crawl, and I'm sure it was because of that crawl. We held it, and we beat PVI. We were probably gonna beat them anyway, but we beat them with that.

Glenn Schwartz, Meteorologist, WCAU:
The whole controversy about it goes back to Wednesday night, when our station ran the crawl in primetime. The wording of it said, "one of the strongest storms of the past century." It never said, "the storm of the century." That phrase was never used by anybody before the storm. That phrase was written by our news director [Steve Schwaid], not by [John] Bolaris. So, Bolaris ends up getting blamed, and when things happen in this city that are big controversial things, they tend to be remembered, and people still remember it.

Harry Holmes, Weather Producer, WCAU and WTXF:
The storm was legitimately something that could happen. It was one of those storms where it was a high risk of not happening. Even though John [Bolaris] and I, when I was doing the graphics and stuff, we would always point out storms in the past that were similar to the storms that could happen. I just always remember going back to the one graphic of the blizzard of 1988, where New York and New England got pounded with several feet of snow, where Philadelphia, I believe, only got an inch, I don't remember the exact number. It was basically, we were on the back edge of the storm. It so happened that this storm behaved the same

way; if you look at the numbers from New England and New York, they had a lot more than what we had, which was virtually nothing.

I just remember [Steve Schwaid] making us do a crawl for the storm. You know, it was a Thursday night before the storm that was coming by the end of the weekend. We were still several days out. John and I tried to push caution, to say, "This is worth a lead and all of that, but we have to be careful to not push it too far." It was a lot of battle back and forth between what the news director wants. That happens all of the time. It's not just one specific event. It's just the fact that it was near the end of sweeps. Pressure was on a little bit more for the news director to push it through, so to speak.

Beth McDonough, Reporter, KYW and WCAU:
The feeling in the newsroom was really energized after that happened because we definitely did rise up to beat PVI for the first time in forever. In fact, the news director created this board with everyone's name on it to kind of recognize everyone who put in the effort. The storm of the century, I remember, we were in the conference room where we had news meetings every morning. We were all having a news meeting, and they brought John Bolaris in early because they knew it was going to be big. Actually, there was a lot of really—I would say—heated debate about whether or not to call it "storm of the century" at the time. The news director did not want to scare people. You don't want to be too dramatic but also to give it enough attention if it deserved that. We all know that weather can change on a dime. We were hammering out all of the different angles of what we were gonna cover and who's gonna go where. There was really a debate about what we slugged the story, what we put on the banners up on the screen, because that kind of defines it. If people are just walking by their TVs and see "storm of the century" on the screen, that's all they are going to remember. What if it isn't the storm of the century? There was a lot of debate about that. I remember John was talking about it, and Glenn "Hurricane" Schwartz, and they were really confident this was gonna be the one, this was gonna be the deal. I remember, we sped out, each of us, at our different posts. It was "take everything you have, grab your go bag, and cover everything you see"—meaning, shoot video, take notes, do interviews, talk to people. Anything where weather was happening, cover anything you see. Then, news was whatever was in front of you.

Vai Sikahema, Sports Reporter and Anchor, WCAU:
I remember there was a heated discussion between [Steve] Schwaid and [John] Bolaris about it. I didn't know why they were arguing. I'm only going by memory, and I could be totally wrong about this, and I will admit that. My memory is that Bolaris was trying to be more restrained on the storm, and Steve Schwaid wanted to say, "Hey, if this thing is coming, it's on us. All hands on deck. We need to be sure people know about it." I don't know whether it was [Glenn] Schwartz or Bolaris or the two of them together that came up with the "storm of the century" moniker that has since, I think, probably dogged us for the better part of the last twenty years.

John Stehlin, Chief Forecaster, KYW:
It was a Wednesday night before [the ratings period ended]. I was sitting in the weather center, but the executive producer calls me and says, "What about this storm this weekend?" I said, "What are you talking about?" He was like, "Channel 10 is running a crawl: 'storm of the century.'" It was a ratings ploy no doubt by Channel 10, who spent an exorbitant amount of money to promote their weather department. I looked at the models, went to the models, and I said, "I could see what could possibly be a storm, but I'm not sold on it at this moment," because it was five days away, and it was not formed. The storm wasn't a storm. It was something that we were forecasting to develop and become a storm. I wasn't convinced at the moment and wasn't sure what they were doing over there [at Channel 10].

Like I always do with my career, if I see something down the road, I don't like to scare people. I'm not very sensational. I'm just a matter-of-fact kind of guy. I said, "Something could be brewing this weekend, but we still have a few days to figure that out. We will keep you posted."

Tom Lamaine, Sports and Weather Anchor, KYW:
I looked into it deeper to see what the possibilities were for this storm to miss the Philadelphia area, and I wanted to see what the data that was being ingested into the guidances or the models as they call them, that saw that this storm had the possibility of missing. If you do your homework and look into it a little deeper—and you can go along with the crowd, but if you think something else is going to happen, it's more than

your gut—it's just that there is something staring you in the face that may be the long shot to happen. However, if it isn't a long shot in your mind and your study of the whole situation tells you that this is going to happen, then you go with it. It's more than a lucky guess. You're looking at information that is a little more detailed, and you have looked into it deeper than maybe the others have.

Rob Guarino, Chief Meteorologist, WTXF:
The first thought I had, ten days out, was it's kind of odd, but that time of year, the patterns start to change from winter to spring, and you can get some freaky stuff like that.

From what we were gathering, [Channels] 6 and 10 were in a deadlock for the February [ratings] book. Channel 10 had never beaten 6. PVI was the king. They had [Jim] Gardner there, and they were just the king for the longest time. Well, Channel 10 had that powerhouse Thursday night, *Seinfeld*, *Friends*, or whatever show. They had three shows in a row leading up to the news that just everybody watched. The biggest night was that couple of hours on TV because *Seinfeld* was hot at the time and number one. Now it becomes, "Wait a minute. There is an opportunity here," I felt. I wasn't in those newsrooms, but this is just me from what I believe and heard. This was a promotable event to push one of them maybe over the top to the viewers. All I remember is a crawl coming up about five or four days out on Channel 10. I didn't catch it at first, but I saw at the bottom, "Historic 40-inch storm could impact the area." I went "WTF," so to speak. Who runs a crawl on a storm five days out and calling for the biggest storm in history, basically? That's like saying the Eagles are going to win five Super Bowls in a row.

Frank Cariello, Meteorologist, WTXF:
Of course, when you have a beast of a storm coming, management loves it. They want you to be out there giving worst-case scenarios because it brings in viewers. Lucky, when I was hired, and I know when news directors hire other meteorologists, they temper [expectations] and get an idea of what sort of meteorologist they are. I don't like to cry wolf because it can kill your reputation. We saw that with John [Bolaris] for a while. I like to be a little more cautious when I forecast.

Rob Guarino, Chief Meteorologist, WTXF:
Any weather guy in any market has never done that, put a crawl out so far out.

It was a "paper storm," as I call it. It looked great on paper, but, dynamically, it didn't look like it could happen. It just didn't look like it was set up for a storm to go to Boston, go to Maine, and turn around. Like, a hurricane could freakily do that, but this wasn't a hurricane. It was a nor'easter. Nor'easters get pushed up north, and they just keep going. They could go right or left up there.

Terry Ruggles, Reporter and Anchor, WCAU:
Weather is really big, and I am not sure whether [John] Bolaris was told to goose it and make it more than it was, but there were companies closed, schools canceled, people changed their shopping plans, and it was like kissing your sister—it just didn't happen. People were pissed, and they were justified to be pissed.

John Bolaris, Meteorologist, WCAU and WTXF:
We were number one in the ratings, and I walked into the studio, into the building—they were celebrating with cake and champagne.

Steve MacLaughlin, Meteorologist, WPHL:
My boss [news director Rich Scott] came to me and said I had to talk about [the storm] on the air. I was like, "I don't know, it's five days from now. I don't know if we should be talking about it yet." He said, "We have to talk about it. Channel 10 talked about it, so we have to talk about it." As we got closer, it looked more and more certain, and it just didn't happen. That Sunday rolled around, and we got some couple inches of snow. That was it.

Frank Cariello, Meteorologist, WTXF:
I didn't go all wild on it, and I'm glad I didn't. I do see the models [John Bolaris] was looking at [that] thought potentially it could be a two-foot snowstorm. If I remember right—and again, this was quite a while ago—I might have gone on the air and said, "Here's what I think is going to happen, but here is the potential." A worst-case scenario kind of thing.

Roger LaMay, General Manager and News Director, WTXF:
If one guy is saying there is gonna be a really big storm and the other one is minimizing, there's a lot more pressure for you to be right if you are minimizing. The one who is calling it bigger is gonna attract more audience. On one hand, weathercasters get an unfair thing because it's based on computer models and probability. They are kind of preparing you for what can happen, but sometimes they [get] carried away with their own bullshit. [John] Bolaris clearly walked to the end of the pier and decided, "I'm gonna jump in."

Bill Henley, Meteorologist, WCAU:
I remember Glenn [Schwartz] coming in and getting all excited about a potential storm. I did the morning show, so Glenn came in around midday and started getting ready for who knows what in the afternoon, working with John Bolaris. I know Glenn was very excited about a potential storm, and I'm sure he relayed that to John, about the storm being potentially a huge storm. I went home, and I don't know what transpired afterward, but the next day I came in and I had voicemails from a little old woman who was saying, "Do I need to cancel my travel plans this weekend. How bad is it going to be?" And I'm thinking, "What are they talking about?" I looked at the data, and I was not impressed. I said, "They don't have to cancel their plans, it's going to be fine." I downplayed it, and the news director later that morning came to me and said, "We had a great number last night, a lot of people tuned in." I guess apparently they said, "Here comes a storm, and it could be worse than the storm we had in 1996." Everyone knew how bad that was.

Other people kept forecasting it was going to be bad, and I kept saying I didn't think it was going to be bad. Then, my news management at the time was mad at me because I wasn't agreeing with everyone else. I got in hot water because I wasn't stirring up the pot because I didn't think it was going to be bad.

It was definitely hyped, and it didn't happen. I was vindicated, but I don't think [Bolaris] was solely responsible for the forecast, but he was the face of that forecast.

John Stehlin, Chief Forecaster, KYW:
I remember going in the newsroom, talking to producers, and I said, "I don't see this happening. I am not going with what they say. At this moment, the data is not there for me to say that."

I did concede to the fact to show two scenarios on Friday. The Friday before the storm, I showed the two scenarios. I said, "Here is scenario one, where we get a major amount of snow, and here is scenario two, where we don't see anything." I literally said, "I think this is going to be halfway to London by Monday and not affect us."

I got all of this pressure, and they made me do the eleven [o'clock newscast]. I walk into the weather department, and the fill-in guy is there. He turns to me and goes, "I had a feeling they were gonna call you in." We went over the data together, and I was absolutely right.

Rob Guarino, Chief Meteorologist, WTXF:
I absolutely pulled the plug on this storm. Larry Lewis was my producer, and we were doing weekends. I said, "Larry, I need you for a minute. This stuff is not happening." Meanwhile, [Channels] 3, 6, and 10 are still going balls to the walls saying this thing is coming. Now, they backed off a little from "twenty to thirty inches," but still—Jesus—this is crazy. I said, "Larry, you have to let me do this. I'm telling you, this will give us credibility. I can explain to them why it's not going to happen. I will explain each detail, but I need more time." As a producer, you are always fighting for time with news stories. I went straight through my time cues. He tried to give me more time. I didn't even listen to him. I basically blinded out my earpiece and just said, "I don't care if he goes to color bars. I'm gonna explain this and do it." Kathy Orr came on at eleven [o'clock], and it came back to me. I could tell they wanted to change their maps because they were starting to [say at the] top of the show that this could change. I went [on for] four minutes. Larry got a little upset, but he understood afterward because he saw the way I explained it. I won an [Associated Press] award for that. I got a standing ovation by all of the news directors and [general managers] when I won that award in Pennsylvania. I basically stopped, put the brakes on, and pulled the plug on the storm before anyone else did. That was a big moment for me in my career, personally.

John Stehlin, Chief Forecaster, KYW:
It was probably one of the low points of my career, but a high point too. I stood my ground, and I said I was right. I knew I was right. I had high confidence that we overshot as a station for prepping people and being sensational. We followed Channel 10's leap because, at that time, they were extremely sensational with the weather department. We were running weather promos on the air saying we were kinder, gentler, and we weren't going to try to scare you. We were just gonna tell you the facts.

Harry Holmes, Weather Producer, WCAU and WTXF:
I just remember each run starting through the weekend, there are computer-model runs that would come in, and they would print out precipitation amounts that could possibly happen. Each run kept coming in and kept cutting back the amounts. We were like, "Uh-oh, something is not right." Even though there was [still] a chance by then, the problem is, when you are heading into a weekend in the news business and the weather business, everybody was in on the storm by Friday. It was the lead in the 6:30 *Nightly News*. It was the lead story there too. It just wasn't a local hyping the storm or whatever: It was national. What happens is there's a disconnect when people are heading into the weekend and the last thing you hear is whatever you heard on Friday. So what happens is everyone on Saturday was starting to plan for the storm.

John Bolaris, Meteorologist, WCAU and WTXF:
On Saturday, I'm going over the computer models, and I call Glenn [Schwartz]. I'm looking at the computer model at home and some extractions. I said, "I don't like what I am seeing. I see some erosion. Right now, if this trend continues, I would be pulling back the throttle some." So the next run comes out, and I want to pull back the throttle. I called the news director [Steve Schwaid], and I said, "Listen, Steve, I'm a little bit concerned. The models are hinting that we are getting some drying, maybe a little jolt, not certain yet, but I would start hedging and bringing it back. I know we still have the storm warning and . . . blah, blah, blah . . . I would like to come on this weekend and take it over and start controlling what was going to go on this weekend." He said, "Absolutely not." I said, "What are you talking about?" He said, "I got Kathy Orr in there, and she needs the PR."

I go in, and it was a Sunday. I'm looking at the models, and I said, "This shit's not gonna happen. This is not gonna happen." Now, I'm talking to Kathy Orr, and we are pulling back on this. We are pulling way back on this.

Steve comes in and says, "What are you doing?" I told Steve, "I'm not comfortable with this. I'm not gonna do this." I said, "If you want a used car salesman, you need to go down to Don Rosen [builder of a successful group of Philadelphia automobile dealerships] and hire yourself a used car salesman. I'm deeply concerned this is not gonna happen. I don't think this is gonna happen."

[Steve said], "Kathy, you throw to John. John, you will say the history and how much snow we are gonna get. Don't be insubordinate."

Anyone watching the Sunday news of 6:30 that evening [saw] Kathy threw it to me, and I walked away from the weather desk. They go back to Kathy, and they say they must be having some technical difficulties. I was not gonna say something that was not true.

I'm in the makeup room, and I'm getting ready for some teases, and my guy [weather producer] High Pressure Harry [Holmes]—we waited to see the new computer models come in—he comes in the makeup room, and he hands me the data in hard-copy form. I'm looking at it, and my jaw drops. I go, "Holy shit, we are gonna get nothing—maybe an inch to three."

I told [anchor] Monique Braxton, "It's not a blizzard warning. This is not gonna happen. I'm gonna come on and, just so you know when you throw to me, don't throw to me as, like, hell is breaking loose. Say, 'Hey, we got some breaking news here that's a big reduction in the storm. John, what's the latest?'" What does she throw to me as? "Hey, John, so this blizzard is really gonna strike, right?" I go, "There is still a blizzard warning, but that's not my thinking." I went into the whole thing where [I said,] "I think it's gonna be less snow—one to three inches. The thirty inches of snow is gonna go across along eastern Rhode Island and eastern Connecticut, but not Philadelphia or New Jersey." That was my whole thing.

I asked Steve Schwaid [whether I could] do a live kind of back-and-forth show with the viewers to answer their questions on what went down. He said, "Absolutely not." In the fishbowl in that newsroom, I actually tore apart his office. I threw his computer down, books down. You know, saying totally, "You destroyed my credibility and my career because of your alarmist attitude in what you did. What you did is just unforgivable." He never said anything and just sat there at his desk. He knew it.

I got death threats. Howard Stern, who I was friends with, he gave me a call, and I was living in my house with Lauren [Hart], and he gave me a call about what's going on.

I was deathly sick to my stomach about what went on, and [the story] just became that I was rogue. Someone wrote, "Bolaris is worse than a hypodermic needle washing along the Jersey shore." I remember seeing that somewhere. Death threats from businesses saying I created this.

I called it early and pulled back early. If I was allowed to go on, it would have been much better. I was definitely getting buried by everyone. Anyone that was a meteorologist knew what track I was on, and I was right. Other ones . . . because of all of the avalanche that went on with that and not happening, it became an avalanche of bad press that I couldn't control. It just went out of control.

Harry Holmes, Weather Producer, WCAU and WTXF:
We must have had at least a twenty-four- or thirty-hour warning of "This thing may not happen. Be prepared." By then, it was too far gone. The one specific memory I have is the night before the event, it was one of the last runs, and once you get between twenty-four hours of the event, you pretty much have a lock on it. It was right before the event. John [Bolaris] went to go get prepared and put makeup on and get ready to go on the air. The new computer run always came out fifteen minutes before we went on air. I grabbed it, took one look at it, and I ran down to the bathroom to where he was and opened the door, and he looked at me. I didn't have to say anything, and he goes, "It's over." He knew it, and so did I.

Elliot Abrams, Senior Vice President, AccuWeather:
It turned into a big storm for eastern New England. I remember that storm specifically because my wife and I were visiting our son in Norfolk, Virginia, where he worked for a newspaper there. I got so worried about the storm. People thought we were short-staffed, so I cut the vacation short. As we drove home from Virginia on the first day of the would-be storm, there was five or six inches of snow in central Maryland, and I thought to myself, "Well, here it comes." I got home and said, "There it goes."

Paul Deanno, Meteorologist, KYW:
From a meteorologist's perspective, the biggest snowstorms in Philadelphia and the immediate area always have the highest potential to bust and not even be anything, and here's the reason why: To get that much water in the atmosphere you need for a two- or three-foot snowstorm, the temperature has to be really close to freezing. Because the colder it is where you know it's going to snow—and there's no question, typically those storms for Philadelphia are drier—so maybe you'll get half of a foot or a foot of snow. It's a lot, but not a huge deal. To get the kind of snowstorm that's going to give you two or three feet of snow, the temperature's got to be thirty-two degrees, but here's the problem: Once it hits thirty-five or thirty-six degrees, that's not snow falling from the sky, it's rain. So, anytime you see a prediction for a ton of snow in Philadelphia, there's always a really fine line of it being a complete bust because if it's just a couple of degrees warmer, then you're talking rain and not snow, and that's exactly what happened in that storm.

Dave Roberts, Meteorologist, WPVI:
[Monday], I made a determination with the AccuWeather people. We went over everything. I was saying just the opposite: The worst of the storm is over. I can remember my general manager and my news director coming up to the weather corner that I had, saying, "Dave, everybody is saying that this storm is still going. You are saying that it's not?" I said, "Yup. It's basically over with." That, fortunately, that's how it turned out. I don't mean to brag here, but it was the beginning of what you see a lot of today—they hype up storms and overplay things. I just couldn't go down that road. I have never gone down that road.

Glenn Schwartz, Meteorologist, WCAU:
It was upsetting before, during, and after. It was a storm that, in the middle of the week, we were fairly excited about for the weekend, but when you are talking about a storm that far away, and especially that type of storm, there's a type A and a type B in winter storms. Type A would tend to start down in the Gulf of Mexico and track upward up the coast. That's what the '96 storm did, and that's what the 1993 "storm of the century" did. The storm like the one that was supposed to develop in 2001 was a type B, where there was something that came

across the Great Lakes, and then a storm develops along the East Coast and then tracks up the northeast. That is a much more difficult thing to forecast because where is that coastal low going to develop? If it develops far enough south, then we get nailed with it. If it waits to develop later, we get spared. That was the one thing that made it not a sure bet like the '96 and '93 storms were.

John Stehlin, Chief Forecaster, KYW:
I basically had to apologize for what happened, saying that I, too, thought this would happen, and I said, "Sometimes these things don't happen."

Steve MacLaughlin, Meteorologist, WPHL:
We all got put on probation from the American Meteorological Society. I got a letter that said I had failed to do my duties as a broadcaster.

Steve Schwaid, News Director, WCAU and WTXF:
It was not the end of the world to me at all. I mean, the intention was actually right, based on all the forecasts, to warn viewers. Should we have done a crawl? The primetime crawl can be debated. Stations crawl stuff all of the time to drive people to their eleven o'clock newscasts. It is what it is. John [Bolaris] and I both are with that one because I would never know to write that, and John came to me and said, "Hey, this is happening."

What's funny is that it's a joke phrase now, like, "We're going to have a storm; it's going to be the storm of the century." It is what it is.

Larry Mendte, Anchor, WCAU and KYW:
There were big stories in the papers about how we beat PVI. It was on the front page of the *Inquirer* that we beat PVI, and I was scheduled to go on [radio station] WIP. I call into WIP, and I'm on the air, and they ask about the storm of the century. I was defending John [Bolaris]. I got on the air and said, "Look, if we have information on a storm that big that can shut down the area, of historical proportions, do you keep it to yourself?" I said, "Of course not." We were lucky it didn't hit us. I was defending him so much, and then they said, "Do you know he is in the

paper apologizing about it?" My heart sank because I have no idea why he did that. My belief is that he probably did it because he wanted the attention from it. I have a hard time believing he got death threats like he claims he did. I still think [the crawl] was the right thing to do. I don't like the way John reacted to it, but I defend us doing the crawl because we said there was a storm that had potential, and it was absolutely true, and it just didn't hit us and didn't materialize. It hit up the Massachusetts area hard. It just didn't hit us.

Marcellus Alexander, Vice President and General Manager, KYW:
Yes, ratings are important. No one would deny that, but there is a point, I believe, where you have to draw the line and say, "Are we sure this is going to happen?"

We focused on again doing what's right, building on the credibility that we had, and looking to serve our viewers.

Elliot Abrams, Senior Vice President, AccuWeather:
Stubbornness is fatal in weather forecasting. If you hold onto a forecast after it's no longer right or going to be right, you are dead.

I don't think it's a good idea to overhype any storm or cheer for them. I'm especially annoyed about that because I don't like when people cheer for a storm that can kill people or cause damage.

Bill Henley, Meteorologist, WCAU:
I don't want to be wrong. If I make a forecast, I want it to be right. I'll be watching it the entire time. There are certain levels of stress beyond what the viewers think. I'm as hard on myself, and I want that forecast to be right. If it isn't and I told somebody something that they made plans on, people were scared of that kind of language. I'm glad the storm didn't happen. I'm glad. We better [not] get a storm like that.

Dave Warren, Meteorologist, WCAU and WTXF:
I would go to schools. I got there in April of 2003. So I was after that, but even years past that—and these are elementary school kids—I would go do a weather talk, and one of the questions would be "What happened with that storm?" These kids didn't even remember it. It was, obviously, they were talking about it with their family, or they might

have said to their family, "Hey, a weatherman from Channel 10 is coming to talk to our school," and someone might have said, "Ask what happened with that big storm."

Frank Cariello, Meteorologist, WTXF:
I do feel sorry for John [Bolaris] in that respect. He went for it, and it cost him. It really did cost him. When you are forecasting a storm and you are seeing something really big, you have to tell yourself, do you temper it and release what you think in little spurts to see if it happens and grows, or do you go for everything? He went for everything, and it just didn't work.

Gail Shister, TV Columnist:
It was so embarrassing for him and the station, but the promotion of it didn't surprise me at all because I think it still holds true today that local news, especially, tends to get hysterical over any kind of two snowflakes on the ground. That's because it gets eyeballs. What do people care about more than the weather? It didn't surprise me that there was this huge ratings spike because all of the stations, at least back then, became apoplectic about weather because people loved to watch it, especially back then. You have to remember, it was pre-big-Internet and pre-lots-of-things. A lot of people were dependent a lot about school closings. By hyping the weather and the so-called catastrophe coming, you are gonna get a lot more eyeballs from parents who are worried about their kid being home.

Neal Zoren, TV Columnist:
There is always a hype. Television makes its money by attracting eyeballs. You promote things and attract eyeballs. It's a travesty, and it did hurt [John] Bolaris a lot, and I'm sure it was the single-most[-important] factor in ruining his personal credibility in Philadelphia. Bolaris was a deeper person than what people give him credit for, but still, the point is, it did hurt him. I think it also showed something about Channel 10 at the time of being so in the Steve Schwaid days and the early days of the ages of NBC. Everything was exaggerated, everything was high touch in there.

SEPTEMBER 11, 2001

On September 11, 2001, the United States of America was attacked by al-Qaeda terrorists who hijacked four passenger airplanes to carry out coordinated suicide attacks ending at the World Trade Center in New York City; the Pentagon in Washington, D.C.; and Shanksville, Pennsylvania, altogether resulting in nearly three thousand deaths.

Following the attacks on 9/11, all Philadelphia television stations allowed their on-air talent to wear American flag pins or ribbons during newscasts. The following are reactions to the coverage of September 11 on the national and local levels through the eyes of Philadelphia broadcasters.

Rob Jennings, Anchor, WPVI:
I was off that day. My wife, Karen, and I were having breakfast at the Shady Maple in Lancaster County. Two women who worked there came over to our table and told us that two planes had crashed into the World Trade Center in New York. We stopped eating and ran out to our car to listen to KYW radio. We sat in silence as we listened and tried to make sense of it. I turned to Karen and said, "This is worse than Pearl Harbor."

Beth McDonough, Reporter, KYW and WCAU:
We were just in the commercial break [out on location], getting ready for them to toss to me, and we have a monitor sitting out. In the monitor,

Matt Lauer broke in and they were showing video of the first plane as it was flying into the building. John [my photographer] and I were standing there just in shock, obviously, because it was like, oh god, that's horrible and a terrible accident. Then, in our heads—I bet that we were dropped. Like, why would they come to us after that? Matt kept going, and then a few minutes later you see the second plane coming in. When John and I saw the second plane on the monitor, we looked at each other, locked eyes, I dropped the microphone, we put the camera on the ground, and we just instantly knew that was it. We started rolling up our cables, breaking down the live shot, we were in a live truck and waited to get the call. When I say "waited"—that was just seconds to where we were going. We knew this was bigger than the first plane. This wasn't an accident anymore. We broke down completely; the assignment desk called us immediately and said, "Head north. We will tell you what you will be doing." We didn't have anything with us other than our daily stuff, meaning, whatever, our computer or notebooks, the equipment, the batteries that we had with us at the time.

Janet Zappala, Anchor and Reporter, WCAU and WTXF:
I wasn't normally anchoring *Good Day* at that point, but Tonya Archer, who was, was on vacation in Europe. So I was called to coanchor with Mike [Jerrick] that day. I'll never forget: it was about 8:46 when the first plane went into the World Trade Center. I think that was the first one, and we didn't know what was going on, but I was on the desk with Mike for about four to six hours that morning because it happened right before we went off the air. We [normally] went off at nine, and we were on for about three or four hours covering it.

I was really shaken, and I'll never forget. Finally, we had to go to a break, and I broke down. I mean, not ridiculously broke down, but I started crying and was like, "What is happening to our country? What is going on?" We were all really moved by what was going on.

Dawn Stensland-Mendte, Anchor and Reporter,
KYW and WTXF:
I remember I called Larry [Mendte]. I called him and said, "Turn on the morning news." All of the networks were covering it. This was before the second plane went into the tower. We were on the phone together when that second plane went in. We both just kind of said, "Got to go."

He was at home; I was at work. I was one of the reporters who went to city hall, and we were being briefed by the mayor. At one point, they said we needed to evacuate because they were fearful—remember, there was one plane still in the air. The plane that we learned ultimately was headed for [Washington, D.C.] but crashed in Shanksville. Nobody knew for sure. I just remember the panicked feeling. On one end, you are covering the story, and it's all happening, and you are worried about your job, but on the other hand, I was worried about family. Everyone's cell phones couldn't get through because the whole system was inundated. Everyone was calling everybody. It was that feeling of being fearful and wondering if everyone was safe and then, at the same time, thinking about the job and the strategy and all of that.

Larry Mendte, Anchor, WCAU and KYW:
I hung up the phone with my wife, and I turned the radio on. I had WIP on, and Pat Croce was talking about his book, he was selling his book, and he kept going. I was on WIP with Angelo Cataldi a lot, so I had the number. I called Rhea Hughes [on-air radio personality], and I said, "What are you doing? Do you know what is going on?" She said, "We know, we just can't shut Pat up." She said, "Hold on for a second—would you go on the air with us?" I told her, "I just woke up, and I don't know much, but I can do play by play for you." She said, "Fine. Stay on." As I got dressed, I was on the air describing what was happening to WIP as I got dressed to go into WCAU. To this day, people come up to me and say, "I heard about 9/11 from you on WIP," as they were driving into work.

Angelo Cataldi, Radio Host:
I'm getting a signal from Rhea Hughes in the newsroom: Cut—get out of Pat Croce. Larry Mendte is on the phone. I'm going, "I'm not getting out; Larry Mendte is a TV guy. I like him, and we have a good relationship with his station but. . . ." Rhea is freaking out in there. Finally—I don't even think I cut short the interview with Croce—I said, "Larry Mendte is on. Let's see what's going on." He comes on and says, "You're not going to believe this: The country is under assault," or something like that. They are flying planes into the World Trade Center. It's not like you can ever be prepared for something like that, especially on a sports station, but Larry took over. From that point until the end of the show,

Larry was using us to report what was happening. I believe when we were on the air, one of the towers collapsed, and Larry was reporting it. He was reporting it by watching the TV. We had TV monitors in [the studio] there, but frankly, we were completely out of our element. Larry talked us through to the end of our show. It was close to an hour where Larry just broke the news on our show, at least to our audience, and then really did a great job kinda detailing what was going on in New York.

Scott Palmer, Sports Anchor and Reporter, WPVI:
So I came in [to the station], and they sent me to the [Cathedral Basilica of Saints Peter and Paul], which was a great idea. I think we were the only station there. Obviously, people were mourning, but there was a religious note to it. So, I worked that, and then I got back to the station, and they said the next three days, you are gonna be going to 30th Street and doing live reports on the early-morning news. That was the only way you could get from one place to another, was by a train or car.

Robin Mackintosh, Reporter, KYW:
We at that point absolutely knew it was an attack, so I said, "Here is what we are going to do." We had done it before on high-profile stories. We got a big-screen monitor downstairs in the studio, and we were on 5th and Market at the time, near Independence Hall, so we put the screen outside. We plugged in the sound, and for a lot of these people [passing by], they had no idea what was going on because they were on vacation and they were touring the different historic sites. We put that out front, and people were absolutely glued. We had a crowd out there of about fifty to sixty people. If we were able to get a speaker hooked up, we probably could have gotten everyone in the place over [to watch]. Many people started crying, and it was quite a moving experience. We did a story of that on the noon show, of local reaction, and actually, I asked the people which state they were from, and they were all responding to this thing.

Ukee Washington, Anchor, KYW:
I can still remember feeling incredibly numb, blanketed with overwhelming sadness and disbelief. I will never forget walking outside of the station, on what was a beautiful day and a clear blue sky, wondering if "we" were next. "We" as in Philadelphia. We had the birthplace of America.

Our former station location was right across from the Liberty Bell on Independence Mall. My eyes were glued to the skies, with occasional tears obscuring my vision of what could and thankfully did not come. Being on air that night, and for quite a while afterward, when speaking of the horrific events, without a doubt, was one of the hardest moments of my young news career.

Larry Kane, Anchor, WPVI, WCAU, and KYW:
All I remember is driving into work at nine o'clock in the morning. The minute it happened, the news director and general manager told me to get in there. We didn't go on the air for hours because the network was on. There are two things I remember: Number one, there was a reverse commute. As I was driving in, there was nobody on the highway. All of the cars were leaving downtown Philadelphia to go home. People were going home. When I got to 5th and Market—I guess it was a little after 9:30—the whole place was empty. Just empty. There was police all around Independence Hall. There were no soldiers there at that time, but there were a lot of people around the Liberty Bell. There was fear monuments were going to be attacked. No one knew what was going on. What you didn't know really scared the hell out of you.

Jim Gardner, Anchor, WPVI:
At that point, just as everybody else did, there was this realization that this was not an accident. This was an attack. It was mortifying. You had a physical reaction to that. Again, the immediate reaction was to get dressed and get into work. When anything happens, an immediate reaction is to get to the television station. That's where we belong and need to be without even knowing what it was we were going to do. Just get there, and that was the same reaction. By the time we got to the television station, within minutes, we watched the first tower come down. As I recall, we started making assignments, and our reporters started moving and deploying.

Carla Carpenter, News Director, WPVI:
I sent crews and live trucks toward New York, but I opted to put the live truck—via satellite—I opted to leave that in New Jersey so my crew would not stay in New York. I was afraid that there was going to be more. If this was gonna be a war situation, then it would just be the be-

ginning; it wouldn't be the end. Since you don't know anything, you have to go by the best decisions you can make under these circumstances to keep people safe, but you still have to cover the event. We sent a crew to the Pentagon and also to western Pennsylvania.

Nora Muchanic, Reporter, WPVI:
We started going up the [Pennsylvania] Turnpike, heading up that way, and they closed down the turnpike. The only things going north on the turnpike were emergency vehicles and news vehicles. At one point, when we got up near New York, we pulled over to the side. You could see the skyline, and my photographer was taking pictures looking south of the ambulances coming, and I am looking at the towers, and I see one of them start to fall. You can't believe that you are seeing this. I start screaming down to him, and I finally get his attention, and he whips his camera around and gets a shot of the tower falling. While we had been driving up, we had the radio on so we could get informed as we were going. We hear that the Pentagon has been hit, and this plane is missing in Pennsylvania, or I don't even remember if it hit at the time. Holy shit—we are under attack. Our mouths are hanging open, and then we see the tower falling. It's like, "Oh my God. This can't be happening."

Colin Macaulay, Senior Sports Producer, WCAU:
I got a call from our assignment desk. They said, "You are in the car and on your way in?" I said, "Yeah." They said, "You grew up in D.C., didn't you?" I said, "Yeah, I'm from D.C." They said, "Why don't you just head south and head to D.C." because of the Pentagon. I said okay and they [said they would] call me in a little while on who to hook up with to meet [me] down there. I got on [Interstate] 95 South and started heading that way. It was probably an hour or so in, and they called me back and said, "D.C. is shut down. It's too risky. Why don't you turn around and come back?" I went back to the station, and obviously we were not doing sports, so I started helping out really in any way I could. I started doing the ticker crawls with all of the cancellations and emergency news. I was sort of compiling that.

Dei Lynam, Reporter, Comcast SportsNet:
I landed in the [Republic of Congo] on 9/11 by myself. I was supposed to have a ride, and it did not come. I ended up having to hitchhike to the

Dikembe Mutombo Foundation office, and when I got there, there was a pink slip from the embassy that had my name on it and told me to lay low. The Congo is a third-world country. There weren't TVs. It took until later that day—I finally found Dikembe—and then I found out what had happened.

Art Fennell, Reporter and Anchor, WCAU and the Comcast Network:

I arrived in the studio probably around 11:00 A.M. We went on the air immediately and stayed on the air continuously without fail until after midnight. There were so many moments during the course of that day that were just vivid and moments that you will never forget, two of which are distinct for me. The actual collapse of the towers, the moment they collapsed, was such a massive and awe-inspiring scene that you just can't imagine. Of course, these images—we have all seen them now, but imagine being on the air live when it happens for the first time and the only time. Obviously, you react because you are human, and you can't help but react to what you are seeing. But to try and make some sort of sense of it for a viewing audience: It was a very challenging and a very long day. The second thing I distinctly remember was very early in the day, there was so much confusion going on with the wire services with the news agencies. Air traffic control grounded all flights for the first time in history. All planes were on the ground and accounted for, but there was so much confusion on the wire services that no one could have a good grip on what was happening. There was one plane for the longest time that was missing. They couldn't account for its whereabouts. That was the United flight. As we tried to sort out what was going on with the United flight, we just assumed it was on the ground and lost in the ground clutter with all of the other planes. Then, the trickling of reports started to come out that were unconfirmed. It was unconfirmed that the United flight was down. At first, it was the flight that crashed into the Pentagon, and then they thought it may have been the plane that had gone down in Shanksville, Pennsylvania, but at that point, it was still unconfirmed. At that point, we haven't reported it yet. It was during that time I was friends with the copilot of United Airlines Flight 93. When that plane went down, LeRoy Homer Jr., the African American copilot from Marlton, New Jersey, was a friend of mine. He and his wife were friends of me and my wife. We have been at their home, and they have been at ours. That was LeRoy's flight. I received a phone call at the news desk. The producer said, "Someone is trying to reach you, and I think you should take it." So I took the call on the desk, obviously not on the air. It was Melodie Homer, LeRoy's wife. She was frantic. She was saying to me that she was trying to get some information on her husband's flight, that no one was giving her any information. She had called the airline, and she couldn't get through, as you can imagine the chaos. She wondered if I had any information about the United flight that her husband was the copilot on. Of course, at that point I did, but there was no way in the world I was ever going to tell her that at that point in time. That information couldn't have come from me. I just remember my heart sank with her because, at that point, she didn't know. I think I told her something vaguely as to "Melodie, there is so much we don't know at this point. I think it's best just to wait until you can get some official information from people who are direct sources with what is going on. There is just way too much chaos at this time." Again, these were poignant moments during what was, as I say, a day in history that we had never seen before.

Monique Braxton, Anchor and Reporter, WCAU:
I had two childhood friends working in the World Trade Center. Like any newsie would do, I immediately started calling them. It was going to voicemail. One of them, I was able to reach later, and what I learned was, as they both got to work, one said to the other, "Hey, I'm gonna run down the street and get some breakfast. You wanna go?" The other one said, "No, I have some work to do." He's the one who passed away. The one who passed away did all of the candid shots at my wedding because we grew up together—he was very close to me. Anytime I would look at those pictures, I would just think, "Wow. He is gone." Then, I had to put on my big-girl pants and prepare for the next day, when I was scheduled to return to work. You have to think about everything you have to prepare for at home, because once you go to work, you don't know when you are going to be coming back home.

Marcellus Alexander, Vice President and General Manager, KYW:
When the second plane hit the South Tower, it was clear that this was coordinated and this was much more significant—still horrible, but much more significant. At that moment, there was speculation about

what other sites, what other iconic places, might be involved with this. There was speculation about Independence Mall or the Liberty Bell. Maybe those would become targets. All of this was being speculated on television and on radio. I recall just looking out of my window at 5th and Market, seeing people scampering to the parking lots to get to their cars to get out from this area. I had two focuses at that point: one was the safety of our employees and two was making sure that we were informing our audience on a real-time basis of what was going on. The newsroom was hunkered down, looking for information, trying to make sure we had everything we could, making sure we had good, solid information. There were people in the building outside of the newsroom asking how they could help, and there were others who felt that they would be better served getting back with their families. We allowed for that to happen. It was a day of gathering information, making sure we disseminated it, trying to calm an understandably shaken community as to what was going on. It was at that moment that I felt, really, the weight of the position of those balancing the safety of our employees as well as making sure our viewers got the information that they needed. That was a very big responsibility that I looked forward to helping to execute on.

Kathy Gerrow, Producer, Writer, and Assistant News Director, KYW and WCAU:
I'm standing in the control room, looking at dozens of TV screens on the wall. I remember there was this shot of just the buildings themselves, just burning. I remember thinking, "Wow, look at all of the paper flying out of those windows." I looked closer, and I realized it wasn't paper—it was people. We stopped using those shots.

Larry Mendte, Anchor, WCAU and KYW:
We wanted to get on the air, but I remember Steve Schwaid looking up and [the footage showed people] jumping out of buildings, and people were saying, "Oh my God, there are people jumping out of buildings." He pointed up and said, "We are not airing any of that. If the network shows it and we are on the air, cut out of it." I thought it was a tremendous call because, normally, you never show someone's death on the air if you can prevent it, so why would you show that? Why would you show people leaping to their deaths? People don't need to see that, and you can easily say it's happening, and it's just as awful. I thought that

was a wonderful call. There were people in the newsroom crying. The thing I remember the most was me being upset that I didn't feel that [sadness]. I think there's a mood you go into because I've seen so many horrible things in my life. I've been to so many shootings, I've been with families, I've knocked on doors, and I've seen horrible, horrible scenes of aftermath of carnage in New York, Philadelphia, and Chicago. I think you go into another place. It's almost like a movie to you. You are not experiencing it—you are reporting it. You are looking at it, and you have a responsibility. I felt removed, and I always go back to that moment because I wasn't feeling what people were feeling. And people were really consoled, and people had to leave the newsroom. I was on the air for hours and hours. We were taking phone calls, hearing from survivors, and slowly the names started coming in. The people who had died and were missing. It was more and more people from our area. It was odd, because for the first time ever in my career, I got choked up on the air as we were reading names and seeing pictures of people that were missing and thought to be in the buildings from our area. It became very personal.

David Henry, Reporter, WPVI:
I remember we got to Liberty Park there in Jersey City, and that's where the ferries were bringing people from Lower Manhattan, who were just covered in ash. They looked like zombies and ghost people, just pouring off of these ferryboats and walking up the road toward us. We just kind of stood there with the smoldering rubble in the background and interviewed quite a few of those folks and got the personal stories of several on the air. Having rushed up there, it wasn't until six days later that we finally turned around and went home. At one point, we had to find a mall in New Jersey, a Target store or something, just to buy a change of clothes. We lodged at a hotel in New Jersey and then every day went into Manhattan. We would get as far as we could and then walk the rest of the way down to ground zero. I just remember at one point standing there, looking at the rubble and talking to my wife on the phone in tears. It was so overwhelming. The extent of the damage, the humanity, the thought of all of those people who died in those buildings, and especially the ones who had no choice but to jump to their deaths. I was in one of the blocks where they removed some of the police cars. There was this long line of police cars just lined up along the road that was completely

pancaked and crushed. Those were vehicles of the first responders that had rushed to the scene while everyone else was rushing away. You just had to stand there and wonder how many officers survived, as there was a tremendous loss that day. It's one of those stories that haunts you to this day. The extent of the loss of life, the loss of our national sense of security, and just the personal loss of your own sense of security. Is my family safe? Is anyone safe? What has the world come to? We were obviously at war now. What changes? Everything changed. It was a tough story to cover.

Lauren Wilson, Reporter, WPVI:
We ended up at the airport [Philadelphia International], probably for a week. That was where we were assigned to go. It was a very eerie feeling to be in that airport when there was absolutely nobody there but a bank of media trucks. For me, it was a time when I realized just how important my assignment was. Millions of people travel by air. People needed to know when the airports were going to be safe for travel. After a few days, it was an, "Okay, when is this going to be over?" It still remained important in my mind that this was information that our audience needed to hear. We needed to give them a sense of what it was like at the airport.

Amy Buckman, Reporter, WPVI:
I went up to McGuire [Air Force Base] because they were starting to mobilize the National Guard troops and the reserves, and we spent a couple days up there after that. It was a lot of time up in Bucks County in Yardley and Newtown because they had so many victims from that area who worked in Manhattan and the towers. It really was a tense and intense time of families not knowing what had happened to their loved ones, prayer vigils. I remember a parent of a young man who worked in the towers we interviewed, and there had been a church service vigil for him. It was one of those things where to do your job, you have to shut down, and so I really didn't process anything. I was just going to work, getting the interviews, doing the live shots, putting the packages together, trying to get the next interview, trying to hold it together while doing these interviews with families and people who were devastated by what had happened. I really felt that I could not process anything.

Vai Sikahema, Sports Reporter and Anchor, WCAU:
At the time, I was a bishop in my church. A group called the Chapel of Four Chaplains—they are based in the Navy ship yard—they were gathering local ministers to go to ground zero to provide counseling for the workers. They knew that I was a bishop. They reached out to me and said they would be happy to volunteer. I do counseling in my church. Everybody has dispatched somebody to cover it from the perimeter. Being part of the clergy gave me special access that I got to go into 9/11. I asked if I could take a photographer with me, and they allowed my photog to come, a guy named Steve Gresham, and we documented our way through ground zero and talked to the workers. One of the eerie things happening was there was a bell: A huge bell would ring whenever they would find a body or a body part. What was fascinating was every time they rang the bell, it was dead silence. Everyone stopped. We were in a mess hall where people came and went to eat. We sat there and were eating. The bell probably rung—my gosh, we were there for a couple of hours—it rung every twenty minutes. Two or three times an hour, the bell would ring. When it did, we just stopped and halted.

Don Tollefson, Sports Anchor and Reporter, WPVI and WTXF:
I spent five days reporting live from ground zero. As unbelievably eerie and as sad as being in Manhattan was, especially with that incredible quiet—Manhattan is never quiet, but it was then. The only sound that broke the quiet was sirens on the ground or fighters in the air.

Rich Scott, News Director, WPHL:
Frankly, it's one of the reasons I left the television business. It was such a numbing experience dealing with so much tragedy, so much overwhelming heartache during that week. It really affected me personally, and it affected a lot of people I knew in the news business. It was perhaps the most challenging thing that any of us had ever done, to try and keep our cool, and cover these events as they happened, and try to provide perspective and provide hope to people, and reassure people. It was a really challenging week. Most of us stayed at the station the whole day. We spent the first couple of nights there, but it was a never-ending story that first week. It was just a really amazing week to be in the news business. Philadelphians were more affected than other people in the coun-

try because of its proximity. I'll always remember the people who landed at the airport because the planes were forced to land, and we had a live setup at the airport. We were interviewing people who had no idea what had happened and why their plane was forced to land in Philadelphia, and those moments where those people learned what was going on, you just sat there and watched them on TV, and it was just amazing, and how they dealt with that, and people who were stranded and couldn't go anywhere and couldn't go back home. There were so many elements to the story. It was the most challenging story to cover in my life, and a story that probably affected me more than others. It's one of the reasons I eventually left the news business. It changes your perspective on a lot of things.

Robin Mackintosh, Reporter, KYW:
I came in the next day, and I was prepared to go home. At the end of the day, they said, "No, you are not going home. You are going up to New York." We went over to 30th Street Station with a cameraman, and then we took the hour-and-a-half ride up to Penn Station. We got to Penn Station, and you couldn't get down to that area. Nothing was running, so we walked from Penn Station down to West Side Highway, which is where all the press was, and ended up interviewing people there. The live truck came up and met us, and we parked the truck there. The problem was, once you got into the press area, you couldn't get out, so we were stuck there, and it turns out we were stuck there for five days with the same clothes on my back that I had when I left because I wasn't expecting when I came into work that day to pack a bag and spend some time in New York. We set up our headquarters there, and that was the main route for all the rescue units and all the first responders to be heading south down into ground zero, which was about ten blocks at the time. We ended up trying to localize the response, and there were Philadelphia firefighters there, there were Philadelphia rescue squads there. We ended up talking to ambulances that had been sent up from South Jersey.

Bruce Gordon, Reporter, WPHL and WTXF:
I remember the trip up to Boston was very quiet on the train. As you approached New York, you could see the towers—or what was left of

them—were still smoldering, the smoke was still rising into the sky in the horizon there. I will never forget seeing firefighters who were coming in from all over the place, coming and going, getting on and off the train quietly. In some cases, they were clearly looking to arrive, and in other cases, their gear was filthy, and they were leaving the scene. Just watching these firefighters very quietly—no one said much of anything I recall, it was mostly just observing these guys going into this horrendous situation or coming out of it.

Nora Muchanic, Reporter, WPVI:
I just remember shaking my head, saying, "Oh my God," because you couldn't believe how many people disappeared. I think we were up there at least for a couple of days, and so you would work double shifts, servicing the early shows, the afternoon shows, and the evening, and so you are running around doing stuff like just what's in front of you and trying to turn it around.

Rob Ellis, Senior Producer and Host,
Comcast SportsNet/NBC Sports Philadelphia and KYW:
I remember once we finally got back, we would have people on the air. We had [Phillies manager] Larry Bowa call in. [The Phillies] were on a bus somewhere. I can't remember where they were going, but he was tearing up on the phone, talking to us. It was a big deal. Still to this day, I think about it. It was a difficult time, for sure. It was a time when you really questioned whether we were doing the right thing even mentioning sports after a couple of days, and then we decided to get back at it. I think ultimately we handled it the right way.

Steve MacLaughlin, Meteorologist, WPHL:
The worst thing I was ever asked to do was later, when we were in the Afghanistan war, I was asked to do Afghanistan weather every night. I found that so insulting. I really did. I'm not a military expert, so what is my forecast for—when it's safe to pull off military exercises? I didn't know what I was doing. Are our troops not gonna fight because there is a certain type of weather? I always found the weather in Afghanistan and later in Iraq, giving updates for that weather, I always found that insulting.

Billy Vargus, Sports Reporter and Anchor, WTXF:
I remember the next day, going to [Veterans Stadium] and doing reports on security at the Vet, and you know, that was really what changed everything because, since then, of course, just to go sit at a sporting event, you got to go get searched and go through metal detectors and everything else. Not to mention the airports, but even the sporting events, everything changed, with long, long lines waiting to get in. Everything kind of changed that day.

Carla Carpenter, News Director, WPVI:
I will never forget sending Matt O'Donnell to downtown Philadelphia. By that time, it's probably ten or eleven o'clock in the morning, and the shot was absolutely no one on the streets. The Schuylkill Expressway heading out of town was completely packed. That was a very eerie feeling for all of us. Everyone that could go home went home. Downtown that would normally be buzzing at ten o'clock in the morning was empty. The streets were empty.

Matt O'Donnell, Anchor and Reporter, WPVI:
What really brought everything into focus was when I was standing there at the base of city hall. It was right at the time schools were letting out, and the kids were being told to go home. This child who was probably six walked by me and said, "Mister, is the world coming to an end?" He was completely serious. It was a serious question. I looked at him, and I said, "No." As he walked away, I said, "Maybe it's not going to end, but this is different." Our country was attacked within our borders. Nothing is ever going to be the same again. All of us worked well into the evening. I think I was back at one or two o'clock and maybe got in at eight o'clock in the morning the previous day. I had a newborn son who was one year old at the time. I said goodnight to him, even though he was already asleep in his crib. I remember apologizing to him for bringing him into the world because things were so scary, but things were going to be so not only different but different in a negative way. Our lives wouldn't be as happy as they once were. I wish I didn't apologize to him because as we know, our country was able to get through this, and things did change—some for the better and some for the worse—but that was what I felt at that moment: The world would never be the same, and I will always wish for the world before this day to come back.

AND FINALLY, TONIGHT

Behind-the-Scenes Stories from the Era

In June 1990, Larry L. Mason, a cameraman and postproduction supervisor with KYW-TV, was killed when the homemade airplane he was flying crashed at South Jersey regional airport. The light plane was designed for one person, and Mason was the only one on board. Newspaper reports say that a preliminary investigation indicated that the plane's rudder may have broken loose, causing the pilot to lose control of the aircraft. Mason was not working at the time of his death. The plane crash was the third crash in fewer than fifteen years that involved a member of the Philadelphia television industry.[1]

On March 5, 1991, KYW-TV news anchor Jack Jones passed away after a battle with pancreatic cancer.

Jones attended West Philadelphia Catholic High School and graduated in the class of 1967. He came to the attention of local newscasters when local news reports featured him after he won a high school award. Jones later attended La Salle University. During his time at La Salle, Jones worked at WCAU, later becoming a full-time member of the news staff after graduating in 1971. Jones was featured on mornings, weekends, and sometimes the 11:00 P.M. newscast. He continued his education while

1. Maureen Graham, "N.J. Man Killed in Air Crash: Film Editor Built Plane at Home," *Philadelphia Inquirer*, June 11, 1990.

working, in 1973 receiving his master's degree in education from the University of Pennsylvania. Jones became Philadelphia's first black news anchor at the age of twenty-six, per the *Philadelphia Inquirer.* In 1976, he moved to KYW-TV, sharing anchoring duties with coanchor Diane Allen, then a rookie at the station. He left KYW in 1979 and went to WLS-TV in Chicago. In 1983, he left WLS and returned to KYW.

In 1989, Jones fell ill, and doctors discovered a small tumor in his body, which was later diagnosed as pancreatic cancer. He continued to work whenever he could before his death in 1991.[2]

Bill Elias, a weatherman, was fired by *Inquirer News Tonight* in October 1995 after failing to disclose that he'd recently been fired from WTXF due to his admission in a mob conspiracy trial that he had given WTXF-TV newscast videotapes to a Mafia bodyguard. A former mob hit man testified in court that a tape that Elias had provided was used to pick out potential murder targets. Elias said that he had given two tapes of WTXF newscasts to Vincent Filipelli, a man he met at a gym in Maple Shade, New Jersey, and then-bodyguard for reputed Philadelphia mob boss John Stanfa. Elias told the *Philadelphia Inquirer* that he had provided copies of the Channel 29 tapes as a friendly favor to Filipelli. At the time, Elias said that he had seen news reports of Filipelli's mob ties but had no idea how the videotapes would be used. One of the tapes was of the funeral for Michael Ciancaglini, a top associate of Stanfa rival Joseph Merlino. Ciancaglini had been killed on August 5, 1993, and Merlino had been wounded in the buttocks. The funeral tape was used to study pallbearers and other individuals. Former mob hit man John Veasey testified in the racketeering conspiracy trial of Stanfa along with seven associates. WTXF fired Elias in July 1994 after the FBI told station executives about the funeral tape. Elias joined *Inquirer News Tonight* two months later, when it first went on the air at WPHL-TV.[3]

---

2. Jonathan Storm, "KYW-TV Anchor Jack Jones, 41, Loses his Long Battle with Cancer," *Philadelphia Inquirer*, March 6, 1991; Francesca Chapman, "News Was His Life: Jones Worked until the End," *Philadelphia Daily News*, March 6, 1991.

3. Associated Press, "Weatherman Suspended for Providing Tape to Mob," *Morning Call*, October 14, 1995; Associated Press, "Weatherman Aided Mob with Video of Funeral," *Courier Post*, October 15, 1995; Associated Press, "TV Weatherman Linked to Stanfa Suspended," *News Journal*, October 14, 1995.

In September 1996, WPVI debuted a new *Action News* theme song that lasted for exactly four days. The new theme ran on just eleven newscasts, starting with the 5:00 P.M. show with Marc Howard and Lisa Thomas-Laury. Within seventy-two hours of the new theme's release, the station received hundreds of angry phone calls and emails from 6abc viewers who did not like the change.

The station learned from its expensive mistake and changed the theme back to WPVI's familiar anthem.

Channel 6 had originally debuted a theme song for the evening newscasts prior to the program on April 6, 1970. The song played behind a video showing scenes of the Delaware Valley mixed with clips of Larry Kane and the evening anchors. The original theme music had been written by Tom Sellers, a Temple University student who earned $75 for his efforts. A year later, when Capital Cities Broadcasting took over WPVI, the company changed the song to make the theme more fast-paced. WFIL general manager Gene McCurdy contacted Al Ham, the producer of "I'd Like to Teach the World to Sing," the song that was used in Coca-Cola commercials. McCurdy paid Ham $20,000 to record what would become the official song of *Action News*, "Move Closer to Your World," with the London Philharmonic Orchestra and the Hillside Singers, producing almost fifty-three different versions of the song over a three-day recording period.[4]

In July 1997, WPVI's helicopter flipped over onto its side at the heliport along the Delaware River in Philadelphia. The helicopter lost hydraulic power as it was taking off around 6:30 A.M., dropping fifteen feet to the ground. Two people were in the helicopter: pilot Paul Larsen and WPVI cameraman Bob Kravitz. The helicopter landed on its side on the concrete pad, and the main blade and tail rotor struck the ground and broke into pieces. The impact left Kravitz dazed and trapped in his seat belt. Larsen escaped and helped Kravitz get out. Both men were taken to Thomas Jefferson University hospital and later released.[5]

---

4. Bill Shull, *WPVI Action News Celebrates 50 Years* (Glendale, CA: Disney, 2019), 18–21.

5. Associated Press, "TV Station's Helicopter Crashes in Philadelphia," *Intelligencer Journal*, July 29, 1997; Andrew Lehren, "Chopper 6 Crashes; 2 Aboard OK," *Philadelphia Daily News*, July 29, 1997.

On October 28, 2001, Philadelphia anchor Siani Lee was fatally injured in a traffic accident in Chester County, Pennsylvania. Siani was known to the community as Margaret Englett, but she changed her name to Siani Lee as she began her professional television career. Lee began her career in 1986 at WTKR-TV in Norfolk, Virginia, as an associate producer and continued working in various positions, anchoring and reporting in WTOC-TV in Savannah, Georgia; WMAR-TB in Baltimore, Maryland; and in Washington, D.C. During her time in the nation's capital, Lee received the prestigious Dateline Award from the Society of Professional Journalists for her in-depth reporting on race relations. After two years working in Washington D.C., Lee came to the Philadelphia market in 1993 to work at WCAU-TV. At WCAU, Lee won a Philadelphia Emmy Award in 1997 for her live special news coverage of the 1996 Olympic Torch run. In 1999, Lee moved from Channel 10 to Channel 3, joining KYW as an anchor and reporter.[6]

In May 2002, WPVI *Action News* viewers were greeted with a pornography video on air. According to the *Philadelphia Inquirer*, a Comcast equipment malfunction in its Sellersville, Bucks County, system areas caused the signal from one of its pay-per-view adult movies to "bleed into" Channel 6's newscast with Monica Malpass and Rick Williams from 5:45 A.M. to 6:35 A.M. Built-in safeguards allowed the video portion to be scrambled, and the audio was removed. Comcast said that the signal may have reached forty thousand homes. The WPVI newsroom was flooded with calls from viewers, and the station issued an apology for any inconvenience it may have caused.[7]

In September 2005, WPHL dismissed its thirty-person *WB17 News* staff, including eight anchors and reporters. The move sent shockwaves throughout newsrooms, as WPHL announced it would outsource its *WB17 News* broadcast to NBC's WCAU Channel 10. WCAU hired an unspecified number of *WB17 News* employees.

---

6. Beth Gillin, "TV Coworkers Recall Anchor Killed in Crash," *Philadelphia Inquirer*, October 30, 2001; Rose DeWolf, "Fatal Intersection Was Due for Red Light: Township Had Just OK'd Signal at Traffic Junction, Site of 20 Accidents," *Philadelphia Daily News*, October 30, 2001.

7. Gayle Ronan Sims, "Ch 6 News Viewers Get Unexpected Action," *Philadelphia Inquirer*, May 15, 2002.

WB17's broadcast at 10:00 P.M. in Philadelphia averaged a 2 rating, indicating that fewer than sixty thousand homes watched.

WB17 News had launched in September 1994 as the sixty-minute *Inquirer News Tonight* before shifting to a thirty-minute format in September 1996. The station went on the air in 1965 and was bought by Tribune in 1992.[8]

8. Gail Shister, "Ch.17 Fires News Staff, Hands Reins to Ch.10 of New Show," *Philadelphia Inquirer*, September 22, 2005; Gail Shister, "Days after Mass Layoffs, Ch.17 News Staff's 'Still in Shock,'" *Philadelphia Inquirer*, September 27, 2005; Dan Gross, "WB-17 Brings You NBC-10," *Philadelphia Daily News*, September 21, 2005.

PART III

Philadelphia at the Center of the World

THE PHILADELPHIA PHILLIES WIN THE 2008 WORLD SERIES

On October 29, 2008, the Philadelphia Phillies capped off a victory over the Tampa Bay Rays to win the World Series. The decisive game concluded after having been suspended by rain partway through two evenings prior, on October 27. The 2008 championship was the franchise's first World Series win since 1980. Phillies pitcher Cole Hamels was named the series' Most Valuable Player.

On October 31, the Phillies held their championship parade, traveling south from city hall in the Center City area of Philadelphia to their stadium, Citizens Bank Park, for the championship ceremony. Between one and two million people showed up for the parade festivities.

Ukee Washington, Anchor, KYW:

I still have a pic of Pat [Ciarrocchi] and I on a trailer at the Phillies parade! Growing up here and seeing my hometown team win a title was magical! Covering it was even better than that! We had reporters everywhere leading up to the final out. Stories from when the postseason began to the clinching moment. While still covering the hard news of the day, week, and month, we all knew that "sports" brings people together, and it was what everyone was talking about, so we made sure to put a little extra in our coverage.

Lou Tilley, Sports Reporter and Host,
KYW and the Comcast Network:

I was out of CN8 [the Comcast Network] by then, but I was doing the Phillies pregame show on the radio. I never saw anything like that in all my time in Philly. Citizens Bank Park for three or four years was hotter than anything. It was like the Flyers in the seventies—you couldn't get in. It was the place to be. I think it was more of a dating hangout than a sporting event.

Maureen Quilter, Senior Director of Communications,
Comcast SportsNet:

It was the first time in the history of [Comcast SportsNet] that they had a championship, but also the city was starved for a championship as well. I think it gave us an opportunity to not do the show that we were doing but to expand on it. I'd have to look back at that year, but the ratings were [so] crazy that I felt like I was doing a press release every day—one like, "Okay, now we have the highest rating ever," and then the next day it would be like, "Last night's game was the highest rating ever." It felt like every day, I had to write a press release about ratings.

Ron Burke, Anchor and Reporter,
WCAU and Comcast SportsNet/NBC Sports Philadelphia:

To me, it was a coordination of a team that worked so hard. Jimmy Rollins being in place when the team isn't playing well, and he ended up being there as a major part of the success they had. [Second baseman] Chase Utley having that working attitude. [First baseman] Ryan Howard being the draw with the home-run swing. You had all of these different kinds of pieces, and it came into place. [Pitcher] Cole Hamels was a guy who was easy to love, and you could wrap your arms around him. [Pitcher] Brad Lidge coming in and being exactly what they needed him to be. They had a real collection of guys who grew up, parts that were put together, and it all clicked.

Howard Eskin, Sports Reporter and Anchor,
KYW, WCAU, and WTXF:

I could have managed that team and won. They had a great—and I mean *great*—core of players. There were some additions that they made that really helped. When you have Ryan Howard, [shortstop] Jimmy

Rollins, and Chase Utley in their prime, that's not bad. That is really good. They had some really good pitchers. They had four or five players playing for contracts, which motivated them to play harder. They were a fun bunch of guys. All of them played hard. Every one of them played hard.

Leslie Gudel, Anchor and Reporter, Comcast SportsNet/NBC Sports Philadelphia:
They get to the playoffs, and the celebration of getting to the postseason is not as euphoric, because obviously, you know, you are trying to get to the next step and get further. There was a real "business-as-usual" approach to it, led by Chase Utley's demeanor and the "act like you have been there before," "we have work to do" mentality. I think [coach] Charlie Manuel's day-to-day approach was really important at the time: It was not to look ahead. He really preached that. I know Charlie takes his lumps for his managerial moves, but from keeping the team together, keeping the team focused on the right thing, that was really big. It's one game at a time, and not going beyond that. The other thing was, Charlie lost his mother. [Outfielder] Shane Victorino lost his grandmother. I think somebody else had a loss in the family. There was this real feeling of destiny with that team. I'm not sure if I would have believed that if I hadn't felt it or been a part of it. There was a belief in themselves that I just knew was going to carry them to where it was needed to go.

Marshall Harris, Anchor, Reporter, and Host, Comcast SportsNet/NBC Sports Philadelphia:
I was covering the games, but for the clincher—Game 5 and a half, as we called it—[the network] said, "We need you on the streets." I left the building, and I walked to Broad Street, and I just started walking up Broad Street. The fans who were watching at home were insane. They all just started to pour out into the streets. I was just interviewing fans and their reactions, and people were, like, so overwhelmed with joy. That was my first "Ah, this is how much Philly cares" moment. I think talking to fans, some who were in tears, they were talking about growing up, watching baseball with their parents when they were young. They were talking about just their whole adult lives back in the eighties, if they were older. For a lot of Philadelphia fans, that was their first championship they could remember and celebrate. It was insane. One

man came up and kissed me. He was just so overwhelmed with joy. That was a unique moment. I remember I was just working there a year. It finally clicked about how much these fans cared. They cared more than any other fans in my estimation, ever.

John Clark, **Sports Reporter and Anchor, WCAU and NBC Sports Philadelphia:**
I was actually in the tunnel or the pit area next to the dugout of the Tampa Bay Rays, waiting to go onto the field if the Phillies had won. There's a whole bunch of media. There's a whole bunch of police and people that were right there, looking at it. I couldn't see the entire field, but I could see Brad Lidge, and I could see all of the fans and the outfield and different things getting ready to go on the field. When they won, I could see everybody in the stadium going crazy, jumping up and down. We ran on the field, and it was awesome. It was awesome to see everyone in the stands going crazy. And interviewing these guys. I will always remember Jamie Moyer, in the celebration, he was digging out the pitching rubber. He wanted to keep the pitching rubber on the mound for his house as a memento. He always told me it was in his bedroom up on a mantle or something—not that his wife really wanted it in there.

Leslie Gudel, **Anchor and Reporter, Comcast SportsNet/NBC Sports Philadelphia:**
We didn't get to see that final moment until later. We had a TV down underground where we could watch what was going on, but there was a delay. You are hearing the roar of the crowd, and you are feeling the stadium shake, and you are not seeing any of it. As a broadcaster, I didn't enjoy that aspect of it. Obviously, the celebration afterward was awesome, but we weren't let on the field until after the umpires had cleared the field and the network got their time in. It was a bit of a delayed celebration, but, from a broadcasting standpoint, the relationships I had built over the years and not coming in there cold but having actually covered the team building up to that was really valuable. As much as it was a job, I was also a fan, which, of course, you walk that fine line when still covering the team. I liked all of those guys and liked them personally. I wanted to see them win and wanted to experience what they were experiencing. I got a front-row seat to that.

Billy Vargus, Sports Reporter and Anchor, WTXF:
I remember the celebration in the locker room, spraying up the bubbly everywhere, and somehow [outfielder] Pat Burrell still manages to be surly, get angry at somebody spraying champagne on him.

John Boruk, Anchor and Reporter, Comcast SportsNet/NBC Sports Philadelphia:
It was one of the first two games in Tampa. One of the things that stood out was [outfielder] Jayson Werth was picked off on a play, and I think it was a double play. He was picked off, and I was critical of that. Somehow, it got back to Jayson. He absolutely refused to speak with me for the rest of the World Series, even after they won the championship. He said, "I'm not talking to you." I was like, "You just won! You are a world champ. All of that is meaningless now." He said, "Yeah, I'm still not going to talk to you." People are critical of situations and plays and the events that go on throughout the course of a game. That something like that was still stuck in his head, that he would still harbor any resentment, blew me away.

David Murphy, Meteorologist, WPVI:
My season-ticket plan just happened to be Game 5. I had worked the morning show, and it was all hands on deck during that, of course. There was no taking off. My son and I sat through a very rainy, cold night, and they suspended the game, and a couple of nights later, I was down there later for the winning game. If you recall, that game started out with a game-tying home run by somebody on the Rays. Funny thing is, the ball landed a couple of rows in front of [my son and] me, and we were the only two who had white Phillies home jerseys on. The next day, I told [the station] about this, and the editor put a little highlighted circle around us, and during the broadcast, I was able to say, "There's that home run, and there's my son and I." It was kind of a fun little [moment], being able to be on TV and point out a very personal, passionate moment with my son and I.

Jamie Apody, Sports Anchor and Reporter, WPVI:
Philadelphia police snuck me onto the field. I was actually in the third-base camera well on the field for that final out, standing with some po-

lice officers, making sure that I was okay to stand there. It was literally the coolest thing ever because you knew it was going to happen. We were underneath the stadium, waiting to storm the field. This is the power of *Action News*: One of the police officers recognized me and literally dragged me out with him into the third-base camera well. That was the craziest, most surreal moment for me. It was my first major championship I covered, but also everything surrounding that. The city hadn't had a championship in a long time and—securely and privately for Channel 6—we kinda knew [sportscaster] Gary Papa was on his last legs. To know that he was there for that made it even more special and even more emotional for me, that they were able to do that for him. Everything encompassing that whole run was like magic. I got to travel with that team the whole way. I was in the locker room for four champagne celebrations because they clinched the division and then three rounds. In Milwaukee, I forgot to take my sweater out of my locker from my suitcase, and I found it months later with mold all over it from being drenched in champagne. It was disgusting. To have come here never having covered a championship and to be with them for that whole ride and then the parade was absolutely insane.

Billy Vargus, **Sports Reporter and Anchor, WTXF:**
People started showing up really early, hours and hours before the parade, and they were just walking by—like, I was positioned on the east side of Citizens Bank Park on the sidewalk, and people just kept coming by in droves, and they were all yelling nice things to me: "Billy V! My man, Billy V!" And that, in itself, was something nice and maybe a little unusual, that all the fans were celebrating me. So everybody was in this incredibly good mood, you know.

Neil Hartman, **Sports Reporter and Anchor, WPHL, KYW, and Comcast SportsNet/NBC Sports Philadelphia:**
I was at the beginning of the parade. I saw Pat Burrell coming down [in a wagon pulled by] the [Budweiser] Clydesdales. I walked up to him and asked, "What is this like?" He said, "This is awesome" and gave a pretty exciting answer on just seeing the sea of people that he was witnessing at the time. The plan was for me to go from the beginning of the parade to the middle of the parade [route]. That did not happen. There was so many people. The thought was, I would jump on a subway and go over,

and that didn't work. Nothing worked. It was so crowded with people. We didn't know what to expect. You can't plan on how many people are gonna be there, what's going to break down, the communication, the trains. It was a mob scene. I never made it to the other location.

Beasley Reece, Sports Anchor and Reporter, KYW:
We had anchors up and down the line reporting on everything that was going on. That is a military precision that you have to accomplish in order to pull that off, and it went brilliantly. We had two or three people inside the stadium itself. I was on the first-base line. We had reporters in the stands with the fans, and we had reporters along the route of the parade. The logistics, coordination, and the planning of all of that is intense. At the end of the day, it's rewarding when you pull it off without major glitches, and even how you cover up the glitches is remarkable within the scope of the business.

Jim Gardner, Anchor, WPVI:
Gary [Papa] and I did the Phillies parade together at Citizens Bank Park. We were stationed by the third-base dugout. We voiced over the parade, and when the event came to Citizens Bank Park, that was our assignment for the day. It was an incredible treat for me because I'm a huge baseball fan, and I felt like I was ten, being on the field at Citizens Bank Park. Someone said, "Jim, it's not a huge a deal." Well, it was for me. Gary was in desperate pain that day. Getting off the stool and in between being on the air, he would go into the dugout and sit on the bench. Getting off the bench, climbing the steps of the dugout, getting back on the stool was really painful, and then when the light went on, it was like a switch, and he was brilliant.

Michael Barkann, Anchor and Host,
KYW and Comcast SportsNet/NBC Sports Philadelphia:
My goodness, it was insane. As many as who were at that parade, there were many who couldn't get off of work or couldn't get out of their house. We were their conduit for what was going on and the vibe that was coming from South Philadelphia. It was awesome. That was a huge responsibility to me. That's why I got into television. To be able to take people places where they can't go or might not otherwise go. In this case, it was South Philadelphia in 2008.

Angelo Cataldi, Radio Host:
Literally, when you got to the World Series, TV had probably 50 or 60 percent of its coverage just on the fans and everything that was going on, which was promotion for radio, for what we were doing. We had sportscasters on, and it was an all-time cross promotion, the biggest one we've ever had. Our best numbers were in '08 and '17–'18 when the Eagles won. These were the best ratings we've ever done because everybody cared. Even the people that otherwise would not care about sports, we lead to sports though TV news, the games themselves. It was the best promotion we could ever have done and the best fun I ever had. '08 was just spectacular. The excitement on the streets that day and the looks of the people and how many people were immortalized on TV, like the little kid who raised his arms. So many people became famous because of the celebration that the city had. And in 2018 [when the Eagles won the Super Bowl], it was even bigger.

THE PASSING OF WPVI'S GARY PAPA

Gary Papa joined the Action News *team in April 1981 as a weekend sportscaster and weekday sports reporter. Before coming to Philadelphia, Papa was a weekend sports anchor at WRGZ-TV in his hometown of Buffalo, New York. Papa hosted 6abc's* Primetime *magazine show from 1983 to 2008 and was named the WPVI sports director in 1989.*

In 2004, Papa revealed to the Delaware Valley that he would be receiving treatment for prostate cancer, a battle he faced publicly for three years through intensive chemotherapy and hair loss. For the Philadelphia region, Papa was the face of cancer's impact, a public figure battling cancer who used his battle to inform others to get checked and to raise money for cancer research. After a courageous five years battling the disease, Papa passed away on June 19, 2009. The day Papa passed, 6abc devoted its entire 5:00 P.M. newscast to remembering him.

"It is a chair that will really never be filled. It's as empty tonight as our hearts. Gary Papa died today. While his mind said, 'Never,' his body finally surrendered to cancer," Jim Gardner said, as the 6abc telecast showed an empty sports chair in which Papa had routinely sat.

The following are remembrances or personal stories about Papa's public battle with cancer from colleagues and friends who knew him best.

Dave Roberts, Meteorologist, WPVI:
I was doing a kids' show in Buffalo, New York. Gary Papa, as a kid growing up, used to watch that show. I never really had any real contact with him in Buffalo, but he was aware of me and knew me, so that when he came here [to WPVI], it was like getting together again. We struck up an immediate friendship.

It was a long personal relationship, in addition to working with him on things. Not a lot, because I wasn't in the sports department, but I was always in the sports department, saying, "Hey, Gary, what's going?" We hung out a lot. [Jim] Gardner, myself, and Gary were very close. I knew of his struggle, and I knew what he was battling, and what he went through was a long, long struggle. I know his parents, his brothers, and everything. I was personally attached to the family and to him.

Phil Andrews, Sports Reporter and Anchor, WPVI and Comcast SportsNet:
Jim [Gardner] went to Columbia, an Ivy League guy, and Gary [Papa] went to Cornell. So I remember Jim used to come into the sports department, and they would rib each other, like whenever Cornell would beat Columbia in football—which back then used to happen a lot—or whenever Cornell used to beat Colombia in basketball. They used to have this friendly little Ivy League rivalry thing going on that they would come in and joke with each other about whenever their two schools played each other. I thought that was kind of neat.

Jim Gardner, Anchor, WPVI:
[Gary Papa] had so much charisma, but he sort of sometimes verged on the point of not being controllable. He was out there, and that was his brilliance at the same time. People felt like he was just sorta doing his thing. If you looked at his scripts, he didn't handwrite his scripts, he had some kind of scribble on it, and who the hell knew what that meant? Directors couldn't follow his sportscast until they got to know him and knew his rhythms and knew what he wanted to do. That was Gary. I didn't take him under my wing. You couldn't take Gary Papa under your wing. He was fiercely independent, and, again, kinda almost out there a little bit. He took Jamie Apody under his wing. He absolutely did.

Jamie Apody, Sports Anchor and Reporter, WPVI:
My job interview was in November of 2005, and [Gary Papa] was on the road with the Eagles. I didn't meet him on my job interview here. They actually flew me back a second time before giving me the job, just to meet Gary. When they flew me back a second time, I was a nervous wreck. All I had known was he is this legend in town, and I didn't know much about him or his personality. He walked into the sports office—his jeans were filthy, covered in Sharpie—and he comes right up to me and goes, "Hey, Jamie! Want some pistachios?" And he reaches into his pocket and hands me some nuts. I take them, and he goes, "You don't want to eat those; they have been in there way too long." That was the first thing he ever said to me. I was like, "Man, this guy is crazy." From there, it was so easy. It was almost funny to me that they flew me to meet this guy. I was like his little sister on the first meeting. I ended up sending him a thank-you note and saying, "Thanks for the pistachios."

Lisa Thomas-Laury, Anchor, WPVI:
When he told all of us that he had prostate cancer, we just knew if anybody was going to beat this, it would be Gary [Papa]. We were sick at the same time, and when I had to have a bone-marrow transplant—because my disease was not accurately diagnosed for two or three years—Gary was at stage four prostate cancer. He would call me up and tell me to get my butt back [to the station], and everything was going to be fine. When I did come back, he would give me such hope. He would lift my spirits when I would come down the hallway and see him. He was a real inspiration to me. I always held myself to his standards.

Phil Andrews, Sports Reporter and Anchor,
WPVI and Comcast SportsNet:
I remember [Gary Papa] telling us that he was going to have to do the chemo. Gary was one of those people that wanted to work. He had to literally prove to [management] that he could still do the job while taking the chemo. I remember the day he decided to shave his head because his hair was coming out because of the chemo. He would literally come to the station after his chemo, so they put a couch in the sports department so Gary would have a place to lay down. I remember the first time he went through it and had the remission: It was good news. That was

the first time I had seen anybody up close and personal with battling cancer. If you know anything about Gary Papa, he was always upbeat, joking around, life of the party. So to see him go through that and still get on the air and do his job . . . it was very brave of him to do that.

Carla Carpenter, News Director, WPVI:
How that newsroom took care of Gary [Papa], I will never forget. I will never forget seeing one of the photographers almost carrying Gary to his office because he got to a point where he insisted on coming to work. He was too sick to come to work, but this guy was almost carrying him to his office. Then, they would literally pick him up and put him in the chair, in the anchor chair. Somehow, in the moment the camera came on, he might have still looked pretty bad, but he'd give every bit he had to be upbeat in being able to do the stories. He did them basically without scripts. Gary was always difficult for directors to follow because he didn't write whole stories out. He ad-libbed so much because he really knew his stuff. He knew it better than anybody.

Jim Gardner, Anchor, WPVI:
[Gary Papa] said he had metastatic prostate cancer. So, I called a friend, and I said—a friend of mine—said he had metastatic prostate cancer, and the doctor said, "That's not good." I said, "So, what is a five-year survival rate?" and he said they were not good. He gave me a number, and I knew for all intents and purposes, the minute that Gary told me about this, that he was in big trouble. He survived for five years, which was a triumph if you were aware of the survival rates, which were for three, which isn't surprising, knowing what kind of a fighter Gary was. It was devastating, but the last person I could talk to about that really was Gary. He talked about his cancer, and he would tell me about his Gleason score [a grading system for prostate cancer], which was very aggressive, so it was clear that he was in trouble. I don't know if he felt that way. I think he felt like there was all kinds of possibilities out there for him to fight this. He set up a strong medical team at Penn [Hospital], and he was also talking to people at [Johns] Hopkins. He was obviously going to fight this with everything he had. My view was that it was a fight he probably couldn't win. I don't know if he ever really let me in inside, you know, in terms of his most innermost thoughts about this. Gary didn't do that very much, even with people who were close to him.

I could be wrong, but I certainly felt that way in terms of our relationship. He let you in to a certain point, but not beyond that. It was very hard watching this whole process take place, but there were moments where there was tremendous triumph. Chemotherapy helped, it worked, and he felt better. There was a point where he felt a whole great deal better. And then it came back. It's not like from that day on, it was a relentless march to death. It wasn't that way. There were moments of fun, laughter, and great spirit, the way Gary had interacted with people prior to that.

Scott Palmer, Sports Anchor and Reporter, WPVI:
I just admired so much, in an appearance-based business, how [Gary Papa] didn't mind how he looked. He was the face of cancer for so many people. I could tell you how tough it was for him to get from the newsroom to the TV studio. It would be about a minute-and-a-half walk, and he would have to rest three times against the wall to get into the TV studio. It was getting kind of late in his life, and [sports commentator] Harry Kalas passed away, which was another blow to all of us. Gary, by that time, was near the end, and he wanted to come to the service. Jamie Apody had brought him in the wheelchair, and he asked me if I would take him by the coffin. I did. I got him through the special entrance of [Citizens Bank Park], and we made our way past the casket to pay our last respects. Then, in the back, it was one of those moments when it was the last time I saw him. We just broke into tears together and cried for about five minutes.

Art Moore, Publicity Director, WPVI:
I think [Gary Papa's] bravery, truthfully, in sharing that whole cancer process with the viewer—not only was it important for other people to potentially get tested and do some of the obvious when they heard about stuff like that, but I think it said to the viewer, "I'm being let in on something very personal here with someone who I like and watch."

Rob Jennings, Anchor, WPVI:
Someone has said that Gary [Papa] was like everybody's little brother. That's an apt description of our dear friend and colleague. When he first came to PVI, he worked weekends with me. I took him under my wing for a while, then he sprouted his own wings and became a legend, not

just in sports but in Philadelphia broadcasting. We all suffered in silence when he was diagnosed with cancer, then rejoiced when he was in remission. A few months later, the disease returned. The chemo was making him violently sick, and he could barely walk. He asked me to help him put his coat on, then he sat down very slowly at the anchor desk. When I tossed to him, Gary was transformed into his old self for four minutes. It was like a light had come on, then gone out again when he was through with his segment.

Jamie Apody, Sports Anchor and Reporter, WPVI:
We became very close very quickly. I don't think I was here more than a couple of days or a week, and [Gary Papa] told me I gotta get rid of my agent. I asked him, "What are you talking about?" He said, "No, you are here and one of us now. People don't leave *Action News*." I said, "Yeah, yeah. I'm from California. I'm not here forever." He said to trust him. My parents flew into town, and he told them he would take care of me, and boy, did he ever. My first weekend in town, it was actually the first time I saw snow fall from the sky. It was January, and I didn't know a soul, and it was a Saturday night. He called me up and said, "You are coming to dinner with me and my friends." He picked me up in the city, and we went to Barclay Prime. There was this table at Barclay Prime, a huge table, with, like, this crazy cast of characters. His best friend Larry, Larry's new baby, a pregnant girl that actually lived with him that he used to employ, and I was so confused. It was all of his friends at Barclay Prime. He ordered basically the entire menu. They brought out dessert, and the plate said, "Welcome to Philly, Jamie" on it, which I thought was amazing. When the check came—I'll never forget—the waiter came back three times to say thank you for whatever tip he had left. I don't know what it was, but it had to be huge. We shut the place down, and we went out to get the car and valet because it was snowing. There was no valet guy to be seen, and he drove around the block five times to see the valet guy to make sure he got the tip. That was Gary.

Amy Buckman, Reporter, WPVI:
It was the day of the [Phillies World Series] parade and, at that point, most people in the public didn't know how sick Gary [Papa] had become. So my job . . . I went with Gary to Citizens Bank Park for the parade and the ceremonies at the ballpark. We were sitting in the dugout, and it just

took every ounce of energy for him to stand up and do the live shots. So, I was doing the running around, the reporting, producing, and then handing it off to Gary. I made sure he had water and was taken care of because, again, it got chilly by October, and we were really worried about him. He was just the consummate professional, that he didn't want to make his own battle like a downer in this amazing moment in Philadelphia. Everyone was on such a high, and it was so wonderful when the Phillies won. He amazed me. He stood up and turned it on when the camera came on, and no one knew how sick he was. He would sit down after the live shot, completely drained, but he had that ability and his dedication and his devotion to not just his craft and his career but, really, to Philadelphia.

David Henry, Reporter, WPVI:
[Gary Papa] would just have some scores written down, and he would go into the editing booth with one of our editors and pick plays: "Okay, give me that one. Okay, edit here." He would just have this highlight reel from one sport to the next with a few highlight plays. He would have some notes but not a script.

Jack Brayboy, Sports Reporter, Anchor, and Producer, WPVI:
[Gary Papa] just typed a few words and just went with it, and that's what the best of them do. You don't have to type in every word if you know who you are and you have command of the subject matter. You don't need to write it all down. You just need the facts in your head and to be able to look at a highlight and make it live. He was the best at doing that.

Matt O'Donnell, Anchor and Reporter, WPVI:
[Gary Papa] had energy that was bottomless. He had a photographic memory. I was filling in for Jim [Gardner] one day. I think it was the six [o'clock newscast]. It was almost time for sports. Gary comes raging in—this was before he was ill. He sits down, and I'm looking over and saying, "Where are his scripts?" He is just doodling with his Sharpie on white pieces of paper. I tossed to him to do the sports, and I look at the teleprompter, and there is really nothing in it. I don't think a lot of people know he ad-libbed every single sportscast because he knew everything, and he wanted a conversation, and he wanted it real. He loved the

play-by-play aspect of sports, and that's what he brought every single day. That's what made him unique, I think, is how he just went—red light went on, and let's go.

Jim Gardner, Anchor, WPVI:

Gary [Papa]'s sportscasts were not packed with a lot of content, but they were compelling, and people loved him. They loved him. I've sort of seen my experience in three phases. There was Jim [O'Brien] and Don [Tollefson], and then there was Gary and Dave [Roberts] and now Ducis [Rodgers] and Cecily [Tynan]. There have been three very distinct kind of segments for me. It's not that one is better than the other, but they are different. Gary and Dave was the time when, if they wanted to crack me up, it was easy. Gary and I had some moments and incidents that were hysterical, at least for us. There was this certain chemistry on that set with Gary and Dave that was different, for sure. It was quite an experience.

Don Tollefson, Sports Anchor and Reporter, WPVI and WTXF:

We used to joke about this: As announcers, if we would have an intern or two, [Gary Papa] would have ten interns. He wanted to help college students get into and succeed in this business. Scott Palmer and I would joke because the three of us worked together. Sometimes, we couldn't get into our own offices because Gary had too many interns in every chair. The reason for doing that was to help people get into and succeed in this business.

Neil Hartman, Sports Reporter and Anchor,
WPHL, KYW, and Comcast SportsNet/NBC Sports Philadelphia:

[Gary Papa] really helped mold a lot of future broadcasters. There are a lot of guys out there that interned or did intern over the years with Gary that are now in the business.

John Clark, Sports Reporter and Anchor,
WCAU and NBC Sports Philadelphia:

When I was in West Palm Beach, I would send my demo tapes to [Gary Papa], and I would ask him to critique, and he did critique and helped me along the way. We bonded over the show *Seinfeld*. We were both huge *Seinfeld* fans, and I think we both have a little bit of ADHD in us.

We kind of connected, and he became a great mentor to me, and then we became good friends.

Pete Thompson, Sports Director, WMGM-TV Atlantic City:
[Gary Papa] made everyone feel special. He would return your calls. He did care about you succeeding. He was the guy, and he was taking time out to help you. The number of people that he helped and the number of people that went on to get into the business—I don't know if that happens anymore, to do that or not. He meant the world to me. I loved the man, and I would tell him that.

Lisa Thomas-Laury, Anchor, WPVI:
When I decided I wanted a little bit more experience anchoring a newscast by myself, I volunteered to do the *Monday Night Football* broadcasts after the *Monday Night Football* game. [Gary Papa and I] developed quite a bond and quite the friendship. One thing he liked to do when we would leave is that he would race me on the Schuylkill [Expressway], coming home at night. At first I would ignore it, because I wanted to be the good little girl that doesn't speed. Then, he sort of brought me into it. I came to be known to have a little lead foot myself.

Jamie Apody, Sports Anchor and Reporter, WPVI:
The last couple of weeks, we had to physically put [Gary Papa] in the chair, which was insane. At that point, I didn't know how he was doing it. The light went on, and the guy was Gary. Nobody would know that he literally couldn't even walk onto the set. The minute the show was over, his wife, Kathy, would pull up to the back—at that point, he couldn't drive anymore—and we would carry him out and physically put him in his car. It was incredibly sad and incredibly inspiring that he was doing that. It was unbelievable. I remember even before that, for the last year, I remember I was dressing him without him even knowing it. He used to wear the same tie every day. Every day. I realized he was color-blind, and it was the first one he saw, and he just grabbed it. I would see what he was wearing, and I would go down in his dressing room, and I would hang a matching tie on the door knob, and he would grab that one, and he had no idea I was doing it. The end was pretty horrible, and when he stopped working, he died not a little while after

that. It was crazy how we had the run schedule [Gary Papa run], and all he wanted to do was make it to the run and died like two or three days before the run.

Mark Meany, Sports Producer, WPHL and WPVI:
I do feel like the work was really keeping [Gary Papa] going. Work and family were keeping him going. As long as he could work, he felt he had a chance to beat it. We had a number of Eagles trips, both flights and just local trips. He was in really bad shape and in a lot of pain. That game in the Meadowlands required a lot of running around. You are on the field, the press box, and you are literally chasing people to get interviews. [Philadelphia Eagles Safety Brian] Dawkins had a great game, and the Eagles were going to give us a one-on-one with him after the game. Gary is literally in the lower concourse but halfway around the stadium and was sitting in a chair with his head in his hands and just needed a break. I'm there producing the show, and I got Dawkins here, but [Gary's] easily a ten-minute walk away. They finally brought Dawkins out to me to get him to Gary, and Dawkins could barely walk because of the game he played. He was a mess and was limping. His head was down, and he was in really bad shape. I remembered I looked at Ryan Nissan, who was the [Eagles] PR guy then, and he kinda made eye contact, and [we knew] this was a disaster. We have two guys that are literally barely able to walk, and how are we going to do this? I told Dawkins, "This is for Gary, and he's not doing well. He's up the concourse a little bit." Dawkins said, "Let's go" and didn't even hesitate. It was immediately, "Let's go." We literally walked silently around the stadium, and he gets to Gary, who is still in the chair, and Dawkins just hugs him. It went on for a couple of minutes. It was an unbelievably long time. It was not just one of those "hey, brother" type of hugs. It was a long, long embrace. I knew we were on the clock and they had to get going, so I edged a little closer to see what's going on, and I could see Dawkins whispering in Gary's ear the whole time. He is intensely whispering into Gary's ear. Gary's sobbing into his shoulders. Dawkins was giving him a pep talk to raise him up a little bit. Amazingly, they break the embrace, and Gary takes all of ten seconds to pull himself together and does the interview with Dawkins. You could never know if you watched that interview what had happened just twenty seconds before. You would never know.

Charles Barkley, NBA Superstar and Broadcaster, TNT:
Everybody liked [Gary Papa]. There's a certain media personality that if they didn't like him, they wouldn't have treated him so good. It just goes to show you how much people liked Gary. If there was a media person in Philadelphia who people didn't like, they wouldn't have supported them like they supported Gary. Everybody liked Gary. I admired him for the simple reason that when you are going through something like that, you try to handle it the best you can. That's all you can do. I don't tell anyone how to handle their situations, but he probably handled it as well as anybody I've ever been around in that situation. I just felt bad because I hate when young people die at an early age. It was tough for me and all my friends. I was glad I got to spend a lot of my career with him.

I didn't look at him as a media guy, I looked at him as a friend. I can't even count the times we went to dinner together and things like that. I could say this honestly, I went to dinner and out drinking with Gary probably more times than he was interviewing me.

Cecily Tynan, Meteorologist, WPVI:
[Gary Papa] lived life to the fullest. He once told me a story about being at a restaurant with his son, who is grown now but was young at the time. I think someone shushed his son Nathan, who was talking and was all excited. I remember Gary said he turned to Nathan and said, "Don't be shushed. If you are enthusiastic about something, you just let it out. Don't be afraid to be loud and bold." That's just the way Gary lived his life.

HURRICANE SANDY

On October 24, 2012, Tropical Storm Sandy developed in the Caribbean Sea. Five days later, Sandy strengthened into a Category 1 hurricane, with sustained winds of ninety miles per hour. New Jersey, Connecticut, and Massachusetts declared a state of emergency.

The New York Stock Exchange, casinos, train stations, airports, and Broadway shows were all put on hold as Hurricane Sandy hit the East Coast. An estimated 4.8 million people were without power in fifteen states, and more than thirty thousand people needed housing. New Jersey governor Chris Christie estimated that Hurricane Sandy caused $36.8 billion worth of damage in his state: $29.4 billion in repair/restoration and $7.4 billion in supplemental mitigation protection and prevention coverage. Hurricane Sandy was the second-costliest hurricane in the United States until it was surpassed by Hurricane Harvey and Hurricane Maria in 2017. According to the National Hurricane Center, 147 people died as a result of the storm, which touched down in the United States, Canada, and the Caribbean.

Glenn Schwartz, Meteorologist, WCAU:
This was an especially unusual situation because the hurricane was developing in an area where they virtually never threaten our area. Some of the computer models, the American models especially, were predicting Hurricane Sandy to do what storms normally do in that area, which

is eventually curve to the right and out to sea. The European model, which I have been a fan of for years, did the opposite. It had it tracking to the north and then making a fairly sharp left turn into the coast of New Jersey. Now, that's something that has never happened before. The weather pattern was favorable for something like that to happen. I went more with the European [model] and got criticized for that on the air and on social media for hyping up the storm that was going to miss. This was days ahead of time. Of course, eventually it did make that left turn, and it really was the biggest example of the European model beating the American model ever. People still talk about that difference. I remember that very, very clearly. It goes to show—and I tell younger meteorologists—just because something [hasn't] happened before doesn't mean it can't. If the weather pattern is right, then something rare or unprecedented can happen. We had a conference call with the NBC-owned stations up and down the East Coast with the head of the division in New York. She had Miami on the phone and Washington, us, and New York and Connecticut, I believe. They were discussing each city. A meteorologist would get on the line and say something. By that time, she asked, "Well, what is the worst-case scenario?" Again, this was a few days ahead of time, and I said, "They worst disaster in the history of this part of the country."

David Murphy, Meteorologist, WPVI:
It was one of those instances where recent improvement and model data over the last ten to fifteen years really came in handy. There was a model called the European that, days out, had this very unusual turn of this low-pressure center going up the northeast, up along the coast, and turning right into us. It was unusual. In my experience, I'd never seen that happen. You could see what the models were buying into. There was a big high-pressure blocking area up to the north that was naturally, because the flow always goes around it, stirring the storm inland. It was a scenario that doesn't happen that often. Your gut at first was to wonder whether or not that model really had the right idea. True enough, six days out, five, four, it really was playing like that. The folks at AccuWeather and those of us in the studio began pretty quickly early on to feel confident enough to start warning people about what was going to happen. We weren't sure where the turn was going to be. I think at one point I was thinking it was going to be down near the Delaware Bay or

it could be closer to Atlantic City, and it turned out to be up in Jersey where it made that turn.

Adam Joseph, Meteorologist, WPVI:
As time moved on, other computer models started to pick up. When we realized, "Okay, we have a very unique hurricane," at the time it was named [a hurricane], "We have a unique storm that was going to move in a very bizarre pattern, something we have never seen before. This is something we need to really hone in on. Tell the public about it and warn them. Give them an early warning and let them know what may unfold with this." The biggest concern was the storm surge because of the way that storm curved in, the way it turned and the way our coast is lined up in that angle of southwest and northeast. All of that water gets pushed up on that northern side of it. Wherever that eye was going to land, the northern extent, it was going to be where we were expecting devastating storm surge. Now, originally it was supposed to make landfall somewhere near, like, Stone Harbor or Avalon, a little farther south. It jogged to the north a little bit, and it actually made landfall more north of Atlantic City. That kept the worst of the storm surge in what we saw in North Jersey, where we saw those images of Seaside Heights, with the roller coaster in the water. Our area wasn't spared, but we were spared from the worst of the storm surge.

Cecily Tynan, Meteorologist, WPVI:
I remember I was in the weather office, talking to Adam [Joseph] about it and to Paul Trombello, our producer. I remember Adam saying, "There is no way," that storms don't do this. We decided five days ahead of time that we can't discount it, because the European [weather model] typically is incredibly reliable, but all models have their biases. I remember as we got closer and closer to the day of the storm, all of the other models started to jump on board, and it became very clear early in the game that this was a storm that was going to devastate some area along the East Coast. I think Staten Island really took the brunt of it. We knew pretty early that this was a storm that was going to have a huge impact on the northeast. That's when we go into—before it hits—we go into twenty-four-hour mode, where we have twenty-four-hour coverage and we would work twelve-hour shifts on and twelve hours off. They could put us up in a hotel nearby.

Adam Joseph, Meteorologist, WPVI:
I just remember us working 24/7 and being on the air constantly. I worked different shifts than Cecily [Tynan] because they wanted one of us always on the air. They split us up. We were on at 1:00 A.M., 2:00 A.M. in the morning. It was like snow coverage. It was never-ending.

Brian Taff, Anchor, WPVI:
I was on the air all night long. I was on the air at 11:30 P.M. and didn't go off the air until 6:00 or 7:00 A.M. the night Sandy came ashore. We were broadcasting live as it was happening. Of course, in the middle of the night, you can't see anything. You are limited to what you feel at the moment.

Jesse Gary, Reporter, WCAU:
I remember just working long hours and being out in the elements and just driving wherever you had to go, where there was either power outages, damage, flooding, or boats in the street. It was wild—it was almost like an apocalyptic event.

Chris Cato, Anchor and Reporter, WCAU:
I walked into the building on day one [of working there]. You think you are going to do HR, the paperwork, and new employee training stuff. I walked into the newsroom. I got to [WCAU news director at the time] Anzio [Williams]'s office to let him know that I was there. I'm there early because I am the new guy, and I am eager. He hands me an NBC10 rain poncho, which is two sizes too big for me because it was his. He tells me to go to the Jersey Shore for storm coverage. He says, "Go to the shore," and I said, "What's 'the shore'?" This was my first northeast, mid-Atlantic experience. I grew up in the South, and we call it "the beach." I don't know what the shore is. He was like, "the Jersey Shore." I was like, "Oh, I get that!" because that's a common thing in pop culture now: the "Jersey Shore." There I am, day one, on the Atlantic City boardwalk with Superstorm Sandy.

Next thing I know, they are like, "We are going to lead with you, and also *NBC Nightly News* is gonna lead with you too." I was like, "What, ah, okay? How did that work?" So there I was—first day of work, in the raincoat that doesn't fit—I'm on the Atlantic City boardwalk, which, in itself, I've never been to Atlantic City before. I've only seen it in media and also what I know about it from [the TV show] *Boardwalk Empire*. This is a whole different world for me, and then it's this storm, and the water is not only the storm surge coming in from the shore but the bay is getting sucked out, so the bay is, like, sucking toward the ocean. I was literally on an island. The boardwalk was an island because there was water on both sides. Water was splashing up on the boardwalk. Then, all of a sudden, Brian Williams is tossing to me as the lead story of *NBC Nightly News*. It was all a fog. My photographer and I spent the night on the boardwalk sleeping—not really sleeping much—in the news vehicle. We couldn't get off the boardwalk.

Doug Shimell, Reporter, WCAU:
You had to pretty much plant yourself. We had no cover, so you had to angle yourself so your lead shoulder was pointed inward toward the wind because if you didn't, you would fly away backward. Your adrenaline sort of powers you throughout the entire day. You really don't think about the elements after a while—you want to make sure what you are saying can be understood because you have wind hitting you at seventy-eight miles per hour, and I see a lot of people out there in hurricane coverage who—I don't want to criticize, but you want to make certain that you and your coverage are not a distraction to what is happening and the reliance of useful information. Sometimes, you have folks dramatizing things, and they actually put themselves in positions to blow away, get knocked over, or in some way overdramatize the impacts of the effects of the storm on them. That's not what I am watching TV for as a viewer. At the end of our twenty-hour shift, as we got back into the van, and my photographer and I were driving back up to the studio, I realized I was partially deaf in my left ear because that was the side that was pelting my hood and hat the entire time. It was almost like going to a concert and only listening on the one side, and I realized my entire body was soaked on the left side.

Rosemary Connors, Anchor and Reporter, WCAU:
I can say this with full confidence: My photographer and I were placed in the hardest hit of our viewing area, which was LBI, Long Beach Island. We were the only ones there as far as we were aware, based on talking to other officials on the island and roving the island. We were the only news crew there. It was by far the hardest hit of our viewing

area because hurricanes are unpredictable—we obviously didn't know that going into it, nobody knew that. Because it's a small island, just about everything was closed. I was working with photographer Jason Ryan, and we ended up going to a bed-and-breakfast at LBI that really wasn't opened, but there was nothing opened. The innkeepers agreed to let us; of course, we told them we would pay them. They were staying there. They were riding out the storm, so they agreed and let us stay. All of the windows were boarded shut. The bed-and-breakfast was on high ground, so it did not endure any damage. This storm was unlike anything anybody has ever seen.

Lu Ann Cahn, Investigative Reporter and Anchor, WCAU:
I watched people looting stores. We were stuck in live trucks when we couldn't find a bathroom. We were stuck where we couldn't get any food, or we couldn't get any communication, or we would drive around all night to find any place with electricity where we could spend the night.

Nora Muchanic, Reporter, WPVI:
A big army truck brought us over to Stafford High School. They were very nice to us because they put us in a classroom so that we were not sleeping in the middle of the gym. So, we tried to set up signals over there, but we were having a hard time. [WPVI photographer] Andy [Doane] and I are sleeping on cots, and that was his birthday, and he spent it on a cot with no power in some classroom. We were down there for several days after that, and we moved eventually from sleeping at the school to some hotel that didn't have power, which was fun.

Amy Buckman, Reporter, WPVI:
We tried to make our way back to Absecon Island. At one point, we were on a road and came upon a boat in the road. We were having problems getting a signal. That's when we'd just gotten technology called Dejero on our cell phone, and so I remember doing a couple of Dejero live shots, just sitting in the van and turning my phone around to do some live shots early in the morning show. We drove into Somers Point, and we stopped at this little park on the bay where there had been a gazebo, and the park was gone. The gazebo was completely under water. We did a couple live shots there, and then we went over the bridge from

Somers Point into Longport, and it was so weird. It was pitch black: no electricity anywhere. There were wires down on the bridge, so we were trying to avoid all of that. We started driving up from Longport, trying to head toward Atlantic City; the storm was pretty much over by then, but the streets were full of sand. It looked like there had been a snowstorm because if you looked down all the little streets and went toward the ocean, they were full from the third step of the one house on the one side of the street all the way to the third step to the house across the street.

Brian Taff, Anchor, WPVI:

Whether it was that day or the next day, I can't remember, but the first day we were able to fly the helicopter, I was on the air. We were all watching at the same time. Everyone in the newsroom, me at the anchor desk, and our audience at the same time were all learning the extent of the damage. I was watching Chopper 6, and I was trying to keep up with where it was. At the time, we didn't have street-tracker technology to tell us where it was. I was looking at the outlines of the roads and trying to match it up with Google Maps to find out exactly where they were. I remember really trying to be as detailed as I could. I would say, "Hey, this is 34th and the beach in Lavallette," or wherever it may be. I knew people were tuning in to see if their house was still there. Are the people that I love gone? I really felt the weight of that moment, recognizing this was the first time people were going to see it with their own eyes.

Kathy Orr, Meteorologist, WCAU, KYW, and WTXF:

With Sandy, we were so close to having the devastation that they had in the northern shore towns in Seaside Heights, when we saw that view of that Ferris wheel and the devastation of the roller coaster. That could have been us. It wasn't that far off. In fact, the storm crossed over Brigantine, but the real significant damage was to the north.

Adam Joseph, Meteorologist, WPVI:

People just remember seeing homes off their foundations and ships inland, the roller coaster in the water. It's an everlasting image that everyone has in their heads, I think.

Nora Muchanic, Reporter, WPVI:
I did a solid full month of Sandy stories after that storm hit. Every day, there was some new angle, something new going on. It was unbelievable.

Ted Greenberg, Reporter, WCAU:
It impacted me and my family and many of my neighbors in the fact that my family was evacuated. We live in Atlantic County, at the shore. We were evacuated for days. My middle child was due right when the hurricane came. We [area residents] all had a lot of pressure and a lot of tension and an unbelievable amount of damage and lives ended and disrupted. We were lucky that our house was not damaged, but many of our neighbors were not so fortunate. It's still a story to this day. Some people are not back in their homes [as of June 2020], which is tremendously sad. That was 2012. It's a story that has had a lasting impact for thousands and thousands of people. To see the damage and the days that followed the storm, to see portions of the boardwalk washed away, even though it was an old section of the boardwalk, to see that floating in the streets in Atlantic City was surreal.

AMTRAK TRAIN DERAILMENT

On May 12, 2015, an Amtrak northeast regional train from Washington, D.C., bound for New York City derailed in the Port Richmond section of Philadelphia. More than two hundred people were injured, and eight passengers were killed.

The National Transportation Safety Board investigators concluded that the train's engineer, Brandon Bostian, lost situational awareness on the train tracks as he accelerated from 65 to 106 miles per hour, which was twice the speed limit on the track's S-curve. Investigators later found no evidence he was impaired or using his cell phone at the time. Bostian was arrested and charged with 1 count of causing a catastrophe, 8 counts of involuntary manslaughter, and 238 counts of reckless endangerment. In March 2022, a jury acquitted Bostian on all charges.

Amtrak took responsibility for the crash, agreeing to pay $265 million to settle civil claims filed by victims and their families. The 2015 Amtrak train derailment was the deadliest on the northeast corridor since 1987, when sixteen people died in a wreck near Baltimore, Maryland.

Bruce Gordon, Reporter, WPHL and WTXF:
I was probably the first one on the air from our station. It was one of those classic news experiences. I had done a story that night that was kind of a goofy piece about a woman who got a bad haircut at one of

these beauty salons that doubles as a training facility for those looking to get into the haircutting business. My original story was kind of this kooky, weird little story about how this woman got a bad a haircut and was outraged at this salon. The piece was more or less put together when the call came in that there had been this tremendous train crash. Out the door we went. For the next several hours, I was live on the air at the scene there. It was a surreal kind of experience to see what we could see. Frankly, that night, it was tough to get close enough to see much of the wreckage—that was mostly more of the next day's aerial view, when you really got your best view of the extent of the damage. I was on the air for several hours that night. It was a surreal experience to see these people being dragged away from the scene and cared for by the first responders.

Lucy Noland, Anchor, WTXF:
Everybody wanted to know what was going on. It was a devastating and horrible night. We were so lucky to have [reporters] Dave Schratwieser, Bruce Gordon, and Jeff Cole and the amazing photojournalists that were with them that night out there on scene. Those three guys know this town through and through. I remember Bruce telling me the history of the area on air around Port Richmond and where that curve in that track was, what was there before, who lived in that area, how close residential areas were to this area, the problems and past they had.

Dann Cuellar, Reporter, WPVI:
When you get a story and an assignment like this, you don't know what to expect. At that point, we heard there was a train derailment, but we didn't know how bad it was. We didn't know if it was minor or major. We just headed out there like we normally would do. When we get there, we realize, "No—this is big." There was so many police cars and firetrucks. We started going to where they were going down this embankment, where they set up ladders to bring people up who had been injured. We realized this was major and a big thing. We finally got the helicopters up, and we could see the extent as to what had happened. It was surreal. The police and firefighters seemed shell-shocked at what they were seeing and trying to help people. There were people walking on their own in a daze from those trains, coming up and looking to get away, but they also seemed shell-shocked and not all there—like, what

did just happen and what did they just go through. They were not completely sure themselves. A story of that magnitude, the station wants you on right away.

Keith Jones, Anchor and Reporter, WCAU:
Everything was dark. It was darkness where this train derailed. I remember walking toward the train tracks that I couldn't see and being met with dozens upon dozens of passengers and firefighters walking the opposite direction from the train with some gruesome injuries—broken arms, broken legs with horrible cuts and wounds. That was crazy to me. We were eventually told to stop walking and turn around. By the time we returned, triage tents and a staging area for the victims had been set up. They were all laid out on the street on cots, blankets, huddled together.

Jesse Gary, Reporter, WCAU:
I was there the next morning. I was a Philadelphian and born and raised in New York; you ride Amtrak all the time. This was another one . . . all the carnage, the amount of damage, the bodies, it was a little overwhelming and mind-boggling. In the moment, you kind of focus in on facts and basics of who, when, where, why, and how. If you pick your head up and just focus on the enormity of it, it is just so staggering. That's why you try not to pick your head up.

Doug Shimell, Reporter, WCAU:
The most uncomfortable call to get was from those family members saying that yes, they could meet us for an interview, but it would be over at the medical examiner's office. There was one family member of a victim, that we found out through our crew at the scene that their loved one was a father who was among the victims, and we were already over at the medical examiner's office, and I had to call him and let him know. They were gracious enough to do an interview with me. I don't know how families in that emotional state would ever agree to talk to media. I wouldn't talk to me under those circumstances. I am always heartened and amazed by the amount of composure and tolerance families of victims in horrific circumstances like that exhibit when we come around.

Denise Nakano, Anchor and Reporter, WCAU:
In a breaking-news situation, you don't know what the heck is going on until you are there and you assess the situation, and you try to pull in from what's going on all around you. I was in the area where everyone was gathering—law enforcement and, kind of, media were in the front line, and you couldn't go past the area where the accident had happened. I remember all of these shuttle buses with people, walking injured, coming out through shuttle buses that they were trying to take elsewhere to interview and things like that. It was like utter chaos, as normally breaking-news situations can be. I just remember just running on fumes and adrenaline.

Monique Braxton, Anchor and Reporter, WCAU:
I was watching it on TV on the ten o'clock news that night. Then, I got in at 3:00 A.M. the next morning. I was sent to the neighborhood. We were ground level for a little bit. Then, we climbed on a roof where you could see some of the cars over my shoulder. That ended up being the spot where *Nightly News* was for the next few days. I went to the hospital, trying to find victims and their families. It was amazing how all of us take the train, and I think I've had flashbacks: Could this happen while I'm on the train? For one, they have no seat belts, luggage that is not strapped down. There was a lot of unsettledness about that derailment. Did someone, in fact, throw something at the train? Did the conductor blink out? Things like that make you think, "How many people get on the train in the northeast corridor?" and "Could that happen again?"

Chris Cato, Anchor and Reporter, WCAU:
We went on early that morning. Our start time at the time was 4:30, but we went on an hour early, at 3:30 A.M. At the time we went on the air, we still didn't know the full scope of the tragedy and the number of people involved, the number of people affected, how it happened. We were just starting to get some images in with our crew getting there and kind of kept back for a while. Then, we were getting a lot of decent viewer pictures, actually, that lived close to the area. Once the sun started to come up, we started to get good aerials and all of that stuff. We knew it was a passenger train. Obviously, it was Amtrak, but you are still thinking, "Maybe there weren't as many people in those cars that

were affected, and maybe a lot of them just had scrapes and got out okay." But then you realized how many people it affected. It was one of those really difficult moments in delivering news. You try to be human whenever you cover any tragedy—whether you are covering it there in person or if you are on the desk and talking over live pictures, you have to think of the human element first. Then, you just think of all of those people that were going about their daily routine, just like we do every morning when we are headed to work, and because of whatever reason, moms and dads aren't coming home to their families. Spouses aren't coming home to their wives and husbands. It is sad. That struck me the most, when we realized how many lives were involved in this and the human toll.

Matt O'Donnell, Anchor and Reporter, WPVI:
The biggest question I had was, how in the world did this train crash the way it did? As much as we are a modern society, especially in this country, with modern transit infrastructure and safety precautions and the NTSB [National Transportation Safety Board] and all sorts of other precautionary agencies, to have a train crash like that is terrifying. To think of what people were going through, the survivors on the train, it was just awful. It was a small-scale 9/11 for them.

Steve Keeley, Reporter, WTXF:
I just remember how awful it was and finding story after story. I remember meeting a woman who just became a paramedic, and that was her first shift. The first patient she had was a woman, and she goes, "Can you help me find my arm?" I will never forget that story. This paramedic's first shift, and that was the first victim she got to, a woman who lost her arm, and she said, "Can you help me find my arm?" I just thought, "Oh my God."

POPE FRANCIS VISITS PHILADELPHIA

On September 26, 2015, Pope Francis began a visit to North America with stops in Havana, Cuba; Washington, D.C.; New York City; and Philadelphia. Pope Francis was in the City of Brotherly Love for two days, saying a Mass at the Cathedral Basilica of Saints Peter and Paul, visiting Independence Hall, and celebrating at the Festival of Families. During his stay in Philadelphia, Pope Francis resided at Saint Charles Borromeo Seminary in Wynnewood, Pennsylvania; visited prisoners in the Curran-Fromhold Correctional Facility; and toured Saint Joseph's University. Pope Francis concluded his visit to the United States by holding Mass on the Benjamin Franklin Parkway, with more than two hundred thousand in attendance.

Every Philadelphia TV station provided wall-to-wall coverage of Pope Francis's visit to the city.

Jim Donovan, Anchor, KYW:

Pat [Ciarrocchi] and I were about two hours into our portion of the news coverage when Pope Francis's plane landed in Philadelphia. As he walked down the jet stairs to be greeted by various officials and dignitaries on the tarmac, the Bishop Shanahan High School band led by Chuck Keating was playing in the background. After a few minutes, the pontiff got into a little black Fiat known as the Popemobile and headed to his first event of his visit. But as he was leaving the airport, he spotted

Keating's son, Michael, who has cerebral palsy, and asked the driver to stop. Michael was in a wheelchair, and Pope Francis bent over a barricade to kiss his head and bless him. As we were watching this unfold and talking about it on live TV, we showed a close-up of Michael's mother, Kristin. I looked at her eyes, and that's when I lost it. It was like I was hit by a wave of emotion, and I started to get all choked up. My eyes started filling up with tears, and I was having difficulty speaking. Plus, it was having a domino effect. Suddenly, Pat started getting weepy; our floor director in the booth started crying. At one point, even the burly cameramen started passing around the Kleenex box, and live on TV, I asked them to hand me some tissues. We all knew that it was an extraordinary event and that the Keating family would remember it for a lifetime.

Bruce Gordon, Reporter, WPHL and WTXF:
The one day, we got up early and covered [Pope Francis's] festivities for *Good Day* in the morning in Washington. By then, he had left [Philadelphia] to New York, and I believe he gave his address to the United Nations in New York. While my photographer and I were driving from Washington to Philadelphia, I'm listening to his speech on the radio, and I logged the speech the best I can with a mini recorder, writing a package, a story, based on that speech. We get to Philadelphia, we pull off the highway, and I run into the station and record that. It gets edited while we are driving from Philadelphia, continuing to New York. By the time the late newscast comes on at 5:00 and 6:00 P.M. I'm in New York for that part of the coverage with a story on his U.N. speech. We were in D.C. for the morning, Philly for midday, and New York for the evening newscasts. When he actually came [back] to Philadelphia, I was part of the overall coverage, the comings and the goings of when he actually arrived and left.

Jim Donovan, Anchor, KYW:
CBS 3 spared no expense on the coverage. In addition to field reporting on the streets, the station had multiple field anchoring locations. Among the remote spots were a room at the Embassy Suites Hotel with a balcony that overlooked the Ben Franklin Parkway and a broadcast booth directly in front of the stage where the papal Mass was held. The main anchor teams were assigned to that booth, and I use the word *booth*

very loosely: It wasn't a high-tech studio like you'd imagine, it was more like a fifteen-foot-by-fifteen-foot wooden box with an open wall, sort of like a booth you'd see at a carnival where you shoot a water gun to win a prize. The booths were lined up, one next to the other. There were eight of them, four in one cluster and four in another. *Eyewitness News* and *Action News* were the only two local stations with booths. The rest were occupied by network news operations, like CNN and the Associated Press. Below the booths were two levels of risers where reporters and anchors could stand for live shots.

Jeff Cole, Investigative and General Assignment Reporter, WTXF:
It was like an armed camp. There were fences everywhere. You could barely move around the city. It was a maze of fences. To be in the city when that fencing went up and to move around the city was remarkable.

Mike Jerrick, Anchor, WTXF:
They put up a perimeter: Once you got in, you couldn't get out. That was really electrifying to actually see the pope. He drove by our TV station. I could see him take the left onto 5th Street and in his Popemobile, and it was just thrilling to be a part of that. We had a setup outside, and people were walking by, all celebratory. That was a special moment.

David Henry, Reporter, WPVI:
I stood there doing live shots from one of the checkpoints, remarking on how slow it was [to enter through the security] and how, as far as the eye could see, the block was choked with people trying to get in. I predicted early on that most of these people would never make it in in time, and they didn't. It was a huge disappointment for so many people. In the end, was it a successful operation? From a strategic point of view, if your mission is to protect an individual, then yes, it was very successful from that point of view, but from a public relations standpoint and a potential feel-good moment for the city, it was ruined by the overcautious security measures.

Bob Kelly, Traffic Reporter, KYW and WTXF:
I was a papal usher when the previous pope [John Paul II] was here, back in 1979. In 1979, I was a sophomore in high school. And back then, they enlisted people to be an usher. You wore this yellow hat, and

you were almost like security, in a sense. They had thousands of free security guards, I guess you could call them. It was pretty cool to be right there on Eakins Oval where they built the altar in front of the cathedral. I was a part of that visit.

To be able to cover the recent papal visit was pretty cool. Totally different, black-and-white scenario of how freely the pope came to town in '79 [compared] to the security and the changes that happened in the world to cover the pope here [in 2015]. To be right there as the Popemobile passed was really, really cool—to have my son Austin on my shoulder, standing on the corner there and having the whole thing go by.

Keith Jones, Anchor and Reporter, WCAU:
What happened was, and we never expected it, but the pope and his Popemobile entered Eakins Oval when I was live—during my live shot. I will never forget being the one for NBC10 to call the play by play of the pope making his rounds that night all around the Parkway. Around Logan Circle, coming back around, setting the stage and describing to people what it was like. For me personally, for the Catholics in attendance, for people who didn't believe but were there for the spectacle, it was very special for me, and I was very honored to serve in that role for NBC10.

Ukee Washington, Anchor, KYW:
Two weeks prior to [Pope Francis's] arrival and maybe a week after his departure was such an experience. First and foremost, as a United Methodist, I learned so much of being Catholic. I anchored the events of each day with anchors Jessica Dean and Pat Ciarrocchi. We covered everything from the pontiff's travel plans to his message, the security, the entertainment, and special guests who were in town to celebrate this momentous occasion. I did a number of individual stories concerning some of the things I just mentioned while anchoring from our stage setup on the Parkway. Having a front-row seat to history was extremely cool!

Mike Jerrick, Anchor, WTXF:
It was challenging to come up with enough stories and different angles. One of the stories I did was, I went over and interviewed the archbishop of Philadelphia. And in his office in the rectory was a chair that was

used in the seventies that came here to Philly. He had the chair that Pope John Paul II sat in in 1979 when he visited Philly, and he kind of had it roped off in this office. "What are the odds of me sitting in that chair?" I said, joking around. He said, "Go ahead." He moved the rope and let me sit in it. We took pictures. He said, "We better get up before lightning strikes." It was very funny.

Jesse Gary, Reporter, WCAU:
I am glad I got the chance to do it, but it was disappointing because that was also when the union photographers at WCAU went on strike. It was difficult to work and get the job done. We did the job, but we had to alter how we did our work. We had people coming in who were not from Philadelphia but were from other NBC stations who we were working with, and it was kind of a tense, uncomfortable feeling. That aside, I really liked the fact of seeing all these people, all these Philadelphians, that are all united.

Doug Shimell, Reporter, WCAU:
That was all of our photographers, editors, technicians, and engineers. They had been without a contract for some time, and I guess they felt like their negotiations with Comcast were going nowhere, and so they took a vote to strike and did. I covered the pope's visit with nonunion scab photographers that were brought up from Telemundo, South Texas, and elsewhere. Not only was it a worldly sort of visit from the pope; it was an otherworldly three-and-a-half weeks of my professional life.

Denise Nakano, Anchor and Reporter, WCAU:
We had random people from other markets show up and say, "I'm your photographer," and we would say, "Who are you?" It was a very difficult time, not only [because of] the chaos of covering the event but also at the same time there was some angst happening within our station because our photographers and other members of IBEW [International Brotherhood of Electrical Workers union] were striking and were not there. It was this huge event. That was pretty chaotic and an exciting time, where this was a once-in-a-lifetime event and drew a bunch of people and drew a different kind of crowd than we were used to, compared to sporting events or the Mummers Parade.

Jim Donovan, Anchor, KYW:
At any given time in the booth, there were six to eight people and lots of equipment, two cameras, several large lights, a big monitor, printers, a large glass table, and several barstools. To say it was cramped would be an understatement. I remember just as we were about to go live for the first time, Pat Ciarrocchi took my hand and said, "This is going to be amazing. We will be fine." In our newsroom, I often referred to Pat as "Sister Pat"; her knowledge of the Roman Catholic Church is unmatched. By the time we went on TV, I think she knew more about Pope Francis than he knew about himself!

Pat Ciarrocchi, Anchor and Reporter, KYW:
We cried our way through the whole thing because it was just so moving to know that all of these people of faith were there to welcome [Pope] Francis to the United States and to Philadelphia. That really was a very special experience to be able to do that. To be there and to explain what he was doing and why he was doing it was an important moment for me in terms of my career.

Jason Lee, Host and Producer, WPHL:
Everything I did was behind the scenes. This is going to sound strange, but I didn't think the pope coming to Philadelphia would be that big of a deal to me. I am Jewish, so this is not my religious leader, but I found myself envious of everybody who was down there and everybody who got to experience it because I realized it doesn't matter what religion you are—this is still a really big deal, and especially Pope Francis: He just seems like a great guy. Wherever he is, he lights up the room, and he just makes everyone happy. Even though the crowds were insane and the entire city was shut down, basically, I really found myself wishing I could be down there and a part of it.

Chris Cato, Anchor and Reporter, WCAU:
This was coming at a time when the Church was trying to heal from scandal and some very negative things that had happened. The mood of the community—not just the Catholic community but the outward judgment of the Catholic community—was at a negative place at the time. I thought this [visit] really helped people put that behind them somewhat and celebrate what is at the center of the Catholic faith.

Rosemary Connors, Anchor and Reporter, WCAU:
What I remember most and what was so interesting about it was that there was a great sense of positivity, it seemed, throughout the whole city. Regardless of your religion, there was this religious leader that was here to celebrate us, to celebrate Philadelphia, to pay attention to us, to our region, and give importance to our city. I think, to me, that was the bigger picture of the story. It all sort of was happening during the time of a great wave of notoriety for Philadelphia. There were a lot of big events happening in Philly. Philly was getting a lot of attention nationally, and then we had this incredible visit from a global religious leader. There seemed to be a great sense of positivity across the region.

Monique Braxton, Anchor and Reporter, WCAU:
The excitement was definitely there. For the first time, I realized how many Catholics are in our market. It was so cool to see people come from all over the world. They wore their native clothing, what represented their heritage and their culture, coming from all over the world.

Brian Taff, Anchor, WPVI:
The idea of several hundred thousand people on the Ben Franklin Parkway for an event of that kind—everyone is unified for something good. They are there for a spirit of camaraderie and joy. Even if you want to take out the religiosity of it, just the brotherhood and sisterhood that was there that day was awesome. To be in the middle of that crowd and to watch the pope make his way down the Ben Franklin Parkway and to watch that Mass, it was magic.

Alicia Vitarelli, Anchor, Reporter, and Cohost, WPVI:
I was positioned—the day the pope was here in town in Center City—I was positioned right at the Basilica of Saints Peter and Paul and was able to be with the people who had the absolute honor of sitting inside the basilica, which was a story in itself. But then to be part of the Mass! The hairs on your arms stood up when he arrived. This was particularly special because he just had a very human way about him and just always made it about the people. Just being able to talk to the Philadelphians who played a special role in the Mass, whether they carried the gifts up or they did readings, you could just tell how powerful it was. It was such a healing presence that he had, a feeling of peace. Philadelphia has host-

ed some major events, and this one shut down almost all of the streets of Center City for security and passage. It almost became a walking city for this event. You would just see floods of people in the streets, but there was a peace and, like, a hope and loving excitement. The overall vibe, whether people were Roman Catholic or not, it didn't matter. It was just, like, a global event taking place here in the city with a historic gorgeous landscape.

Steve Highsmith, **Anchor and Reporter, WPHL and WCAU:**
Not to have a pun, but [the pope's visit] was special. Major events like that don't happen all that often. When you have someone that has the ability to have such influence throughout the world, in a positive way, that's something that I am always interested in covering.

Some of those things about broadcasting don't change, regardless of what the event is, but it was obviously a very, very big deal. I think it's one of the high-water marks for the city in the modern era.

THE PHILADELPHIA EAGLES WIN SUPER BOWL LII

On February 4, 2018, the Philadelphia Eagles defeated the New England Patriots, 41–33, in Super Bowl LII at U.S. Bank Stadium in Minneapolis, Minnesota. The Eagles' backup quarterback Nick Foles was named the game's Most Valuable Player. The win was the Eagles' first Super Bowl victory in the franchise's history. The big game was broadcast on NBC and pulled in 103.4 million viewers, the lowest Super Bowl audience since the 2009 Super Bowl.

The City of Philadelphia threw a championship parade on Broad Street and the Benjamin Franklin Parkway that started at Lincoln Financial Field and cruised up from Broad and Pattison Streets to the steps of the Philadelphia Museum of Art. Reports say that somewhere between seven hundred thousand and more than one million fans attended the parade.

Brian Monihan, President and General Manager, Comcast Spectacor and Comcast SportsNet/NBC Sports Philadelphia: It was an amazing experience to see everybody pull together and be so focused on such a great opportunity. Combining that with everybody's fandom because as much as you try to be an outside sort of source or you try to pull yourself out of it, the Eagles just hadn't won in so long. I guess everyone, in some ways, was like, "It will never happen again." It was just an amazing ride, and [I was] happy to be a part of it. After each round of the playoffs, we would have a station meeting, and we would give out T-shirts after each one or we would give out little mini footballs to keep everybody positive and focused. That two-week run up to the Super Bowl was just amazing, from a content standpoint to a camaraderie standpoint and an opportunity standpoint. We have a station in Boston, so we were able to do a lot of programming that was, like, Philly versus Boston, which always works. The two towns are just huge sports rivals. It was really a transformational experience when [the Eagles] won and then they had the parade. That whole week was just . . . it's hard to put into words. It was an event that brought everyone together, made everyone feel so good, and you just felt like you were making a difference in Philadelphia.

Derrick Gunn, Reporter,
Comcast SportsNet/NBC Sports Philadelphia:
You look at the volume of bodies [the Eagles] lost along the way. They lost their franchise quarterback, Carson Wentz. They lost one of the best special teams players in the history of pro football in Darren Sproles. They lost a future Pro Bowl left tackle in Jason Peters. And we are thinking, "Okay, they are not gonna go very far." Then, they hold on and beat the Atlanta Falcons. Everybody is still saying, "I don't think they are gonna beat the Minnesota Vikings," and they not only beat them but blow them out. We are thinking, "Maybe we got something here." Then, you have to go up against the Evil Empire in the Super Bowl in the New England Patriots.

Ukee Washington, Anchor, KYW:
We put a lot of emphasis on traveling with the team and bringing the viewing audience not only football stories but human-interest stories involving the environment around the team both at home and on the road. Going to schools, from kindergarten to major universities, to senior homes, to restaurants and gas stations. Eagles pride was everywhere, and we wanted to bring it home!

Mark Meany, Sports Producer, WPHL and WPVI:
I was there [in Minnesota] for nine days. They sent us down a little early, and I was there the whole time. It was the most incredible experience,

and I'd covered—it was my third or fourth Super Bowl—but I was never there covering a local team in it.

Part of being at Channel 6 with a big event like that, we figure out ways to be different and try to give viewers as much as we can possibly give them. One idea I had was to bring [former Eagles running back] Brian Westbrook with us. We paid to bring Westbrook with us to be part of our [broadcast] team. We already had [former Eagles quarterback Ron] Jaworski working with us, too, but we literally had Brian there every night of our coverage. It just gave an element that was incredible.

I can't stress enough how cool it is to work in that newsroom when everybody is in there because we are all on the same page. We are all living and dying on every play. A lot of these guys that are working in the back—editors, production assistants, and [associate producers]—they grew up here and only worked here, and they are obsessed with Philly sports. That's why they wanted to work there, and it's just so cool.

Brian Taff, Anchor, WPVI:
I covered the Super Bowl in Minneapolis. We went to Minneapolis for a whole bunch of days in the lead-up to the game. We were there, obviously, for the game itself. We would walk into a bar where Eagles fans were gathering, and the bar would explode and say, "*Action News* is here!" It was as if members of the Eagles had walked in. It felt like home.

I'm on the air, and I notice that my photographer, born and raised here and an Eagles die-hard fan, is literally sobbing. He's doing his job and keeping us on the air, but he is also crying. I signal to my executive producer Nick [Paine] who was with us, and he instantly got what I was putting down. I said on the air, "Nick, would you do me a favor and grab that camera?" Nick took the camera from the photographer, Mike Niklauski, and I pulled Mike on the air, and we did a live interview with him. He was so emotional about it. It was like this guy literally encapsulated what so many fans were feeling at that moment. Relief! A whole lifetime of fandom, and it just came out of him. It was this awesome interview and a really special moment. I will remember that forever.

Maureen Quilter, Senior Director of Communications, Comcast SportsNet:
Logistically, we were blessed that year because NBC had the Super Bowl. Luckily, on a production side, we kind of relied on a lot of the stuff that

NBC already had in place for the Super Bowl. That was a good thing. After every game, *Eagles Postgame Live* ratings were just doing gangbusters.

It was the talk about what do we do for the Super Bowl? Of course, we had to do a pregame show, but we decided to do a postgame show. I believe we were live on the air, like, all day that day, from like noon to, I want to say, until the end of the game. Our talent was fantastic. I remember Amy Fadool had an evening gown on when they won and had champagne.

Amy Fadool, Anchor and Reporter,
Comcast SportsNet/NBC Sports Philadelphia:
Rob Ellis and I talked ahead of time the week prior because we knew we were doing this. I told Rob, "We have to do something big and something huge." I said, "If they [the Eagles] win, I'm going to wear a full sequined gown, and I'll bring champagne," and he said, "If we lose, I'm bringing Mad Dog 20/20." We had to get the clear to drink on set because, technically, you're not supposed to do that.

Jamie Apody, Sports Anchor and Reporter, WPVI:
We worked our tails off. Everyone says it's the most amazing thing, and yes, it is, but it was also the hardest work I've ever put in in my career. We worked eighteen-hour days every day for ten days in very, very poor conditions, but it was worth it and so cool. We did it the right way and had so many crew and people. We had that thing covered. Ducis [Rodgers] and I worked out of the mall. I said, "This is cool, the Mall of America." By the eighth day, I said, "Get me out of this freaking mall!"

Derrick Gunn, Reporter,
Comcast SportsNet/NBC Sports Philadelphia:
When [Eagles defensive end] Brandon Graham made that strip sack, it was like euphoria in the Philadelphia-contingent press box. You felt the adrenaline rush throughout that stadium that was filled with Philadelphia fans. That stadium just erupts, and it was just like electricity in that place. Then, we get down to the field. Running around and getting interviews with so many different players and team officials. Tears streaming down peoples' faces. Grown men—just tears coming down their

faces, and them trying to regain their composure and consoling each other for what they are trying to accomplish. The curse was finally lifted. No more does this city have to hear that the NFC East has twelve Super Bowl trophies, but the Philadelphia Eagles had zero. To me, it was as if I played that game with them and won that Super Bowl with them.

Jamie Apody, Sports Anchor and Reporter, WPVI:
I'm on the field for the trophy presentation, and people are crying. I grabbed Brian Dawkins and [Brian] Westbrook, and Dawkins grabs Westbrook and is throwing him in the air on live television on our cameras, and they are hugging. Joe Biden comes up to me and finds me. I'm like, "What? He recognized me?" It was insane, and it was awesome.

Ray Didinger, Football Historian and Author:
My son was shooting the game for NFL Films. I knew he was going to be there. During the week before we went, before we both flew out there, we were talking and he said, "Listen, if the Eagles win this game, when it's over, I'm going to find you, and we are gonna celebrate together. I'm gonna give you a big hug!" I said, "Dave, come on. Don't bother. You are going to have stuff to do. You are going to be shooting postgame, and you will have a lot going on." You've seen the end of a Super Bowl. It's like Times Square on New Year's Eve. Trying to find any one person in the mob scene is just impossible. I said, "Don't even bother. We will celebrate back home." He said, "No, no, I'm gonna find out where you are, and we are gonna celebrate right then, after the game." It came Game Day, and the Eagles, of course, win. We are doing the postgame show, and they set us up in a box on the mezzanine level behind the end zone where [Patriots quarterback Tom] Brady's Hail Mary came down. Postgame show begins. I guess we were maybe a half hour into the postgame show, and I see the door to the box open and—lo and behold—who comes in but David. He had found us. He's sort of standing there behind the cameras. At that point, what was on the air, we were downstairs with Derrick Gunn doing some interviews. I leaned over to Michael [Barkann] and I said, "Hey, Mike, when's our next break?" Mike said, "Why—do you have to go to the bathroom?" I said, "No, David is over there, and I owe him a hug." Derrick was getting ready to throw it back to us upstairs. Michael said, "No, we will do that

on camera." I said, "No, Mike, I don't want it do it on camera." By then, he had already started to introduce us and say, "Folks, we have a special guest here in the booth with us," and he introduced David and brings David on. David and I hug, and I got all emotional and teared up. I felt a little uncomfortable with it, to be honest with you. We had been on the air for a half-hour—maybe even more. I really kept my emotions very much in check. I was clearly happy they won, and I was really happy for the city and the fans, but I had really kept my emotions in check. I felt that's what professionals do. I'd kind of always been that way, and I kind of felt like even on this day, when the Eagles had the biggest win of the franchise, still, you kind of have to maintain a certain level of professionalism. I did that for thirty to forty minutes, but when David came, we had that hug. When I hugged him, I said, "That was from Grandpop," talking about my father. That's when all of the emotion that I'd kind of been holding in check and the floodgates opened. I just started to cry. I sat down, and I was really crying. I know this is being televised live to this huge audience in Philadelphia, and I just was really not comfortable with it, but when I sat down, Governor [Ed] Rendell was next to me, and he saw that I was a little uneasy with it. He leaned over and said, "Listen, that moment with you and your son, that's happening in homes in all of Philadelphia right now. Don't worry about it. They are all Eagles fans, and they all get it and know what they are feeling, and they are feeling it themselves." He was 100 percent right.

John Clark, Sports Reporter and Anchor,
WCAU and NBC Sports Philadelphia:
I don't think there will ever be a championship in Philadelphia like that to that magnitude, because it was fifty-seven years since the last NFL championship for the Eagles, but the first Super Bowl in Philadelphia where older people were saying, "I can die now happy." Families coming together and families remembering their grandparents who died who didn't see a Super Bowl. I don't think there will be another championship celebration of that magnitude.

Marshall Harris, Anchor, Reporter, and Host,
Comcast SportsNet/NBC Sports Philadelphia:
It was like an entire city had been bitten by radioactive spiders because everyone thought they were Spider-Man, and everyone was trying to

climb everything. It was a party. An outdoor party—bring your own everything. It was insane. It was something to behold, it really was. I think celebrating with the fans and celebrating with the players are two different things.

Lesley Van Arsdall, Sports Anchor and Reporter, KYW:
They were trying to throw to reporters, and I'm not kidding—it looked like they were getting swallowed up. I remember watching [reporter] Joe Holden, who was out in the field, and he had to climb up almost on a pole to try to get his story. You could barely hear him. People were just screaming so loud and were so excited.

Maureen Quilter, Senior Director of Communications, Comcast SportsNet:
The things that people don't think about, and it goes back to the Phillies, too, when they win: "Yes, this is awesome and so exciting" to "Okay, what about the parade?" There is really no time to rest. It's like, "Okay, fantastic, they won. Okay, when is the parade, and what are we doing for the parade? What are the logistics?" The teams are so superstitious, they don't want to talk about it. As much as you are like, "Do you have any idea or plans?" they won't say a word because they are superstitious about saying anything. You can have some planning or conversations, but you really can't do anything until after they win. So, there is really no rest for the weary.

Ukee Washington, Anchor, KYW:
The parade was a sea of Philly pride! Eagles fans from not only here but from all over the world converged on Center City for a scene I have never seen before.

Jim Donovan, Anchor, KYW:
At the beginning of the football season, a clothing company sent me an Eagles suit as a promotional item. Just for kicks, I decided to wear it the morning after each Eagles win during our sports segments. The suit was made of some sort of polyester and fortunately was several sizes too big. I would slip it over my actual suit during commercial breaks. After a few wins, the suit had a following of its own, with the hashtag #JimsSuit. When covering the championship parade, I was assigned to

broadcast from along the Ben Franklin Parkway. I decided to wear the suit on my walk to the location but eventually had to take it off and carry it because so many people stopped me, wanting to take a picture with me wearing it.

Derrick Gunn, Reporter,
Comcast SportsNet/NBC Sports Philadelphia:
That parade was like no other parade I ever covered. Listening to Jason Kelce at the podium—I will never forget that speech. Then, talking to players about that speech on the steps of the Art Museum, former and current players—Brian Dawkins, Todd Herremans, the Jeremiah Trotters—they were just as proud as the guys who actually fought the battles that season and stood tall. How that team adapted that underdog mentality with the [dog] face masks, it was like nothing I'd ever seen before.

Howard Eskin, Sports Reporter and Anchor,
KYW, WCAU, and WTXF:
It's number one. I told [former Phillies third baseman] Mike Schmidt. I said, "Schmitty, your [World Series champion] '80 team was my team. That was the most enjoyment I have ever had, but the Eagles Super Bowl team just passed you." Being on the field, there is just something so special about that. It was unbelievable. It was truly unbelievable. That was the greatest moment in covering anything in my career, without question.

COVID-19

In December 2019, the first case of COVID-19 was discovered in Wuhan, China. The disease quickly spread worldwide.

In March 2020, the spread of COVID-19 in the United States and the rest of the world resulted in businesses, schools, professional sporting events, and other gatherings shutting down temporarily. As of 2024, COVID-19 has killed more than seven million people worldwide. To help protect against the contraction of COVID-19, the World Health Organization coordinated development of multiple vaccines with research groups and pharmaceutical distributors around the world, and the U.S. Centers for Disease Control and Prevention (CDC) set guidelines and released public health information in the United States.

Even as many offices and schools transitioned to remote work to minimize spread, television news crews continued to operate in newsrooms across the world and in Philadelphia, but with huge changes. The following are personal stories from anchors, reporters, and meteorologists as they persevered to cover the pandemic during the 24/7 news cycle.

Ali Gorman, Health Reporter, WPVI:
Myself and my producer [Dawn Heefner] I worked with kind of saw it coming months before. There was a lot of talk, and we were following what was going on in China. We covered a lot of stories of the MERS

epidemic, SARS, Ebola. . . . We covered a lot of epidemics that happened globally but didn't really hit the U.S. or impact the U.S. that monumentally. We were listening to a CDC press conference, and we had been listening to them, I think, every Friday. Then, all of a sudden, I still remember when one of the experts started talking about, "Well, I think we need to start planning for if businesses need to shut down and we need to close schools." It was a completely different tone. It wasn't "Hey, this is coming. We need to do this now," but it was the first time we heard from an official saying we need to start making plans if we need to shut down. All along leading up to the pandemic, it was kind of "No, there's only a couple of cases here, and we have it under control, and it's in China." I just remember that meeting and being like, "Woah. This is going to be really big." We were in different offices, and Dawn came out of her office, and we both looked at each other like, "Woah—what was that?" A month after that, it just kind of spiraled.

Tamala Edwards, Anchor, WPVI:
It became more and more clear that [the virus] was something that wasn't [just] going to be a story somewhere else, and what did that mean? I think experiencing it in real time, [I had] the same questions everyone was experiencing: Can you take a walk or go for a run? If you're gonna be in someone else's foot stream outside? Do you need to wipe down your groceries? What can your children do or not do? Are you prepared to just go to your house and live at your house? I think within a couple weeks of this getting serious, [people from the station] came to my house and set it up for me to broadcast from home. It was interesting: In a way, it affected you, and it proved that you could do things that you couldn't do. I would've never told you you could work from home. Well, you can if you have to. I think the world has been remade in a lot of industries. I learned I didn't have to, and I liked having work at work and home at home.

Adam Joseph, Meteorologist, WPVI:
I remember saying to myself, I was like, "They will never send us home. There's no way of doing the newscast from home." It was never talked about, never an option or an opportunity. I was always jealous of people who worked from home. You get to wear comfy pants, don't have to

leave or travel or fight traffic. I remember the day my boss came to me and said, "We need to send you home." I was like, "Woah!" How was this going to happen? Society as a whole—whether you are talking about TV or other industries—everything was in person and face to face, in an office, a conference room, on a news set, or if you're live. Yes, we have the capabilities of going live, but now we are talking about trying to put a product together without having to have a photographer with you in your house, professional equipment, or how do we get in and run the weather computer and make the weather graphics? Things had to get put together rather quickly. I was sorta really impressed with how we as an industry adapted to that change so quickly. When I was home the first time in 2020, I used my cell phone and dialed in on Skype. I would dial in on the cell phone and use earbuds to hear the producers and to use the microphone. I didn't have any professional equipment. People didn't realize I was literally using my cell phone to go live from the basement of my house. I also had a laptop where I found a program where we could get into our weather computer and update the graphics from my house into the computer at the station. When I was on the air, I was running the graphic from my computer in my basement. We found ways to do it.

Jim Donovan, Anchor, KYW:
Over the course of my thirty-year-plus career, I've seen a lot of technological advancements. Typewriters replaced by computers, videotape replaced by video cards, studio camera operators replaced by robots. I guess it's inevitable. But I never in a million years would have imagined that one day I would be anchoring a newscast from my house, using a six-year-old iPad and a mix of lights that I bought on Amazon. But that's exactly what happened shortly after the COVID-19 pandemic hit our region. In an effort to keep the staff safe, our management team scaled back our in-house operation to only essential personnel. Practically overnight, the TV station became a ghost town. For over a year, most of our news producers, writers, and video editors worked remotely from their homes. Our field reporters and photojournalists drove to assignments in separate vehicles due to social-distancing concerns, and month after month after month, most of them never even stepped foot in the newsroom.

Dann Cuellar, Reporter, WPVI:
I had one photographer, and we had masks, gloves, sanitizers, and Lysol that we would [use to] spray the van down every day before and after our shift. We only used one van, but we didn't trade vans. We were assigned one van, and that was it. We didn't get to go in our building. They had this portable restroom for us outside. Again, they were trying to stop the spread of the virus. Many of our colleagues that work behind the scenes—the producers, editors, assignment editors, managers—we didn't see them for two years.

Jennaphr Frederick, Reporter, WTXF:
I was working harder than I ever worked. I was more scared because I didn't know how to protect my family. I would come home at eleven or twelve o'clock after the show was over, take my clothes off in the laundry room, and completely change my clothes. Hand wipe in each hand and wipe down everywhere when I came in. I would brush my teeth, hands, and literally change my contacts, and I didn't know what the rules were at the point. I would immediately get mad at my family at that point because they were eating Dunkin' Donuts as they DoorDashed, blowing off Zooms. The spring of 2020 was not my favorite.

Matt O'Donnell, Anchor and Reporter, WPVI:
There are so many things I could say about it. I would wake up in the middle of the night and just have this terror of "Did this really happen? Are we still three weeks into a shutdown? What's gonna happen in the future? Am I going to get sick?" But Jim [Gardner] said it best. Someone asked him, "How do you approach this story differently?" [He replied,] "You don't. You approach it just like any other breaking news story. You get the facts, and you tell people what is happening. Tell people what we know."

Jim Gardner, Anchor, WPVI:
I was really glad when Ducis [Rodgers] came back into the studio. He did a great job from home, and it was what it was. Was I delighted that he came back? Sure. Would I be disappointed if my compatriots in the studio have to go back home? Yes, I would be very disappointed. I'm hoping it won't happen. There was a fair amount of conversation: Should I do

this from the station or from home? In fact, they moved in the whole deal and were testing shots and [deciding] should it be in my study or in my living room. I thought it should be in the study, and we checked out the shot, and I guess it was our news director Tom Davis who said, "I don't like that." So, we checked out the living room, and it was a better shot. It was more neutral and ready to go. The question was, "Should I do this from home or work?" I was very anxious about going to work, needless to say, and no one tried to influence me at all, ever. So, I had to make a decision. We [anchors] don't work out of offices; we are all in the newsroom. Someone suggested that I work out of an office, and would that make me feel more comfortable? I said, "Let's try that." So, there's an office right off the newsroom where I've been working almost since then. There was a period of a month or so where I came back out, and then they ratcheted it up with some concern a little bit, so I went back into the office.

I felt like I was taking a little bit of a risk, which was not my normal personality. I felt that if viewers saw me at the station, in the studio, that that might be a little comforting for them. It's normal, regular. I thought that was important, so I said, "Let's try that and see how it goes." We did, and we never stopped doing that. After about eight or nine months, the station said, "Alright, let's get the stuff out of your house. We can use it elsewhere."

Mike Jerrick, Anchor, WTXF:

When [the pandemic] first happened, they came to me and said, "You are kind of the face of this station at this point" because I outlived everybody. "Would you mind staying in the studio and be one of the few people in the building?" So, I jumped at that chance and said, "Heck, yes." I still wanted to get out of my apartment, to come in every day, even though there were very few people here. I was alone in the studio: A producer was in my ear, and the director in the control room. No one was in the newsroom. I was alone in the studio certainly for months and months—probably for a year.

The big hiccup for me was, it was a Monday after Thanksgiving I came down with COVID, and it was a pretty damn bad case of it too. I got the diagnosis and the positive test result at about 9:30 P.M. on a Monday night. I called Jim Driscoll, our news director, and said, "Jim, I have it." I didn't see anybody until the first week of January. No human contact. Just me in my apartment, flat on my back, hoping I wasn't going to die. In the first few days, I said, "This is it." I was way up there in age. "I'm going to be on a ventilator, and I'm going to die, and I'm not going to see my girls again. My career is over, and is this how it's going to freaking end? Oh my God—alone in my apartment." I went into a pity party and [became a] drama king, but obviously, I survived. My doctor just kept saying, "Dr. Mike," he said, "if your blood oxygen level gets below ninety, go to the emergency room." I had that thing on my finger about twenty-four hours a day, checking the oxygen in my blood every few minutes, taking my temperature constantly. It was horrible. My daughter would order food on Instacart and deliver it to my apartment. I had a friend, Joe, who lives in my building, and he would bring up the food and leave it at my front door. I would open the door, pull the food in, and survive.

Alicia Vitarelli, Anchor, Reporter, and Cohost, WPVI:
We did it together. I have never seen people, like, literally step up. There were people at home, and yes, you could be a meteorologist at home, but also on the inside, crew that have to take the signal in, who have to make sure it's working. The workflow was totally different. Between in studio and at home, it got done. That was the amazing part of it. No matter where you were as part of the process, there was no handbook for this. We never did this before.

Rick Williams, Anchor, WPVI:
We were getting tested regularly. There was a regimen of washing hands, using hand sanitizer. We had to wear a mask, except when we went into the studio, we could take them off. Even at the desk, we had to make sure that we were six feet apart from everyone. It was the same, but it was different.

Alex Holley, Anchor, WTXF:
I was sent home first. Mike [Jerrick] never went home. That was interesting because we are such a chemistry-based show, and so much of it—people are surprised to hear so much of it isn't scripted. That was the difficulty. Usually, we just go off our own cues by looking at each other

and going off the cuff. It's hard to do when I'm in a whole other location, I can't see him, and he's on a two-second delay to me. Trying to go back and forth off that took a big adjustment to get used to.

Sue Serio, Meteorologist, WTXF:
I started doing things and making the best of it. I started an Instagram post called "Documenting My Days." If it was National Pasta Day, I'd actually get up early and make some pasta and take a picture of myself with the pasta. I started with my Christmas tree, which started out as my Thanksgiving tree, which I kinda do every year, anyway. Then, it became a winter tree, and I knitted little sweaters on the tree. Then, I had a Saint Patrick's Day tree, and a Valentine's Day tree. Anything to just keep myself and the viewers interested.

I will be honest with you, and I will say it because I also said it on TV—we made a segment out of it. I was experiencing anxiety about it because I really did live inside my little bubble. I didn't go out a whole lot during most of that period. We didn't go out at all, and I was totally fine with being a homebody. I had to deal with that anxiety when I first came [back] to the office. It was a little rough for the first week or so. I don't know what I thought was going to happen, but anxiety really doesn't have to make sense. That's the way I was. This happens to a lot of us on *Good Day*. If we experience something and we think, "This is probably something people are going through," we often make a segment out of it. I was getting anxiety, and I had to make a few phone calls to counselors to talk to somebody about it. I was a little freaking out. I got talked off the ledge and brought back in. We brought in an expert to deal with that because Lord knows so many other people were going through the same thing.

Jim Donovan, Anchor, KYW:
What none of us really expected, however, was the level of fascination about what our homes looked like. I'd often get emails from viewers asking about the color of the paint on my walls or where I bought the drapes that were in the background when I broadcast from my home office. But I did the same thing. I'd watch as my colleagues broadcast from their homes and then text them about furnishings that I liked. We also helped each other out, offering lighting and staging tips to make the

shot look better. Several months into the pandemic, I decided to mix things up and broadcast from a different room each Friday morning.

Bob Kelly, Traffic Reporter, KYW and WTXF:
For me, I remember once, I lost power at my house. I said, "Aw, crap—now what am I going to do?" I grabbed my selfie stick and cell phone camera and went to Wawa because I knew the cops always hung out there. They said, "Power lines are down everywhere." They said, "Come on, we will take you to each [power line that is down]." So, all morning long, I went live with my cell phone camera on a selfie stick. Never before had we ever done that.

Dawn Timmeney, Anchor and Reporter, WCAU and WTXF:
I feel like when you do a Zoom interview, it's not quite the same as being in person with somebody and maybe even insinuating some of the emotions, feelings, and sitting across the room from somebody. But thank God for Zoom because, you know, we needed to get these people. What evolves out of that, sometimes when you can't get somebody, but you really need them for a story, you can say, "What about Zoom?" They are at their home, it's nine o'clock, and they say, "Alright, I will do it." Whereas before, you might not have gotten it. I feel like that's one maybe good thing. We had to wear masks, and our microphones were attached to, like, long rods that they made. We had, like, sixteen-foot poles with the mic on the end that we were reaching out to do interviews with masks outside. We rarely did interviews inside at all because of all of the precautions.

Adam Joseph, Meteorologist, WPVI:
I think a lot of people got wrapped up as an American—we are not working to live, we are living to work. We are constantly having to work, work, work in our brains in order to make a dollar to survive and rush around. I think COVID, I think for me, made me [stop] to take a step back in life and to realize what is important in life, and it's family.

Brian Taff, Anchor, WPVI:
The initial moments of COVID-19 for me were this, like, jolt and reminder that what we do is critically important, and people tuned in in

massive numbers every day because they wanted to know what was happening. How were their lives going to change that day? What was still open? What do I have to worry about with this virus? Do I have to wear a mask? Every day—life-changing stuff. Our numbers were through the roof. We don't do this [job] for numbers, but that was an absolute reminder for me that what we do matters. It gave me a real sense of purpose.

Ukee Washington, Anchor, KYW:
The highs of working during the pandemic were keeping people informed of this deadly virus and what they had to do to take care of themselves and each other. The highs were also actually seeing that we all truly were in this together. I also got a major high when I sang the song "Bridge over Troubled Water" and dedicated it to the frontline workers and what we all were going through. It received a tremendous response on my Facebook page and on YouTube. The lows, naturally, were talking about the number of infections and passings that occurred not only in our area but around the country and the world. It also hit home: I lost a dear friend I grew up with.

Stephanie Stahl, Reporter, KYW:
Pandemic coverage is a prime example of how journalists provide a public service. In the beginning, it was a little tricky dealing with claims of "fake news" and the anti-vax contingent. But again, we stick with facts and science while also making sure to air both sides, when appropriate, to provide comprehensive coverage.

Ali Gorman, Health Reporter, WPVI:
It was the most interesting reporting I've done, to see the research unfolding and learning new stuff. Information was coming out so fast that I would do a report, and it could be completely changed two hours later. I loved that type of reporting. I will say, after two years, I was pretty burnt out because you didn't get the opportunity to do those features that kind of give you a little bit more of a boost or motivation, or maybe it's just a little bit of a break to do a happy story. You didn't get that with the pandemic, at least as a health reporter. You were pushing out what is the latest information with two, three, four reports a day.

AND FINALLY, TONIGHT

Behind-the-Scenes Stories from the Era

In May 2007, KYW news anchor Alycia Lane and television personality Rich Eisen were involved in a controversial incident. The scandal occurred when Lane sent several personal emails to Eisen, who was working for the NFL Network at the time. These emails reportedly contained flirtatious and inappropriate messages, and one of the emails allegedly included a revealing photo of Lane.

Lane said in a statement at the time, "Rich Eisen and I have been good friends for almost 10 years and our relationship has always been purely platonic. I apologize for any misunderstanding that the photos, which were totally innocent shots of myself and my friends on vacation, might have caused."

The emails were discovered by Eisen's wife, Suzy Shuster, a former Fox and ABC sports reporter, who was upset by the nature of the messages. Shuster forwarded the emails to Lane's employer, KYW-TV, which sparked a scandal and led to an investigation into Lane's conduct.

"Boy, do you look amazing in a bikini . . . congrats! Whatever you're doing, (Pilates? yoga?) keep doing it—it's working for you," Shuster wrote to Lane, according to the *New York Post*. "Anyway, sorry but those seven emails you sent to my husband, Rich, well, oops, they came to the e-mail address we both use from time to time, but no worries, I'll forward the beach shots as well as the ones of you dancing with your friends on to his main address. Do you have it?"

The incident received significant media attention, and there were repercussions for Lane and Eisen. Lane was eventually fired from her position at KYW-TV in January 2008, as the network deemed her actions inappropriate and unprofessional.[1]

In August 2008, then–KYW anchor Larry Mendte pled guilty to hacking into the personal email of his then-colleague and coanchor, Alycia Lane. Mendte hacked into Lane's email more than five hundred times from May to June 2008 after the two were involved in a flirtatious, unprofessional, and improper relationship.

Mendte was fired from KYW in June 2008 after FBI agents seized his home computer during the investigation. Lane had been fired earlier that same year after allegedly hitting an undercover New York City police officer in December 2007. Charges against Lane were later dismissed and the case expunged.

Lane sued CBS Broadcasting, KYW-TV, Mendte, and others in 2008, alleging that CBS had failed to stop Mendte from snooping on her, an offense to which he pled guilty and was sentenced to house arrest and probation. Mendte was accused in the suit of invasions of privacy and other related violations. After eight years of litigation, in 2017, Mendte and Lane finalized an out-of-court settlement, the terms of which remain confidential.

"I deeply regret my actions with respect to Alycia Lane and the harm that I caused her," Mendte wrote in a statement included in court filings.

Lane went on to become a morning anchor at an NBC station in Los Angeles, but she left in 2013. Mendte went on to work at various TV

1. Michael Klein, "Bikini Breach: CBS3's Alycia Lane Defends 'Saucy' E-mails to a Married Newsman, Calling Them 'Harmless,'" *Philadelphia Inquirer*, May 2, 2007; Associated Press, "Oops! Philly TV Anchor Sends Bikini Pics to NFL Host, Wife Intercepts," *Daily Journal*, May 2, 2007; "BIKIN-E-MAILS RATTLE TV WIFE," *New York Post*, May 1, 2007, NewsBank, https://infoweb-newsbank-com.libproxy.temple.edu/apps/news/document-view?p=AWNB&docref=news/118DEAC8A5305708; Dan Gross, "Fe-mail Goof," *Philadelphia Daily News*, May 2, 2007; Chuck Darrow, "CBS3 Newswoman Calls Bikini E-mail 'Harmless Pictures,'" *Courier Post*, May 3, 2007; Michael Klein, "Handsome Guy's Wife Isn't Fazed," *Philadelphia Inquirer*, May 3, 2007.

and radio stations, including WPIX, WDPN, WJLP, WABC Radio, WFMZ, and iHeartMedia Delaware.[2]

In March 2010, former WCAU and Fox 29 meteorologist John Bolaris got caught up in an organized scheme to get men drunk and make expensive purchases on their credit cards in Miami, Florida. Bolaris's credit card was charged for more than $43,000 for large purchases of expensive alcohol, caviar, and a $2,500 painting after hanging out with two women for two nights in South Florida.

The FBI later opened an investigation and indicted seventeen members of the Russian mob, who were accused of scamming more than eighty-five men in South Beach, Miami. American Express settled Bolaris's tab and reportedly paid him $100,000 in damages.

Shortly after news of the incident broke, Fox 29 declined to renew his contract, and he left the station.[3]

In October 2012, WPVI's Adam Joseph and Cecily Tynan had an awkward encounter on air. Joseph's microphone was not working, but Tynan's was on. Several viewers took to social media to speculate that they had heard Tynan saying "moron" or something that sounded similar.

Joseph tweeted, "Let me make this clear if you just watch our weather hit. Cecily did not say 'moron' she said 'do you want mine on' (the mic) lol Too funny."

Moments later, Joseph tweeted, "Man, twitter is blowing up over the comment by @cecilytynan! Even if she did say it, its in good humor. We are like brother and sister."

Later in the broadcast, Jim Gardner threw the bizarre matter to further relief with an explanation that Tynan had not insulted Joseph.

---

2. Jeff Gammage, "Mendte's Apology Closes Lane Lawsuit," *Philadelphia Inquirer*, January 6, 2017; Jeff Gammage, "Signing Off: Apology Caps End of Mendte, Lane Suit," *Philadelphia Inquirer*, January 6, 2017; Michael Klein and Larry Mendte, "Mendte's Statement," *Philadelphia Inquirer*, August 23, 2008; "Mendte Will Stay off Air during Probe," *Philadelphia Inquirer*, June 2, 2008; Joseph Gambardello, "Mendte Spied Tirelessly, U.S. Alleges," *Philadelphia Inquirer*, July 22, 2008; Patrick Kerkstra, "CBS 3 Anchor Alycia Lane Arrested, Released in N.Y.," *Philadelphia Inquirer*, December 17, 2007.

3. David Gambacorta, "John, We Really Knew Ye," *Philadelphia Daily News*, January 11, 2012; David Gambacorta, "Drugged, Duped: Bolaris' Perfect Storm," *Philadelphia Daily News*, May 19, 2011; Dan Gross, "Bolaris Boo-hoos about Life after 'Do Shot,'" *Philadelphia Daily News*, December 13, 2002; Dan Gross, "Bolaris Has '20/20' Date," *Philadelphia Daily News*, March 29, 2012.

"Maybe I shouldn't even acknowledge this, but the folks who thought that Cecily called Adam an untoward name when Adam was having trouble with his microphone, that's not at all true," Gardner stated on air.

"What Cecily was saying was 'Do you want mine on?' My microphone on. And then Adam had a chance to fix his microphone before that even became an issue. If you thought that Cecily called Adam an untoward name, that's not the case at all. We don't do that here. We are a family; we love each other," Gardner said.[4]

In March 2014, Fox 29 reporter Steve Keeley became a viral sensation while reporting on snowfall on *Good Day Philadelphia* in Woodstown, New Jersey. Around 6:30 A.M., while live on the air, describing the snowy conditions, Keeley was pummeled with snow as a snowplow rolled past his live shot.

The plow driver, Michael Wyatt, ended up calling Keeley to apologize. Keeley suffered no injuries.[5]

In October 2013, allegations surfaced that Don Tollefson was defrauding individuals and charities for payments for trips to large sporting events. The allegations included misappropriation of funds from a charity event he organized, where money was intended to be donated to various charitable causes.

In 2015, Tollefson pled guilty to felony theft and other charges related to the charity fraud case and was sentenced to prison for his actions. Tollefson was convicted of stealing more than $340,000 from two hundred people who had donated to his charities and another foundation he worked for. He spent two years in state prison, where he got sober.

Tollefson was hired by WPVI in 1975 for general assignment duties and was later named the sports director, where he covered various big Philadelphia sports events, including the 1980 Phillies World Series Championship and the 1983 76ers NBA Championship. In 1990, after fifteen years at 6abc, Tollefson left Philadelphia to start his own nonprofit dedicated to helping young children suffering from drug abuse.

---

4. Dan Gross, "Ch. 6 Offers Moron Sandy," *Philadelphia Daily News*, October 30, 2012.

5. Molly Eichel, "Plow Makes a Fox 29 Snowman," *Philadelphia Daily News*, March 4, 2014; Daniel Rubin, "Sometimes All You Can Say Is 'Oh, Slush,'" *Philadelphia Inquirer*, March 8, 2014.

After a few years of running the organization, Tollefson got back into the television business in 1995, when he was hired by Fox 29. He worked as a general assignment reporter, hosted *Good Day Philadelphia*, and covered sports. He was let go from Fox 29 in 2008.[6]

In August 2014, WPVI meteorologist Adam Joseph announced that he and his longtime partner were expecting their first child.

"While I believe every person reading this article should respect others' privacy, I decided to share this personal moment for my son," Joseph told the *Philadelphia Inquirer* in 2014. "I want my son to be proud of both his fathers. From the day he was born, I want him to understand that families come in all shapes, sizes and colors. In our eyes, as long as there is unconditional love for a child, it doesn't matter who that child looks up to or leans on."[7]

In September 2015, just two days before Pope Francis visited Philadelphia for the World Meeting of Families, sixty-five photographers and technicians employed by NBC10 went on strike following a vote by members of the International Brotherhood of Electrical Workers (IBEW) Local 98. The reason for the strike: Workers had worked without a contract for more than a year before the walkout.

To replace the striking photographers and technicians during the papal visit, NBC10 hired nonunion photographers for the coverage. Weeks later, both sides reached an agreement, with NBC10 and Telemundo62 ratifying a new four-year contract that included wage increases, a ratification bonus, and some job protections.

The union did pressure NBC10's parent company, Comcast Corp, by holding a news conference outside city hall when Comcast officials were meeting inside with city officials to negotiate the company's cable-TV franchise renewal with the city. IBEW also accused the station of breaching security during the papal visit, when a station executive gave

---

6. Ben Finley and Frank Kummer, "Police Probe Sportscaster's Sale of Sports Tickets, Trips," *Philadelphia Inquirer*, October 19, 2013; Dana DiFilippo, "Tolly's Ticket Trouble Sparks Investigation," *Philadelphia Daily News*, October 17, 2013; "Ex-Sportscaster Tollefson Admits Theft," *Morning Call*, October 3, 2014; "Don Tollefson Guilty in Ticket Scams," *Morning Call*, October 5, 2014.

7. Molly Eichel, "6abc's Joseph Opens Up on Parent, Baby," *Philadelphia Daily News*, August 7, 2014.

his media credentials to one of the freelance camera operators. The operator later obtained his own credentials.[8]

On February 15, 2016, *SNJ Today* anchor Cara McCollum was tragically involved in a car accident. McCollum lost control of her 2014 Ford Mustang in slushy conditions along a stretch of Route 55 in Pittsgrove, New Jersey. McCollum underwent four hours of brain surgery the day after the accident but passed away on February 22. McCollum was twenty-four years old.

McCollum had been crowned Miss New Jersey in 2013 and represented the state in the 2014 Miss America pageant in Atlantic City, New Jersey. She was a graduate of Princeton University. In the community, McCollum had created the "Birthday Book Project" at age sixteen, a charity that delivered more than twenty-five books to underprivileged children for their birthdays. At the time of her death, McCollum was dating WCAU anchor reporter Keith Jones.[9]

8. Bob Fernandez, "NBC10: Talking with Union," *Philadelphia Inquirer*, September 26, 2015.

9. Jacqueline L. Urgo, "Ex-Miss New Jersey, 24, Dies from Crash Injuries," *Philadelphia Inquirer*, February 23, 2016; Jacqueline L. Urgo, "A Beautiful Life: Former Miss New Jersey Cara McCollum Is Mourned in Ocean City," *Philadelphia Inquirer*, March 13, 2016.

PART IV

Only in Philadelphia: Covering the City

BUILDING TRUST WITH TV VIEWERS

Journalism plays a vital role in providing accurate, timely, and reliable information to the public. Building trust with viewers is crucial for a TV station to establish and maintain a loyal audience. If a television station can establish trust with its audience, that audience is more likely to remain loyal to the station and continue watching its daily and weekly programs. This loyalty can translate into higher ratings and increased advertising revenue for the station.

Television stations on public airwaves have legal and ethical responsibilities to ensure that the information they provide to their viewers is accurate, balanced, and unbiased. In the end, building trust with viewers is crucial for a television station's success, and that foundation helps build viewer loyalty, establish credibility, and promote a station's positive brand image beyond its legal and ethical obligations.

Following are personal opinions and experiences regarding how some Philadelphia media personalities have built this essential trust with viewers in an age of increasing suspicion of media.

Justin Pizzi, Reporter and Host, WCAU:
You can't bullshit Philadelphia. You gotta tell them the truth, and you have to be fair. You have to make sure that diversity is reflected in reporting.

Derrick Gunn, Reporter, Comcast SportsNet/NBC Sports Philadelphia:
Any market that is highly opinionated, that's highly critical and highly passionate like Philadelphia, initially it was a wait and see: "Let's see what this thing [Comcast SportsNet] is all about." Basically, we were a regional ESPN. I think why people gravitated to us a lot was because we were focused on the Philly market, the South Jersey market, the Delaware market. We were interviewing and getting to know players from the high school level, collegiate [level], and the pro level on a daily basis. We had people everywhere. We had eight or nine on-air talent, and we were covering everything. We were a jack-of-all-trades and masters of all of them. We had to do our homework. We had to learn the background and the history of this team. We knew if we made a mistake, we would get called out on it. We had a collection of people who did their homework. They were not only professional; they were very talented, and very creative, and very thorough in what they did. Because of that consistency, the numbers continued to grow. The following continued to grow. [Comcast SportsNet/NBC Sports Philadelphia] became a pied piper in the region because of what we did consistently.

Jeff Cole, Investigative and General Assignment Reporter, WTXF:
Particularly in a city like Philly, the best way to do it is go hard at it. When folks say it's a rough city and it's the city that threw ice balls at Santa, I think that depiction of the city is somewhat unfair, but I think it is, in fact, a rough kind of—in many ways—sort of working-class, go at it, hard city. You have to play it straight and ask tough questions. Ask high and hard. Throw the ball up and in; and try to ask sharp, tough questions; and elicit revealing responses; and try to show the public that I am out there, trying to dig it up for them and report it straight. I also think you do it by showing that you know the city, you care about the people in the city, that you are in their neighborhood and you are talking to them about problems that they face. It's often heard you hold people accountable. Well, yeah, you find what the problems are in the communities, and then you go back to the people in charge and ask them good, tough and fair, in-your-face questions to see if you can get something done. I think that's how you do it in the city of Philadelphia.

Alex Holley, Anchor, WTXF:
Sometimes, you can rush to be first, and you haven't checked all of the boxes. You have to make sure the video is correct and, now more than ever, we've learned how important it is. Is this correct, and do we have all of the information? I think we learned context. Context is very important about how you are covering stories, especially in a community that is so tight-knit, especially in the Delaware Valley, where they are vocal about what's going on in their neighborhood or what's happening. I do think it's taking the time to accurately get all of that information and to get context. That's an important part that was lost before, and people just used to accept it. Now, people are not just accepting it if you are not telling them the full story or if you are not giving them necessary context.

Dann Cuellar, Reporter, WPVI:
The temptation is always great when a television journalist wants to be first with something. You want to be the first on something, whatever it is. At the same time, you have this *Action News* voice in your head that is saying, "You better get it right. You better have this right and be absolutely sure because if you're wrong, you are really going to hurt this organization." That's the last thing I want to do. You want to be absolutely certain you know what you are talking about and that you have it on solid grounds that what you are about to report is true.

Steve Keeley, Reporter, WTXF:
I think accuracy is the key. That's the most important thing. Being first is also important in our business, but it doesn't count if it's first and wrong.

I think longevity also builds trust. People know you are there. You're a consistent thing. You've had consistent accuracy and you never burned a source, you are fair, and you are only going after people if they are doing something wrong and not just taking a side politically or whatever. It comes with time, but accuracy over years and years.

Kathy Orr, Meteorologist, WCAU, KYW, and WTXF:
I think, over the years, there's been model improvement, and we've learned from storms. Things can happen, and it can look the whole way like it's going to be a huge storm, and maybe a night before. . . . I remem-

ber that 2001 storm. I think the computer models started to change a little, like the night before—very quickly before the event. You have consistency all the way, and then something changes. You say, "Okay, is this a fluke?" because a lot of times it can be a fluke. Or it can be, "Hmm, something is changing," and then you have to wait for the next model run, but that's in the morning, and the storm is starting to form. I think we learn from every single storm, and we know that things can change. I think our audience now knows from those past experiences that things can change. That's why we try to educate them. Like, this is what we are looking at, and this is the decision that we are making, and these are the concerns on this particular storm. We just give them the information we are looking at so they know where we are coming from. I think we give more information out. You're see us giving scenarios: "It might do this, and it might do this. As we get closer, we should have a better idea." Some storms, you just don't know. Some storms, you say, "You know what? I think it's going to do this, but I'm still concerned about this." We hope that doesn't happen, but we try to tell the viewer more.

Carol Erickson, Anchor, Reporter, and Meteorologist, KYW:
I think it's having respect for your audience. I didn't talk down to them. I told them the things I would want to know and the way I would want to know it. If I don't know it's going to snow ten feet, I'm not going to say it is just to hype ratings, just to get a headline out of it. I'm gonna say, "We don't know." I would fess up if I completely missed that one. I treated them with the respect that I would want. I would tell them things I would want to know without treating them like children or whatever else. I treated them like friends.

Sue Serio, Meteorologist, WTXF:
There are some people who, I feel like they have to change when the red light goes on and they go on the air. I think early in my career, I thought that about myself. I was young when I started in radio, but I had to be an announcer. I had a boss who said, "Look, why can't you be like you are around the office when you are on air?" That really changed my life and my approach to my career. I thought, "You know, I just have to be myself. If it's not acceptable, oh well." But I guess it has been because

I've been at Fox for twenty-four years. Just being honest—that's how you build the trust to just tell the truth.

Mike Jerrick, Anchor, WTXF:
I believe in being honest on the air always, being honest with the viewers when they hear about my personal life. I was struggling with some depression in 2017 and—thank God—the station allowed me to do that employee program where they let you go away for a month for an intense therapy, which changed my life. I've had very deep, deep depressing thoughts, and once I got through that thirty-day therapy, that hasn't been an issue with me ever since March of 2017. Those negative thoughts have never come back. I told the viewers all about it. I think they do trust. They know I'm silly, but when I need to be serious, they know I will be. I think just because they hear and see my honesty, I think that is trust.

Brian Taff, Anchor, WPVI:
You have to keep being who you are and not worry about the blowback you're gonna get. I'm not gonna lie to you: Sometimes, when you say something on television, or you repeat it on Twitter or whatever it may be, the response you get is really disheartening, and sometimes it's really personal and needlessly awful. I think the reason people watch us is because we're just gonna tell it to you. Sometimes, I think on television, I think we try to deliver with a certain polish. On Twitter, sometimes you can lose a little bit of that gene and say things a little bit more raw. I do that, and I think I have been doing that over the last couple of years, when the war on truth has been especially amped up. I've come to anticipate some of the response, but it's predictable, and you know where it's coming from. I think the people who follow me—whether the people on Twitter or television—do it because I'm going to tell them the truth, and what they are going to hear from me is not some partisan spin or it's not some agenda version of what people should be . . . the facts. They just are the facts. That's my sort of North Star.

Alicia Vitarelli, Anchor, Reporter, and Cohost, WPVI:
You have to remember why we are here. This isn't about your feelings, emotions, and that's gotten really hard because of the fact that opinions

and emotions have been extremely high. There are a lot of feelings attached. That's not what we are here to do. We literally are not here to tell you how we feel about the world. We are here to tell you what is going on. Consumers also have to understand what they are taking in. That's what I keep saying: Local news doesn't have that agenda. We are here to say, "This is what it is," and that's your little black dress of journalism. It has to be the facts, and that's it. The lines have been blurred, and hopefully the people at home understand the difference. It's two-fold: We have to keep toeing the journalist line and making sure we stay on point and on target. At the same time, we also have to know that people at home have to be better, smarter consumers of what's out there.

Jim Gardner, Anchor, WPVI:
Viewers have much more trust in their local news people than they do in their national and cable news people. I think the reason for that is we [local media and viewers] are all members of the same community. So, they feel a certain kinship. This relationship builds because we root for the same teams. We breathe the same air. We are members of the same community. So, when good things happen, I think viewers know that we are affected by that just as much as they are. In contrast, when bad things happen, we are reacting the way they are.

Michael Barkann, Anchor and Host,
KYW and Comcast SportsNet/NBC Sports Philadelphia:
If a columnist and/or a writer covering a team had something to say, then they would get it off their chest. It would also be a way for the network to continue to legitimize itself. They might have partnerships with teams, but you watch this *Daily News Live* show, and you are gonna get the real deal. I was mindful of that. There were times when I would go into a show and say, "You better be careful here." That was the beauty of it.

Ukee Washington, Anchor, KYW:
Trust in the station among employees is built first and foremost by believing in each other. That also goes into building a relationship with the viewer. Being factual, believable, and showing that you care in storytelling, I think, are key factors in building trust. I've always believed the viewer can spot a phony; personally, I make it a point to be the same

person off camera that you see on camera. When people can watch you and feel like they know you, it's much easier to feel like you have earned their trust.

Tamala Edwards, Anchor, WPVI:
TV is a filter. It clarifies and magnifies what is there. I think your values and who you are as a person—are you benign, authentic, are you putting on a show, what's going on here? Obviously, I don't tell my kids to make your bed, brush your teeth, and I don't use the anchor voice at home. But to the extent that you are speaking to people and how you are coming across to people, they feel a connection. I think over time, people notice things about you, and if they know we will make them laugh even on the worst of days, then they know these people are the real deal, and they are really smart. I think they read and think and do the work, and people can tell.

Jim Donovan, Anchor, KYW:
If a news team isn't accurate, it's like a fast-food place that hands a customer the wrong order. If it happens time and time again, eventually the customer will go to another restaurant, or in the case of a TV viewer, they'll switch channels. News stations are in the information business, and if the information that is broadcast isn't correct, then we have failed at our job. Right behind accuracy, I believe I would list commitment to the community. You have to be committed to the audience that you serve. That's why it's so important that newsrooms be diverse, staffed with people from all sorts of backgrounds. What might be an interesting story to a single parent living in Philly might not be that important to a couple of senior citizens living on the Jersey Shore. But if stations try their best to report on a multitude of topics, I think it's the viewers that benefit the most.

Alex Holley, Anchor, WTXF:
Also, Philly is a diverse city. For journalists of color, this has always been a thing, and it's now more widely thought about and something that people seek. I think people test you, that you are going to accurately represent their communities and tell stories fairly no matter what a person looks like—that is being discussed. That is very important. Even since 2020, that's been put in the spotlight to show how important that is.

Jamie Apody, Sports Anchor and Reporter, WPVI:
For me personally, it took time to build trust with viewers, being that I was the first female they ever hired in sports. I had trouble with that in the beginning. Once people relate, [understand that] you know what you are talking about, they do start to trust you, and you become a valued source for something. I do think that Philadelphia, based on our longevity, does turn to Channel 6 when they want the right answer and right news. We don't do things the wrong way. We don't sensationalize things. We don't say, "If it bleeds it leads." We don't do that, and I think [the channel has] stuck to the format for all of these years. I really think Jim [Gardner] has a big thing to do with that. He will hate me for saying that, but he's the voice of reason.

Jim Gardner, Anchor, WPVI:
In the midst of all of that, we are charged with being neutral. The word *objective* doesn't mean very much. Computers maybe can be objective, but a reporter who is white, grew up in a privileged environment, and went to Princeton is just going to bring certain things to a story or to viewing an event that someone who grew up Black, in the ghetto, and went to John Jay College—forgive me—they bring different things to their experience. Those differences show up in the way they see it and the way they tell it. As far as I'm concerned, that's not just fine; that's a good thing. Objectivity: I'm not sure what *objectivity* means, but if you are talking about being fair and being—within your own capacity—neutral, those things are not only good but they are essential. I think when you prove to the audience, to the viewership, that that is your intent and that is what you do. . . . In blackjack, we say "an infinite number of hands." Sometimes, when we talk in the newsroom and we are talking about stuff like this, I say "over an infinite number of newscasts." That builds trust, but it's more than trust. It's also building a relationship. I don't know that Wolf Blitzer sees that when he's on CNN: Maybe he does. I don't know. That's not in my experience, so I don't know. But as a local anchorperson, not that you set out to accomplish it—it just sorta happens. You build relationships with viewers.

Maybe I am wrong about this, but when you are on the air—and I don't know if there's gonna be a whole hell of a lot of anchorpeople around that are going to be on the air for forty-five years—but when you are on the air for a long time, you're sharing life experience with the viewer. In other words—this may sound corny, but I don't think it is—you kind of go through life with the viewer, which means you go through happy times in your own life and you go through unhappy times in your own life. It's inevitable. You go through the birth of children. You go through divorce, death of loved ones, and the viewer is doing the same thing. So, when you are on the air for a long time, I wonder if a viewer feels like . . . the viewers watching you when they're teenagers, and they ask someone to the prom, and they are told, "No, I don't want to go to the prom with you." This is the most crestfallen experience that a teenager can have, and that night, they are watching the news. The next time, they are getting into the college they want to go to, and that's great, and they watch the news. And then they graduate from college, and they go to medical school, and it's a great thing in their life, and they are watching the news. They ask some woman to marry them and then are told, "No." You go through all of these life experiences, and there's the same man or woman on the news. This viewer has experienced their life sorta in the presence of that person on the news. Maybe that person on the news has also experienced these same kind of ups and downs. That's a unique relationship, and I guess it happens to a broad degree for someone who is anchoring for forty-five years. I think it happens with a television station too. It happens with the group of people who are on the air. It's these relationships—and I guess I'm overthinking it, so people may say this is really absurd—but there is an intimate relationship that forms with some viewers and some people on TV because you are there for each other all of the time for a long period of time. That's not appointment viewing—that's a relationship.

THE MORNING SHIFT

Philadelphia television stations offer different morning programming, including local news shows and cut-ins during national broadcasts, such as the CBS Morning News, Good Morning America, *and the* Today Show. *WPVI has morning programming from 4:00 A.M. to 7:00 A.M., WCAU from 4:00 A.M. to 7:00 A.M., and KYW from 4:00 A.M. to 7:00 A.M.; WPHL has* PHL17 Morning News *from 5:00 A.M. to 9:00 A.M.; and Fox 29's* Good Day Philadelphia *goes on the air from 4:00 A.M. to 10:00 A.M.*

The following are stories from producers, anchors, and reporters who have personal thoughts about the morning shift's effect on the human body and mind and the wacky hours of the graveyard shift.

Matt O'Donnell, Anchor and Reporter, WPVI:
I wake up at 2:20 in the morning. That's the first, second, and third question I'm always asked. It's never "Who is your most interesting interview?" or whatever. Then they ask me, "How do you get used to that?" I say, "Well, you don't." It is not something that you get used to. We as human beings are still governed by when the sun comes up and when it comes down. When you are fighting against that and going against the grain, it becomes somewhat inhuman to act that way and get up at that time of day. By the way, for more than half the year, I go to bed while it's still light out. During the winter time, you do have some

months where it's dark and it's sorta normal to go to bed. Putting the sleep mask on and knowing that stuff is happening outside and that you have to go to bed while everyone else is still pretty much awake is pretty much weird.

Tamala Edwards, Anchor, WPVI:
When you tell people what you do and when you get up, they will go, "Oh my God, it's the worst." You have to make up your mind going in that you're fine with it and that you are glad you are doing it. Otherwise, you won't make it. I think I established that mindset, and I think it's come to work for my life. Yes, you are getting up in the middle of the night, and you're on a different schedule, unlike the majority of the world, but I think having worked the overnight at ABC News and *World News Now*, that was really weird going to work at ten o'clock at night: getting off as the sun was coming up and sleeping during the day while everybody was up. I figured out you could do one thing a day. Go to the gym, doctor, meet a friend, but that was pretty much all that you could get done. That was really discombobulating.

Meisha Johnson, Traffic Anchor, KYW:
People do not realize when they see you at 4:30 A.M., 5:00 A.M., 6:00 A.M., or 7:00 A.M., depending on when you jump on—they see you all hair and makeup ready. What they do not realize is that your alarm is going off at 1:15 in the morning, especially if you are a woman, to do hair and makeup and get all ready. I would get up at 1:15 A.M., and I would be out the door by 3:15 A.M., fully hair and makeup ready.

Amy Caples, Anchor and Reporter, KYW:
I will say for the first year after I got out of TV, I still woke up at two o'clock in the morning every day. It took a year for me to stop waking up at that hour because your body is attuned to it. It was a gigantic challenge because I had two young kids.

Anita Brikman, Reporter, WPVI:
It's one thing when you know you are getting up at that hour, but if there is a call at 1:30 or 2:00 A.M. that you need to get up and fill in for somebody, that's really tough.

Sean Murphy, Reporter and Traffic Reporter, Comcast SportsNet and KYW:
As long as I was able to have the coffee going, I was fine. I think twice in my time, I slept in and was late for work, and on a news headline, weather, and traffic show only, that wasn't very fair to my coworkers, so they had a lot to fill for twenty minutes before I came running into the studio. It was tough at first, but then it was something I was used to. When we were doing rehearsals for our morning show, originally the idea was to start it in March and not go on the air until late May, so we could get a lot of rehearsal time, and that gave me an opportunity to acclimate to that time schedule.

Matt O'Donnell, Anchor and Reporter, WPVI:
I almost get upset when I'm sitting in traffic because I'm not used to it anymore. That's really good. You know you can get up at a certain time, and you can get on the Schuylkill Expressway, and there's an end point you meet every single time. That doesn't happen during normal morning rush.

Carol Erickson, Anchor, Reporter, and Meteorologist, KYW:
Once you are up, after that first fifteen minutes when you just can't stand it, it's not bad. Everybody when you walk in is very aware, awake, and alive. That exhausting and the awful feelings you have in the first fifteen minutes of that shift when you are home, they disappear, and you are really on a roll.

Monique Braxton, Anchor and Reporter, WCAU:
You have to come with your A game. You have to be able to call people for information at four or five o'clock in the morning and know that they won't be mad at you, but they will help you out and go back to sleep.

Connie Colla, Anchor and Reporter, WCAU and the Comcast Network:
You are going to bed knowing when you wake up, you have to get caught up on all of the stories that happened overnight. You need to get a good understanding of them and be accurate. A lot of times, they are writing

the scripts as you are on the air, so you are reading other people's copy, so you are looking at the teleprompter, but you are really kind of ad-libbing the story to make sure there is nothing wrong with it.

Jessica Borg, Anchor and Reporter, WPVI:
The morning reporting shift depends on what station you work at or work for, but it's a long shift because you're reporting not only for the morning show, which are frequent hits, but then you're getting ready for a long package at noon. And then sometimes repackaging, getting new elements for an evening show, so it's a long day.

Mike Jerrick, Anchor, WTXF:
I wake up at 3:56. I don't know why I make it four minutes before, but I do. I flip on our show. I am listening to it, but I'm not watching it too much because I am getting ready. I'm in by 5:00 A.M. and into the newsroom. There is no watercooler talk. At 5:01, we are into the nuts and bolts of the show. We have an hour to talk it over. The whole show is planned the day before, but we get in there and talk about stuff that happened overnight—the breaking news and stuff. There's not a lot of chitchat. We joke around a little bit, but you gotta put your head down and get this four-hour behemoth show ready to go and lined up in that fifty minutes or so we have together. The watercooler and the chitchat and all that happens after the show.

Lori Wilson, Reporter and Anchor, WCAU:
From the minute you hit the door, you are reading stories, you are talking to your producers, you are planning for the show and everything you are going to be taking people through for that day. You are reading scripts, and you are getting your face on. You hit it as soon as that tally light [on-air indicator] goes on. It's like you are helping people wake up.

Jim Donovan, Anchor, KYW:
Anchoring a morning newscast is like doing a high-wire balancing act. You need to have just the right amount of energy and personality to help people start their day, but you can't be too perky, or you'll risk being annoying. As far as the programming goes, it, too, needs to be balanced, just like a balanced breakfast. Most morning-news viewers are creatures

of habit, and they have limited time. They want their news, weather, and traffic in a quick format with some light-hearted banter. Unfortunately, a lot of overnight news is not necessarily uplifting and involves things like crime or fires. The goal is to keep people informed without depressing them as they walk out the door.

Alex Holley, Anchor, WTXF:
We are tasked with the job of [telling viewers,] "This is what happened overnight," and "This is bubbling up. Let's focus on this this morning," or "Let's talk about this," or "Hey, here's a chat or survey we can discuss that is really cool to get people talking." That's kind of a cool element. I always tell people, too, and the phrase always is "Oh, we will be there bright and early." If you are really a morning riser like we are, there's no bright and early—it's dark and early. The sun is not even up when we are up and have to go to work. That's the true "waking up early."

Chris Cato, Anchor and Reporter, WCAU:
To be a morning-news person, you have to be really psycho, really energetic from the moment your eyes open in the morning. You have to have a certain attitude about the day. You also have to have a willingness to grind through exhaustion and reset your body clock. That's what it takes.

Ukee Washington, Anchor, KYW:
Personally, I had no problem with the hours—in bed every night no later than 8:00 P.M. and up at 3:00 A.M. Even during vacation, I'd go to bed at 9:00 P.M. and get up at 5:00 A.M., to keep my body on somewhat of the same time schedule. I had to. It was my job, and I wanted to be the—shall I say—best me on TV, not a tired me. I was and I am dedicated to the craft.

Matt O'Donnell, Anchor and Reporter, WPVI:
If you are trying to maximize most time spent outdoors outside of your work shift, the morning shift is perfect. You can lead a very happy life in terms of doing outdoor activities and all sorts of other things that other people can't because their work shifts are spaced right around the

time they wake up and right around the time they have to slow down and get ready to go to bed. That's good.

Steve Keeley, Reporter, WTXF:
Here's the secret to survival. People won't do what I did, and people will think I'm crazy. I've used this morning shift to all of the advantages to help myself in life. It forces you to live healthy. I didn't start exercising before work, but today I'm in a gym by myself, and I have a StairMaster in my condo. I work out every day before work. When I get done with a high-intensity interval training thirty-minute workout on the StairMaster that makes me want to collapse during the high-intensity intervals, after I get done with that, I'm like, "Alright—the rest of the day is downhill. Nothing rattles my nerves anymore." I will have adrenaline on a story, but I just did the hardest thing of the day, and now I'm going to work.

Jennaphr Frederick, Reporter, WTXF:
The number-one pro as a mom is approximately half of the day I work, my kids are asleep. Unlike [the kids of] my friends who are really successful and lawyers, cardiologists, and everything, my kids are sleeping. The people that I want to spend time with are asleep when I am going to work, so there's less mom guilt. That's the number-one thing. The other really great thing about the morning shift in particular is when you are done, you are done. When I worked news, the performance part of my day was at the end of the day.

Lori Wilson, Reporter and Anchor, WCAU:
You can take a nap, do a speaking engagement, do a luncheon, you can go home or workout. I think it's a different kind of schedule, but it was always my favorite of the schedules—which is a lot because there is no really good schedule in news.

Denise Nakano, Anchor and Reporter, WCAU:
I just think it's the hardest shift for anybody. For some people, they love it because it works for their family life. You get your shift out of the way, and you have your family for the rest of the day. I just find it very difficult and taxing on the body.

Rob Ellis, Senior Producer and Host,
Comcast SportsNet/NBC Sports Philadelphia and KYW:
I think it's especially tough when you are doing sports because the games are happening at night most of the time. You get lucky Sunday afternoon—there's a Phillies game, and that's fine and all of that—but when you are doing mornings, you make the conscious decision to either go to sleep, get up, and read about it or watch whatever you DVR-ed the next day, or you stay up and watch 'em. My quandary was always I felt like I had to see it to talk about it. I would just stay up, and I wouldn't get any sleep.

Lu Ann Cahn, Investigative Reporter and Anchor, WCAU:
There would be times I would leave the station, come up to a stop sign, and stop. I would forget and think the light was going to turn. That's how tired you are. Someone would honk at you. It's exhausting. You had a choice to take a nap to keep your eyes open anymore or power through to about six or seven [o'clock] at night.

Maria LaRosa, Meteorologist, KYW:
Even when you try to get yourself a solid six or seven hours of sleep that make you function as a human being, [that] still never quite feels like it's enough. I think every hour before 5:00 A.M. that you are awake is like three hours. It always feels like you are trying to catch up.

David Murphy, Meteorologist, WPVI:
Probably five or six years after I started doing that morning shift, I was diagnosed with sleep apnea, which explained why I was even more tired. I remember one time in the old building, Carla Carpenter [former WPVI news director] came into the weather office in between the shows, and I had my head propped down on my desk, with my eyes closed. I looked up, and she was looking at me, and I said, "Sorry, sorry. . . ." And she said, "Don't apologize. That shift you're on is crazy." I also used to keep a pillow and blanket sorta hidden underneath my desk. If there was a day that I really hadn't slept the night before, in between the shows, I would crawl under my desk and just grab a nap and put an alarm on somewhere to make sure I didn't go past my time. One time, Carla probably caught me in the office doing that too.

Sue Serio, Meteorologist, WTXF:
I think all of us who work on the show . . . that is part of the camaraderie. We are the only ones who know what it's like to do this. You can have a spouse or a child that is around you every day, but if they don't actually do it, they don't get it.

Mike Jerrick, Anchor, WTXF:
It's not easy, but one thing we have learned to do is don't gripe about it. Everybody is in the same boat. It just brings you down if you complain about the hours. I don't hear much of that at all. The most buoyant everybody is is Friday morning. People do look forward to Friday because you can sleep in. Friday nights are weird. If you go out with your friends, you might start drifting off at nine o'clock out in a restaurant on a Friday.

Dawn Timmeney, Anchor and Reporter, WCAU and WTXF:
We always kind of joked when I was at Fox, like, if it wasn't for the people that we worked with who were so fabulous, it would have been a lot more difficult to get through because we really had a camaraderie, and we really could complain about the same things.

Beth McDonough, Reporter, KYW and WCAU:
The morning-shift people at the other stations, you kind of form your own little bonds versus dayside and nightside. You are competing against each other, and you are looking to get the interview and all of that that the others don't have. I think this is because the morning shift is so hard to suffer through. Even though you are at different stations, you kind of suffer through it together.

THE *ACTION NEWS* MODEL FOR SUCCESS

The Action News *format changed the face of broadcasting in the early 1960s and 1970s. The key elements of any* Action News *format was a high-energy newscast, dual anchors, catchphrases and branding, and a big focus on local news and community. The* Action News *format was first launched in Philadelphia by* Eyewitness News *in 1965, but in 1970, WFIL-TV (soon to be WPVI-TV) adopted the new news format.*

The feeling of an Action News *half-hour or hour newscast is encapsulated in the word* action. *Writing for the* Action News *format involves presenting a series of short stories, carefully and closely written with as much attention to detail as possible. The newscast is thirty minutes, including an opening, close, commercials, and twenty-five to thirty news stories with proper storytelling pacing. The anchor identifies themselves at the start of the newscast and then continues the broadcast by introducing the top story with the famous line "the Big Story."*

Television ratings serve as a measure of how well a television station is performing compared to its competitors through its ability to attract and hold an audience. In Philadelphia, WPVI has consistently held the ratings crown as the number-one station in the city over the period dating back to the early 1970s.

The following are reflections about what makes WPVI one of the most successful and elite television stations in the country.

Rob Jennings, Anchor, WPVI:
First, you must understand that WPVI-TV was owned by Capital Cities Broadcasting, and I was told that the company's unique and highly successful business model was taught as an example at Harvard Business School. When I told a sales rep that I was going to work at WPVI, he said, "There are a lot of whores in broadcasting, and Cap Cities isn't one of them."

Cap Cities treated their employees fairly, unlike some companies today. We enjoyed a profit-sharing plan and stock options. Over the years, we watched in amazement as our company continued to expand, buying more stations and even the ABC network in 1985. The Capital Cities way was to hire a few talented people and let them use their skills, period—no micromanaging, no layer upon layer of managers. As for the incredible success of *Action News*, it boils down to the people. Gary Papa once said to me, "[News director] Alan [Nesbitt] and [general manager] Larry [Pollack] were able to see potential in us that we didn't know was there." I say this with modesty and great appreciation: There were a lot of people who would have given their eyeteeth to have worked at our great station. I am forever grateful to Alan and Larry for giving me my big break.

Dave Roberts, Meteorologist, WPVI:
Two words: Larry Pollack, who I believe came to the station in 1975. He was working at the Caps Cities station in Buffalo, New York. He came into WPVI then. He was the best general manager that I have ever worked for. Extremely knowledgeable, capable man who had an insight into the entire television business and where it was going and programming. He selected a number of people to put them on the air, and then news directors, producers. The team that he assembled from 1978 on: He is the man that made it all work. He was brilliant. He got Oprah Winfrey in line in terms of coming on the air with her new show. He brought *Jeopardy* in. He had a number of news directors that he worked with. He was just knowledgeable.

Dann Cuellar, Reporter, WPVI:
Cap Cities was a very family-oriented organization. When you met one of the major figures from Cap Cities and they would come visit Channel

6, they knew who you were, they asked you how your family was doing and if you needed anything, is everything okay, are you doing okay, are you good? They really cared about you, and that was the atmosphere that Channel 6 was. There was this family kind of feeling that you had.

Ned Warwick, Assignment Editor and News Director, WPVI:
Cap Cities was the best company I worked for in my life. They had a philosophy on how to do their business. They had a philosophy on letting local television stations do what they thought was necessary to be successful in their markets. They wouldn't try to impose an imprint of corporate philosophy on top of the various television stations. The mission was, you do what you think is necessary to be successful. We don't want you to be extravagant in how you use the money. We are not gonna be the biggest station, the best-equipped station, but we are gonna have the best people. That's how we are gonna be successful. Channel 6 along with some consulting help came up with a concept, and then Cap Cities was sure to implore them to stick with it and not begin to change it or tweak it. If what you created works, stay with it. No changing around. Pay the anchors, probably, to be there. Get the best anchors, make this the right place for them to be, and go for it. Channel 6 has known who they are since those early days.

Marc Howard, Anchor, WPVI and KYW:
Very little change of personnel and very little change of format. You could go to Florida for three months, come back, and feel like you didn't miss anything. Nothing changed. No other station does that.

Larry Kane, Anchor, WPVI, WCAU, and KYW:
One overriding factor at Channel 6 over the last fifty-two years without question has been management and the main talent. They have great management. They haven't had one manager who wasn't successful and who didn't maintain the integrity of the product and yet while being innovative at the same time. I believe that the market has changed a lot, and there's a revolution that's about to take place again. I think what happened in 1970 and '71 will only happen once in a lifetime maybe. We [WFIL] went—from April 1970 to April 1971—to number one in one year. That just doesn't happen, and it happened very quickly. Fortunately, they had a guy like Jim [Gardner] to bring in, and he did very

well. He is enormously successful, and he deserves every bit of credit he has gotten. My career has just been a career filled with news.

Harry Martin, Weather Anchor, WPVI:
I think it's the *Action News* format that really resonated with everybody. It wasn't only the format, but at the time, they had people who were just so attuned to that format, with Larry Kane and Jim Gardner. Both of them had this really forceful, powerful delivery. And yet both of them, especially Jim [Gardner], had this wonderful knack with making it friendly. You can get on TV and just yell at people and have a fast delivery. But Jim especially, I think, was able to really nuance it, and run, and kind of walk that fine line of powerful delivery and just really being friendly, and kind of talking over a cup of coffee about what happened that day. That's a rare talent.

Bill Shull, Producer, WCAU and WTXF:
[Jim Gardner] is the dean of Philly TV news anchors in Philadelphia and probably in most of the country; you are not going to find anybody who's been at one station as long as Jim. He is the glue. He is the guy that everyone turns to for the big story every night. [Note: Jim Gardner's final broadcast was on December 21, 2022.]

Jim Gardner, Anchor, WPVI:
When they were creating *Action News*, they did this thing where it was like shotgun news: bah bah bah. And they found someone who could really do that in Larry Kane. The whole idea was that there would be huge story counts. No story or voiceover would be more than twenty-three seconds long. Packages would be a minute [and] ten [seconds] and go bah bah bah. We still like to use a lot of video, but show me a television station in America that doesn't.

Our format is that we like to be accurate. We like to tell stories that we think people should know about and that we think people want to know about. Yes, we are in a television medium, a visual medium, so video is extremely important. We like to be compelling. That's a goal. Yes, we like to tell a lot of stories if possible, but I know for a fact that in 1980, the page number of, as we like to call it, the "coming up"—in other words, "Coming up on *Action News* before the break"—would be pages 22 or 23. Now it can be page 15 or 16. So, clearly the format isn't quite the same as it was twenty-five years ago because we are not doing as many stories as we did twenty-five years ago. One of the reasons for that is that we used to have an eleven o'clock newscast with two reporters. Now we have three, sometimes four. We often do weather in the first segment because we think, and we have reason to believe, that weather is really important. The newscast has changed. We do more investigative work. We do more consumer news than we used to. We do more medical news than we used to. When you add that extra element or two, then it changes the feel of the newscast. Sometimes, we have so many extra pieces that I think slows down the newscast much too much, but that's on a given newscast. My point being, if there is a format, I don't know what it is.

Joe Pellegrino, Sports Anchor, WFIL/WCAU:

It was very simple: [WPVI] covered more stories in a day than anybody else. A lot of these stations could cover stories, and they would stretch them out because, I guess, they didn't have a good-enough philosophy to go out and really dig up stories. We had people who were digging up stories that nobody was seeing. They shot more film for each day at different stories, but what they did was, it was kind of short bursts of news. They wouldn't spend a minute and a half or two minutes on a story. That's what happened at the other stations. [Other stations] were going a minute and half and maybe three minutes on one story. That kind of buried them. People's attention span just wasn't there, especially when they want one thing after another. I called it "Gatling-gun television." If they were hitting ten or twelve stories in half an hour, we were hitting twenty-five. It was just short bursts. We could do a story in twenty seconds. All of the interviews were cut down to get to the heart of the matter. You had a full sportscast or newscast with a number of stories that you were not getting any place else in Philadelphia.

Linda Munich, Public Affairs, WPVI:

As big a star as Jim Gardner is, it's not a star system—it's about hiring people who want to be part of the formula, not work against it or be all about themselves. It is when people say everybody does their part and they do it with a very positive attitude. You could say that's the challenge of hiring the right people.

Channel 6 has a certain humanity about it. Remember Gary [Papa] going on and off the air when he was ill, or Lisa [Thomas-Laury] going on and off the air when she was ill. I think that [is because] the management and the company appreciate the people as much as the people appreciate the station.

Alicia Vitarelli, Anchor, Reporter, and Cohost, WPVI:
I was extremely familiar with the big names and heavy hitters of 6abc: Jim [Gardner], Rick Williams, Monica [Malpass], Lisa Thomas-Laury. She's one of the reasons I knew I wanted to do this job because there was just something so human about her that was different from everybody else. She wasn't talking *at* you, she was talking *to* you. I always knew about the station, and I knew I wanted to get into this profession. I went to go get my master's at Northwestern. I went to New York for a while, and then the news director at the time, she sent me a note on Facebook—which was, like, eleven years ago, and it was very groundbreaking at the time. I was on the air at News 12 in New Jersey at the time. She said she was watching me do a segment about fencing for a show we used to do and take on the road. She sent me a note for me to come in. I knew what the station was. It was an instant yes. The secret sauce here you learn the second you walk into the door is that this is actually family. It's a level of females, especially female camaraderie, that I have never seen and is extremely rare. The second I walked in, there was a big station meeting. Lisa Thomas-Laury crossed the room and told people to personally say hello and welcome me. It was such a wild, full-circle thing. You know that you are part of something special. The relationships I made here, I will have forever.

Lisa Thomas-Laury, Anchor, WPVI:
For the longest time, we were and have been the top in the country. We learned when Jim O'Brien died that it wasn't one personality, it wasn't one or two top people who made us number one—it was the format. It was presentation. It was all of us collectively who fit into that format.

Eliott Rodriguez, Reporter, WPVI:
They also knew when they came back from commercial break, they would say, "You are watching *Action News* with Marc Howard and Lisa Thomas-Laury." They also made sure to show the name of the talent under your face. This is stuff that in other markets, that they don't do.

This is something that Channel 6 knew how to do. They knew how to make the talent, anchors, a household name in that city. People just warmed up to us. I think Channel 6 had one of the greatest promos of all time, the one about "There goes that van again." Everywhere we would go, people would say, "There's that van again." They just have a formula that works perfectly well in Philadelphia.

Art Moore, Publicity Director, WPVI:
Even when there have been changes on air or off air, most of the people that came in there were promoted from within the company someplace. There was a sense of knowledge of what that station's strengths were, and then those people had a sense of how to play to that. The irony of all of this is I worked with Jim Gardner in Buffalo. I directed his first newscast in Buffalo, and I directed his first newscast in Philly. I've known him for a long, long time.

No one had to gear up for something—they were already there. They got it, and they understand the market, and they are very loyal to the market. Again, just because Philly is the way it is, I think the viewers respond to that. My favorite word for this business is *comfortable*. If a viewer is comfortable with what they are watching, and they feel a genuine connection to the people who are giving them the information they need, there's a loyalty factor that builds up. In Philly, it literally gets passed on from generation to generation. I mean, it's incredibly unique.

Don Tollefson, Sports Anchor and Reporter, WPVI and WTXF:
I mean, you talk about the Pittsburgh Steelers having three head coaches in their history, and *Action News* has had Larry Kane and Jim Gardner since maybe the late sixties. Anchor stability is a second aspect that people really underestimate, [people] who are in the business. They never have an anchor off when another anchor is off. They never have two anchors off. If Jim Gardner is off, you will hear the fill-in anchor say, "In for the vacationing Jim Gardner." They always remind the viewers that this person didn't leave because they got fired or something. While that person is away for, usually, maybe a week at a time, all of the other anchors are there, and they mention him or her constantly; they still run their promos about the person who is not on the air. The familiarity comforts people with this anchor stability. There's no other station that has ever come close to it. That's a really big reason why *Action News* dominates it all.

Don Polec, Features Reporter, WPVI:
People would grow up seeing the same people night after night. They could go away to college, go to graduate school, come back, and the same people would be there. It's reassuring. It's like a family, whereas the other stations that are obviously trying to catch up to 6abc in the ratings are trying everything. Every couple of months, they switch anchors, reporters, people are being hired, people are leaving. You never know who you are going to see. Whereas with [Channel] 6, the consistency is the key. It fosters a sense of camaraderie and family.

Chris Wagner, Anchor, WPVI:
When you work at Channel 6 and you are on the air, you feel like you are a part of the foundation of the city. You just do. You know all of the people who are running the city, you know all of the sports figures, you know all of the council people. You know everybody, and they know you because they watch Channel 6 too.

Jim Gardner, Anchor, WPVI:
Over the last five or six years, there's been a great deal of turnover, a generational change at Channel 6.

Yes, I think it is fair to say that when people invite you into your homes, they are more likely to invite you into their homes if they're familiar with you, if they like you, if they feel comfortable with you. So, I do think it has helped that over the years, Channel 6 [has been] with Cathy Gandolfo, with Vernon Odom. Not only were they good, but they were there for thirty years. Does that help us create a relationship with our viewers? Absolutely. So, when you have a situation where over, say, a forty-year period, forty-five-year period—from, say, 1976 to now—how many people were there [on air] over that long period of time, and the answer is "a lot." You would look up at other television stations, all who do a good job covering the news, but you would look up at other television stations and say, "Who is that? Who is that?" You look at our television station over the years, and it's someone you know. Even if it's Dave Henry or John Rawlins, any number of people. When there's a generational shift like there has been over the last four, five, six years, Dann Cuellar is still there, Cecily Tynan is still there, Walter Perez is still there, Jim Gardner is still there. Even when there is a shift going on, there are still a lot of people who are still old-timers, right?

We are a legacy television station. What does that mean? I hear this all of the time. Someone who is thirty-five to forty years old says, "I watched you guys when I was eight, sitting with my parents and my grandparents." You make a certain impression on a family just like . . . if you watch baseball games, I'm a Phillies fan, and I used to go to the games at Connie Mack Stadium with my father. Well, I'm an *Action News* fan because I used to watch *Action News* with my father or grandmother. There is a certain legacy quality to this television station that has served us very, very well. I think the audience trusts us. I think we respect them. I think we should trade our respect for them, and they give us their trust. I think we are empathetic, which I think is really important, while still being neutral. I remember a program director that I had in Buffalo who ended up directing all of the television stations in the group. His name was Walter Liss. I was anchoring weekends in Buffalo, and I would say something like, "There was an accident," and I would say, "Nobody got hurt." He would say, "You know, you can say 'Fortunately, no one got hurt.' You can say that it's a good thing that nobody got hurt and that you are glad nobody got hurt. That's okay, and you can do that." That was a big lesson for me because so much of what we talk about is people's misfortune in one way or the other. To be able to say we are glad that this person is going to be okay, you do that over thousands of newscasts and—excuse me, but—people see you as an empathic person, and I think I am an empathic person. I think over a period of time that served me well, and I think—I don't mean to suggest that my empathy is something that has created something for the television station. I'm saying it has served me well. What's the secret sauce? I don't have a clue and have no idea.

Larry Kane, Anchor, WPVI, WCAU, and KYW:
How many anchors in the last fifty-two years have stayed here a long time? And how many anchors have succeeded in breaking through? Breaking through, becoming a household name? Even at this stage of my career, people know it's "Mr. Kane," and it used to be "Larry" in the beginning. Now, it's an older kind of thing. I also think Channel 6 is not the only station that has personalities that people like. Ukee Washington is very popular; everybody likes Glenn ["Hurricane" Schwartz] because he is a great forecaster, and you like his style because he is very Philadel-

phia. He does not apologize for his local accent, and you recognize him immediately.

Michele McCormack, Reporter, WPVI:
The thing that I loved about *Action News* is they didn't need no stinkin' network reporter to serve their viewers. They really committed to sending people who were from the city to cover national events, to not only look for local connections but just have it be a familiar face instead of just any type of cardboard presence that is easily replaceable and makes no connection with the viewer whatsoever. That is the unique thing, I think, about WPVI. I think it's the unique thing about Philadelphia television, that a cast of characters is desired, not a homogenized safe version of what we think journalists should be like. If you want real stories, it's gotta be real people. That's why Philly will always have a soft spot in my heart because of that.

Erica Grow, Meteorologist, WPVI:
Philadelphians are nostalgic. We like things that we know, and we know that team. It's the same familiar faces but [also] the same familiar music, style. It's part nostalgia and part comfort food on your television.

David Murphy, Meteorologist, WPVI:
They knew not to change the recipe. If it's not broken, don't fix it. It was that sort of attitude. I will say, as the years went on, and certainly in my experience, they did make changes. I mean, the weather situation changed dramatically once [news director] Carla Carpenter came in and realized magnetic clouds weren't going to cut it as we moved into the modern age of meteorology. The station was really big on getting us whatever equipment we needed. They were out front on new technology. Keeping their own helicopter—and I know other stations share a helicopter, or did for a while. Going digital, and all of these things came along. The website too. We adapted to that faster than any other stations did, and that's part of the reason why the website does so well in comparison to the others. I really think a lot of it has to do with not having turnover. The same reason I went for the job there: I knew that there was a better chance of having a long career there than at other places where you were behind in the ratings. New people would come

in, and those new people would want to put their stamp on the program, and that meant changes. We tended not to do that so much.

Rick Williams, Anchor, WPVI:
There was a time when they tried to change the theme song. The audience rebelled. They really did not like it. They tried to jazz it up or make it more contemporary or whatever. That *Action News* theme song is probably from the seventies, but it's a part of the brand that people have come to love and expect. I think that's part of the success. The brand of journalism—and not that the other stations don't do a great job as journalists either—but when there is a big story, whether it's the MOVE fire or COVID, the Black Lives Matter protest in Philadelphia, Joe Biden getting elected, *Action News* is very serious about how we cover such stories. There is a journalism integrity and a journalism excellence that we all embrace. People like Jim [Gardner], our producers, who have been there for years, carry this mantle of journalism excellence that also kind of helped our success as well.

Joe Torres, Reporter, WPVI:
[WPVI] oozes integrity. That generates trust. That builds loyalty. That's one big reason why WPVI was and has been so successful.

WPVI has built up such a level of trust with Philadelphia TV news viewers that it may just be impossible for the market's other stations to wrench that trust away. That trust dates back generations. It's why stories "come" to Channel 6. It's why news conferences don't start until the PVI crew arrives. How did all that begin? Well, I wasn't there to see it, but if I had to guess, I'd say this: the people of *Action News*. High-quality, reverent, and patient people who listen more than they talk. Your typical man on the street gravitates to those types of people. They feel free to "open up" to those types of people, and ultimately they put their faith and loyalty into journalists who will not sandbag you, backstab you, or misrepresent you when that story hits the airwaves. The world needs not only more journalists like that; it needs more people like that.

Nora Muchanic, Reporter, WPVI:
I think it's fast, accurate: [Channel] 6 takes great pride in getting it right, and I think that it has grown into this thing where people are so loyal to

the station. Nobody ever takes that lightly, trust me. It's kind of like, you are always thinking, you're always changing. Dave Roberts used to use happy clouds, magnetic clouds, and now Cecily Tynan is using two different kinds of radar, and they have such high-tech equipment, but it's still all about the people. I think they really figured out that loyalty counts, and you become a family member. Channel 6 does not have the most good-looking on-air people, but Channel 6 reporters and on-air types are like people that you know. They are people that you are comfortable with, and so you just keep coming back, and what the special sauce is, I am not sure, but it doesn't seem to go bad.

Amy Buckman, Reporter, WPVI:
They hired people who were smart, had a good work ethic, who felt mission-driven by what they were doing, and felt really connected to the city, and I think those are things you really can't fake. Philadelphia knows when someone is for real and when someone is going through the motions. They know it when they watch the sports teams, they know who hustles on the field or court—and I think it is the same way for TV.

Matt O'Donnell, Anchor and Reporter, WPVI:
We cover the community. I don't know how many times I've heard people say, "If there's a news conference or there is a community event, if there's one [camera] there, it will be Channel 6." We just cover everything: Philadelphia, Pennsylvania, New Jersey, Delaware, and every single suburb. I was a street reporter for a solid eight years. I've been to every single township, village, borough, city, and talked to someone in all of those places at least once. I can't think of any streets in Philadelphia I have not been to. It's not because of me. They sent me to these places because we felt and always do feel it's important to cover the community. That means everyone. No one is left behind.

Anita Brikman, Reporter, WPVI:
When I was there—and I'm sure it has continued and only grown—the station's consistent presence in the lives of the Delaware Valley was always there. Whether it was the Auto Show, the Thanksgiving Day Parade, I remember countless times being on our 6abc float and just getting off the float and meeting people and talking to them. They were

just so excited. *Action News* was always part of Philadelphia's biggest events.

Carla Carpenter, News Director, WPVI:
When you work at a number-one station, it's very difficult to stay on top. I think the reason Channel 6 was on top when I arrived and stayed on top was because we were very careful about changes that we made because the station was literally really committed to the community. Almost every television station in the country will say they are committed to the community, and to some extent they all do community work. But when I hired people there, in the course of the interview, I would try to get at whether or not these people were a "give-back" type of person or if they would have to be forced to give back. I tried to hire only people who naturally—if they weren't in the business or were in the business—would give back to the community. That makes a big difference, when you really care about what happens. The other thing I look at is, I always look at someone's profile and how they perform, because that's important, but I also look at what kind of person they are and if they are a true journalist. There are a lot of people, unfortunately, today more than ever—there are a lot of places to get news. That is not new; that is dangerous. It's important that if you're in a power position of giving millions of people information, then you have to take it seriously, and it better be fact and not your opinion.

Larry Mendte, Anchor, WCAU and KYW:
One of the ways to compete against Channel 6 is not to compete with Channel 6. Don't do what they do, because everyone comes in and tries to compete against them and does the same exact thing they do, and you will never out-6 Channel 6. Here's what they do very, very well: First of all, they have Jim Gardner, and you start with that. Number two: They cover and they make it part of their DNA to cover community events in every community. "There goes that news van again" is not just a PR stunt—it is real. I made it part of my mission as an anchor to be at as many community events as possible. Sometimes, we wouldn't cover it, but Channel 6 would be there. I had this thing with the Channel 6 photographers where I would go down to them and say, "You want me to get off the stage for a while?" and they would say, "Yeah, please" and

shoot the event so I could get out of the way. They are in your community, and they are known for that.

Ed Schimmel, Executive Producer, WPVI:
One of the key things we always tried to do was be in your neighborhood. It sounds a little corny, but that's why we always made a point of covering some of these community events that some people sometimes would think, "Jeez, is that really news?" The Boy Scouts in Fishtown, or such and such going on in Gloucester County, New Jersey. We kind of gave people the feeling that we were everywhere, and we were in your neighborhood. Someday, you could see yourself or somebody you know on an *Action News* cast. I think that kind of tied everybody together.

Alicia Vitarelli, Anchor, Reporter, and Cohost, WPVI:
We've always been at the one hundredth birthday.

Terri Merryman, Anchor and Reporter, KYW:
You would go out on the street and cover a story, and people would see that [Channel] 6 news van drive by. They would go, "Oh, it's Channel 6." You felt [as someone working for a different station] like, "Oh, I'm chopped liver," and you would be standing there talking to the person! They would say, "I don't watch you guys. I watch Channel 6." I would say, "That's fine, give us a try sometime. I'm on weekends, and try it on the weekends." Everybody I met, I felt like a politician out trying to get a vote.

Scott Palmer, Sports Anchor and Reporter, WPVI:
Other stations I would come to before I got to Philadelphia, they would say, "Scott Palmer is here."

[WPVI] kept me off the air for the first two weeks and said, "Learn the city. Go around and learn how to pronounce names. Go out with our crews. Go out with reporters. Find out what makes this place tick and find out the people that you are going to be talking to. Just go out into the community and just talk to folks. They don't know who you are yet, but find out about them." The first day I was on the air, Jim O'Brien said, "Scott Palmer is here with sports." I might as well have been there for five years. People at home are thinking, "Well, there's a new face," but it wasn't someone who came from Birmingham, Alabama. It was, "Here's Jim's friend, Scott." I was a member of the family. It's like you have been there forever. It was never introducing people from other cities who are coming to live here. It's, "Here's Scott, and he has sports today," and we went from there. If there is anything [that separates *Action News*,] it's that stability factor.

Steve Highsmith, Anchor and Reporter, WPHL and WCAU:
I chalk it up to consistency: to quality and a formula and part of that formula beyond which—consistency and quality are very important, but it is also being everywhere. [Channel 6 is] giving the impression that they reflect the entire community, and you can be everywhere. They are also better than everybody else in the early stages where loyalty is built up. Creating a sense of urgency, "the Big Story" was a part of that. It sounds hokey to some people, but the reality was very early on—combined with that consistency and quality and being everywhere and feeling local—was this idea that you had to watch because you would learn something very important that happened. Everybody tried to replicate that, but this is the other reason, sort of the back-end reason, for their success.

Brian Taff, Anchor, WPVI:
I was actively looking for a job, and I was in discussions with the general manager of the ABC station in Boston, WCBB. We were trying to come up with a situation where I would go work there. When I got the call from [news director] Carla [Carpenter] offering me the job at PVI, he was first guy I called to get his opinion, because we were already talking. He said to me, "Brian, I would love for you to work with this television station, but I would be crazy if I didn't tell you to jump at the opportunity to work at WPVI." He said, in his direct words that has stuck with me to this day, "Those call letters are the gold standard in television." Coming from him, from a guy who I had such tremendous respect for, it just planted this seed within me that this place is something special. When you get here, what you come to understand is that they give tremendous thought to every hiring decision that they make. Philadelphia is a unique market. Trust me when I tell you, because I experienced this as the new

guy back then, first, it's like this arm's length, "Who are you? Who are you here to replace? What are you doing? Do you really talk like that?" Once they find out who you are and you start to show the layers of your humanity, that arm's length becomes a full embrace, like a bear hug, and they never let you go. Sorry if that sounds cheesy, but I really feel that way about it.

Tamala Edwards, Anchor, WPVI:
David Muir was my coanchor overnight [at ABC's *World News Now*]. When the offer came in [to work at Channel 6], he almost functioned as my agent as much as my agent [did]. He was like, "No, no." He was a local guy from Boston and upstate New York. He said, "You need to understand, this is different. This is not just an offer from a station. This is an offer from a powerhouse, and it is a different realm than any other offer." I think he laid the table of "This is what you need to understand, and this is why this is special." Certainly, as soon as you enter Philadelphia—I don't know if there are people who are attached to habitat and institutions the way people are here. The attachment to 6abc is a thing unto itself.

Jamie Apody, Sports Anchor and Reporter, WPVI:
When I got the call saying [Channel 6] wanted to interview me, I was really mad at my agent. I called him, and I said, "What the hell?" He said, "What do you mean?" I said, "I just got a call from PVI Philly." He said, "PVI?" I'm like, "You were only supposed to send my tapes to California or the West Coast." He was like, "PVI called you? Oh my God, you gotta take it!" He said, "It's the best station in the country." I was like, "Why did you send my tape there?" We literally got in a fight, and he interrupted me every five seconds, going "PVI!" I was like, "Okay, I understand." Then, I realized, I'm gonna go to this interview, and if I get offered the job, I'm gonna take it because it's this great station, right? I remember his advice when I got here the night before was to watch the newscast. So, I am sitting in the hotel room, and I hear that theme song, and I'm like, "What the heck? This is not the number-one station; give me a break." And then I did a little more homework and realized all of it. You quickly learn the history behind it and all of that. The secret sauce is the people.

Alicia Vitarelli, Anchor, Reporter, and Cohost, WPVI:
The fact that we truly love each other [is the secret sauce]. The year I had my daughter, two of my coanchors on *Action News at Four* had their first children too. I had a baby, Adam had a baby, Brian had twins. It's like we've grown together from the day we all kind of walked in. There is no beef. There is no smokescreen. We actually humanly love each other and care for our families as well.

THE PHILADELPHIA MUMMERS PARADE

The Mummers Parade is held on New Year's Day in Philadelphia. With well over ten thousand marchers and participants kicking off the start of each new year, the Mummers Parade is the oldest continuous folk parade in the United States. The parade is made up of five unique divisions: the Fancies, Comics, Fancy Brigade, Wench Brigade, and String Band. These divisions offer diverse floats, props, costumes, dancing (or strutting, as the Mummers call it), and musicianship. The tradition of the Philadelphia Mummers Parade started in the late seventeenth century, as a way to usher in the New Year.

In 1941, Philco Television (then Channel 3) hosted the first newscasts from the Mummers Parade. In 1949, WFIL/WPVI broadcast the parade and continued to do so until 1980. WFIL's on-air talent included Phil Sheridan, John Corcoran, Harry K. Smith, Mary Durante, Charles King, Mary Dorr, Jean Sargent, Bill Webber, Roy Nassau, Anita Klever, and Connie Klever. WPVI talent included Dave Roberts, Hank Sperka, and Mummers expert Frank Conforti. In July 1980, WCAU filed a lawsuit in a Common Pleas Court, asking the court to declare illegal a provision in the recently expired contract between WPVI and the Mummers. The provision gave Channel 6 the right to broadcast the 1981 parade if it offered the Mummers a contract matching or exceeding another station's offer. The Mummers Association also filed a lawsuit against Channel 6, seeking additional payments on the basis that the station had misrepresented its profits from previous parade broadcasts. The Mummers Asso-

ciation voted to switch to Channel 10 because WCAU offered to pay the association $100,000 for the 1981 broadcasting rights; Channel 6 had paid the Mummers $15,000 for broadcasting rights to the 1980 parade. WPVI filed a countersuit, and as a result, a Common Pleas judge ruled that WPVI had lost its right of first refusal when it failed to match within two months WCAU's offer to the Mummers. The Common Pleas judge ruled that the Mummers could break their relationship with WPVI and granted the rights for the parade to be broadcast on WCAU.

From 1981 to 1986, WCAU broadcast the parade and featured talent Larry Kane, Bill Baldini, Deborah Knapp, John Facenda, Diane Allen, Alan Frio, and James Donio. In 1987, KYW took over the parade broadcast rights, which it held until 1991. KYW talent included Steve Bell, Pat Ciarrocchi, Jack Jones, Ray Murray, Jerry Penacoli, Dick Sheeran, and Beverly Williams. KYW's coverage included a "Pride of Philadelphia" special, Mummers Eve, hosted by Murray and Ciarrocchi.

After contract complications with KYW for the upcoming 1992 parade, the Mummers had no broadcast agreement just weeks before New Year's Day. Two cable operators—the Lenfest Group and Comcast—agreed to underwrite the broadcast of the parade. As part of the agreement, WHYY (Channel 12) carried the broadcast and helped produce the program live, and KYW provided the on-air personalities. The 1992 parade broadcast aired from 8:30 A.M. to 7:30 P.M., with an average Nielsen rating of 11.5 and a 21 percent share of the viewing audience, beating college football bowl games and other out-of-town parades. The Mummers parade returned to KYW for two more years in 1993 and 1994.

In 1995, WPHL took over the parade broadcasts. In the station's first year, a multitude of on-air talent was featured on the broadcast, including Pat Ciarrocchi, Gene Crane, Mike Strug of WCAU, Ed Cunningham of WHYY, and Steve Highsmith and Larry Cosgrove of Channel 17's Inquirer News Tonight. Former Mummer and judge Jake Hart offered commentary on the WPHL parade broadcast for twenty years. Highsmith is the longest-tenured host of the Mummers Parade, with twenty-eight years; he started in 1992. Highsmith and Hart retired from the booth after the 2020 parade. As of 2023, the Mummers Parade is now televised on WFMZ-TV and WDPN-TV with Larry Mendte and Dawn Stensland-Mendte.

Steve Highsmith, Anchor and Reporter, WPHL and WCAU:
There are Mummers in other parts of the world, but each of the cities that have Mummers has its own little take on it. Philadelphia's take on it is unique. It was joyful, and we continued with that. I got to know a lot of the people behind the makeup, masks, and the sequins. I realized these people were amateurs, and they were not professionals doing this. These are people who are working really hard during the day at some other job, and they were carrying on tradition that they may have begun with high school classmates who carried on from their parents or great-grandparents. The tradition is basically to go out and have a good time on New Year's Day. I think that the vast majority of Mummers who do it simply do that. They want to celebrate on New Year's Day and be a part of a tradition of celebration of fancy display that entertains people. That is the mindset of the vast majority of Mummers that go out there.

Mike Dardis, Reporter and Anchor, WPHL:
I really kind of studied [the parade tradition] a lot because I realized its importance in Philadelphia and at the station. Philadelphia is the kind of city that celebrates its own. Whether it be heroes, big issues, personalities, or traditions, Philadelphia really is the kind of city that celebrates things that are Philadelphia. There is nothing more Philadelphia—obviously—more than the Mummers Parade.

Jim Sinkovitz, Anchor and Reporter, WPHL:
I had gone out and covered Ferko [String Band] and a couple of other string bands that were rehearsing months, weeks beforehand. I was just thinking how amazing and how good instrumentalists these guys and ladies were. To sit in an auditorium and hear them play just gave me a whole new perspective about how talented these people were.

Cherie Bank, Health Reporter and Anchor, WCAU:
When I first came to town, I couldn't understand what a Mummer was or what a Mummers Parade was. I couldn't get anyone to explain it to me. There was no Internet at the time. When Channel 10 got the rights to cover the parade, I was in the booth, which was on the Parkway with Steve Levy. We were a good pair. He was writing down, "This was the best party I've ever been to."

Dick Sheeran, Reporter, KYW:
I grew up on Hick Street, which is a block and a half off of Broad Street in South Philadelphia. I have been watching the Mummers Parade since I was a little child. It was a big, big deal in our neighborhood. All I had to do was walk a block and a half to Broad Street, and the Mummers at the time would do their routines in front of Saint Agnes Hospital, which was at Broad and Mifflin. That was the place to be. People would be six-deep, watching.

Steve Levy, Anchor and Reporter, WPVI, KYW, and WCAU:
I grew up in South Philly, so after the Mummers Parade, a lot of the Mummers would come down Ritner Street, where I lived. They were pretty well-oiled by then—this was after the parade. This was when night was almost setting in, and they would come actually staggering down the street.

Rich Scott, News Director, WPHL:
I can remember waiting outside the office for the [contest] results of the parade so we could get them on at ten o'clock. Now, they release them earlier. But we used to wait there, run downstairs, turn the camera on at ten o'clock, and say, "Okay, here are your winners." It was a huge draw, the biggest numbers ever. Same with the newscast—the biggest numbers ever. It's a huge undertaking. So many people are involved.

Larry Kane, Anchor, WPVI, WCAU, and KYW:
I was the primary anchor, and all of the personalities came on throughout the day. This was Channel 10. For six years, I got up at three o'clock [in the morning] and broadcast until nine o'clock at night. Of course, they did give me a break here and there. One of the Mummers challenged me to be in the parade, so I marched with Klein Fancy Brigade. I was pulling something with large crystals. We marched from Washington Avenue all the way to city hall and then around city hall before the reviewing stand. I just was praying that my family wasn't watching too carefully. It was quite an experience. To this day, I'm the only non-Mummer who has ever marched in the [1985] Mummers Parade in the middle of the broadcast.

Paul Perrello, Host, the Comcast Network and WPHL:
It really did become a fifteen-plus-hour event at that point, so the three stations—3, 6, and 10—they rotated between the three of them. They [the stations] pretty much said no, they're not going to do it, when it came down to the wire. At that point, they [the Mummers] had kind of shopped it around to see who would bite on it. Channel 12 did it one year to sort of bail [the Mummers] out because there was really no outlet, to the best of my recollection. And then shortly, I guess the following year, Channel 17 stepped up to the plate.

Terry Ruggles, Reporter and Anchor, WCAU:
I had a great assignment because Channel 10 broadcast the Mummers Parade for a number of years. I got to be around city hall, where everybody put on their show, whether it was a String Band or the Comics. While we had people like Larry Kane in the anchor booth, I got to be the guy who roamed the audience around city hall with people who came from all over the world to see the Mummers Parade. I got to interview these people, and that was really good because there was an interesting cross section of people.

Thomas Baldrick, Freelance Broadcaster:
I called Ron Jaworski, who I knew, and said, "Hey, Jaws, can we borrow a golf cart for the Mummers Parade?" That's what we did. I remember Dick Sheeran and I were doing a live post-parade show from down on Two Street, and while we were live on the air, some drunken Mummers stole our golf cart. We joked on the air about police doing a low-speed chase to get back our golf cart.

Ray Murray, *Evening Magazine* Cohost and Producer, KYW:
We did a special called *Mummers Eve*. We would produce a bunch of stories about Mummery and about the people who were involved with it, what it meant to them, and the practices they had to go through, and the dedication they had to show to be a part of that. We would put together an hour-long special, and it was live the night before. So, there was an energy about that. We would roll those pieces into the live show. Then, at three o'clock in the morning, a police car showed up at my door to take me to the parade.

In order to do a Mummers Parade well, you have to go through an enormous amount of preparation. You can't just show up. The parade is more than just String Bands and more than just the Comics, it's more than just the Fancies. You just have to know who are the key players and how they've done in the past years, who are the outstanding personalities, what are their routines, and how long did they work on the costumes, and where did those costumes come from? What were their inspirations? There is an enormous amount of research that starts long before January 1. You start studying up for the Mummers in September or October. It also means going to some of the clubhouses to watch them practice and talking to them.

Robin Mackintosh, Reporter, KYW:
The parade was the parade, but the real fun with the Mummers was to go to the clubhouse: the clubhouses before [the parade], when they were getting ready, and everybody was getting themselves set and getting their costumes together and doing some last-minute gluing and so forth.

Mike Strug, Reporter, WPVI, KYW, and WCAU:
I think what I discovered early on was that for Mummers, it is the equivalent of a country club. They are devoted to this thing year-round, and they meet and decide what they are going to do, and they are as devoted as a couple of golfers would be at a golf course. This is their devotion, their hobby.

Thomas Baldrick, Freelance Broadcaster:
I would go visit [Mummers clubhouses], and that's all—you had to have a beer with everybody. I think the formula that worked for me was, if you showed you care, not just said it, but if you showed you care, they opened up doors, they opened up stories, they just welcomed you with open arms to what they cared about. The buildup for me, I would kind of start to put my toe in the water in the summer and find out what people were doing, and then the two months leading up to it, we'd go make visits and work the phones. That day [of the parade] itself was just an adrenaline rush. It was excitement, it was pride, it was beer, it was all those things.

Steve Highsmith, Anchor and Reporter, WPHL and WCAU:
What I also learned about [the Mummers] throughout the years was that so many of them are very giving people and charitable people in their churches and community and in the wider community. They have been goodwill ambassadors. Mayors have often called them up and said that there are dignitaries coming in from the airport, "Can you go to the airport and give them a Philadelphia welcome?" and they did that. There are a lot of ways the Mummers can be appreciated. We all learn about histories and things over time. We need to face those things and have an awareness of how we got to where we are. I think the city has an opportunity if it chooses to seize it, to not put aside but to embrace all of its major festivals, celebrations, parades, and really emphasize the position aspects of each. Share them and educate them and, as I said, make aware and incentivize inclusion and inspire inclusion. That's what celebration and the mosaic of America should be all about. I think that the majority of people in the city want peace, but it begins with humility. Everyone who is a Mummer and everyone who is not a Mummer. I'm not preaching here, but let's start with humanity, and let's talk about self-awareness and about fairness, and just appreciate the celebrations and good dialogues and actions that will come out of it. That's kind of the take on it.

Deborah Knapp, Anchor and Reporter, WCAU:
I remember a line from the parade I would use is, "It's a kaleidoscope of color moving down Broad Street." It's amazing. It's a tradition that has endured. These neighborhoods get together every week all year long, make their costumes, practice their routines. That's a rare thing. You don't see that in many places.

Pat Ciarrocchi, Anchor and Reporter, KYW:
For me to be able to cover the String Bands on New Year's Day in Philadelphia was the greatest moment ever. To do it year after year, and to wait for the late Bob Shannon to come around the [city] hall and to part the waters. His satire, his costumes, to see that for the first time and to see his engaging smile as captain of Quaker City.

Steve Highsmith, Anchor and Reporter, WPHL and WCAU:
The personal memories of it are the people. The late Bob Shannon Jr. and Judge Hart and all of the other people I worked with. The soup

contest at the Mummers Museum. The serenades along 2nd Street, for example. Going into the warehouses ahead of time, many of them cold at the time, or the clubhouses and all of the sneak peeks you get. The sewing that is going on. The gluing that is still going on. The people that get to hang out together. People were always trying to feed me. The best soup, meatball, and gravy that anybody could ever have was because I got an opportunity to emphasize the positive aspect of Mummery.

PHILADELPHIA'S RELATIONSHIP WITH ITS TV BROADCASTERS

The Philadelphia local news teams have provided comprehensive coverage of regional, national, and international events, keeping viewers informed about important issues. The journalists, reporters, and anchors who have covered these stories have helped shape and inform the city of Philadelphia and beyond. Their coverage has left a lasting impact on the television industry and has played a significant role in shaping the media landscape in Philadelphia.

The following are personal stories from producers, photographers, anchors, and reporters regarding what it was like to work in the Philadelphia television market.

Terry Ruggles, Reporter and Anchor, WCAU:
Philadelphia is the bedrock of broadcast history. This is one of the places where it started, where the seeds started to sprout, where it turned into what it is today.

Jim Gardner, Anchor, WPVI:
Now, understand, the landscape has changed dramatically since 1977 or 1978. Philadelphia wasn't wired for cable even when I first got here. The size of the [broadcast] audience was enormous. There was stuff in the newspaper all of the time. The promotion departments were very

aggressive, and it was a very big deal. Yes, it was clear almost from my first day of work that TV news in Philadelphia was a big deal.

Don Tollefson, Sports Anchor and Reporter, WPVI and WTXF:
I think it's the most intensely viewed television news market in the country. You look at the data, the ratings, and all of that. Philadelphians watch local TV news.

Steve Doerr, Executive Producer and News Director, WCAU:
Maybe I'm old school, but that period in the nineties when the television business was healthy financially and we were a competitive market, it was just such an excellent place. We were throwing helicopters at each other, we were hustling for breaking news. There's just something about it. It's an electric feel to the Philly news market. It is very competitive.

Dave Roberts, Meteorologist, WPVI:
The level of competition in this market with television stations is extremely high. I think it's probably better than any other market in the country, and that includes New York and Los Angeles, Chicago. That's just my opinion. It's increased too.

Stu Bykofsky, TV Columnist:
I've often wondered if, in a way, it's sort of like the tradition of, "My family is Democrat, we always vote Democrat." You hit a point when the younger generation wants to break loose of its elders and do something different. PVI seems to be immune to that. In most major markets, there seems to be a continuing horse race where there might be a station that is dominant for a few years and then it falls back and gets overtaken. That hasn't happened here.

Cecily Tynan, Meteorologist, WPVI:
When I was offered the job at 6abc, I almost didn't take it. We were still using magnets in our weather forecast. I was working in Las Vegas, where we had as much bells and whistles as possible, even back in 1995. I realized that we don't have these flashy graphics because we didn't need them. We had those magnets to convey the same info. Obviously,

now we have grown from that and grown with the times. We have our augmented reality and our own radar. I think it comes down to the basics, that everything else is just window dressing. When it comes to the news and weather forecast, for 6abc, anyhow, it's really the substance that is important. Everything else is just extra.

The very first time I was on the air was for an afternoon show. I was filling in for Dave Frankel, who took a vacation. I did the noon show, and I remember my knees were shaking so much, I was afraid you would see them through my green suit. Then, I went to PNC Bank around the corner to open up a checking account because I hadn't done any of that. I literally got off the air and went over to PNC, and I was waiting in line, and a cute little old lady said, "Excuse me. Didn't I just see you on the news?" And I think she said, "Aren't you Cecily Tynan?" and I think she butchered my name, which most people do when they first hear it. I couldn't believe it. I was on the air once for three minutes, and somebody recognized me. I remember telling my news director that, and he said, "Philadelphia is different."

Chris Wagner, Anchor, WPVI:
I remember Larry Kane told me the year I started there, he said, "Washington has its politicians, and New York has its celebrities, and we are stuck in the middle. We're the celebrities, and they like to watch their news celebrities."

Ali Gorman, Health Reporter, WPVI:
Most of the new reporters when they first start would go out with Vernon [Odom] on a couple of stories. I probably was there for a week or two, and I went out on a story with Vern. We went out on the story and went out to lunch at the Reading Terminal Market. Given it's Vern, the people were yelling his name like he was a Hollywood superstar. I was thinking in my head, like, "Oh my goodness!"

Vernon Odom, Reporter, WPVI:
[In] California, everyone is off in La La Land. People in Philadelphia are always concerned about their community and about what's going on around it, in their neighborhood, down their sidewalk, and up their alley. They can decide very quickly if they like you or not.

Justin Pizzi, Reporter and Host, WCAU:
When I was working there, there were two gossip columns in each of the papers. Gail Shister had, I think, a three-times-a-week television column because Philadelphia is like a big city made up of small towns; in a lot of ways, the news people became what we would call "celebrities."

Gail Shister, TV Columnist:
Through the years, we elevated the on-air personalities to the status of celebrities because, when you think about it, outside of sports stars, where are the celebrities in Philly, at least back then? It didn't surprise me at all. Plus, my experience was, readers had a voracious appetite to know about their local TV personalities. Interesting to me is when I wrote, I tried to keep the column for all of those years news-driven. Once in a while, there would be a great personality story I would have been insane to pass by. I remember once I did a story on Jim Gardner's hair color. One day, he showed up on air, and the color of his hair was something I'd never seen in a civilized world. You had to be blind to miss this. I wrote about it and actually got to him. We always had a contentious relationship. I was able to get to him, and I remember him being very defensive, but I actually got him to talk a little bit about it, and then basically he said that the woman doing his hair messed up and left the color on too long.

Neal Zoren, TV Columnist:
Philadelphia has three branches of stars: the athletes, the television personalities, and these chefs. The people who were the celebrities and the people pointing to them on the street and at restaurants were the television people. We were not a movie city, and we were not going to have movie stars here.

Dan Gross, TV Columnist:
When I took over the column from Stu [Bykofsky], I remember even telling him one of the first things people would say: "What are you going to do differently?" or "What are you going to do?" I said, "Listen, I really don't think I'm gonna write much on these Philly TV people." It seemed too much. Do these people merit all of this attention? The funny thing was, as I got on the job, and you get emails and phone calls from readers or even letters from the mail, which was pretty common. They

do care. While I didn't set out to cover television news as much as I did, it became very clear very quickly that people in this area—look, I've never lived or grown up anywhere else, so I really don't know how to compare it to anywhere—but people here seem unusually concerned with or interested in the lives of their television news folks. You got letters: "So, it looked like they gained weight. See if she is pregnant!" Or like, "I noticed so and so isn't wearing a wedding ring—what happened?" Or, "Hey, whatever happened to this one—are they still dating?" You get questions from people and stuff like that or like, "Hey did you watch last night? I couldn't believe they made this dumb mistake." They pay attention.

Alicia Vitarelli, Anchor, Reporter, and Cohost, WPVI:
When I got here, people told me, "Oh, you know, people here care deeply about this station." I was like, "Oh, okay." I worked in New York City and am from NYC. It's cool, and people [there] would say, "Hey, you're so and so," kinda. Here, forget it. People go nuts here, in a cute way. The news director was like, "Heads up, people get excited." I was in the supermarket, and people were waving, making eye contact, and following me around—not in a weird way, but getting close and smiling.

I always say to people, "If Philly likes you, then you're golden." This is all of the viewers. For us, if the viewers care, you know you made it. They knitted blankets when we had babies, they told us intimate stories about their families, they care about us, they send birthday gifts for our kids. It is legitimately a huge city, but a small town with a massive heart. It's the reason we are successful, only because of the viewers. There is no other reason. The viewers are it. If they care, you're good. They care deeply, and they get excited.

Jennaphr Frederick, Reporter, WTXF:
They think and they know we are their best friend. They know it. Just like you're talking crap on your best friend or you are loving your best friend, they've got to know what's up. They want to know what their best friend is wearing, they wanna know what their best friend thinks about the Eagles, Phillies, Flyers, Sixers. They wanna know where their best friends are having dinner, what the new drink is, or if they are celebrating Taco Day. They know that we are their best friend. They have to check in and see what's up. It's like looking out the front door.

Mike Jerrick, Anchor, WTXF:

When I got to Philly, it was almost instantaneous that people would respond to you on the street. I would say to my friends, "If this doesn't seem like a small town, how come everyone knows me?" I worked in these huge markets: Los Angeles, San Francisco, New York. It was never like this. This is like being a movie star. Oh my God. Early on, it was probably three to four months in which I felt that way. This is the most unusual TV market in America. They listen, they watch closely, they care, but you better be one of them. I guess I was savvy enough to just throw myself into the city. I rented a car and drove all over the place, getting out and about, trying to meet everybody, and trying to understand who these people are. They are not New Yorkers, they are not people in D.C. or Los Angeles that I've met. These Philly people are different. They are kinda like me. I'm from Kansas. I'm not a sophisticated New Yorker, even though I love New York. I'm not an L.A. guy, and I was never comfortable out there, but I felt comfortable the minute I ended up in Philadelphia.

Alex Holley, Anchor, WTXF:

When I came, Mike [Jerrick] took me and my father out to dinner. He said, "Your life is about to change." I looked at him and said, "Yeah, I'm going to a different market." He said, "No, you don't understand. Your life is about to change." "What you think it's going to be?" "I'm telling you, it's not going to be the same." I said, "Oh, okay," and I was like, "Thanks for the heads up." I can't tell you exactly when it hit me, but I get little reminders throughout the years, whether I'm off for a couple of days, okay, "What's going on, Alex? What is happening?" Or "I just saw Mike [Jerrick] the other day, and he was doing this" or I'm in the grocery store, and people are like, "Hey, Alex," as if we are friends. The familiarity of it is really something special. Literally, my grandfather comes to visit, we will be walking down the street, and people will yell out of their cars, "Hey, Grandpa! Welcome to Philly!" It's a special family feeling that I haven't seen anywhere else.

Amy Fadool, Anchor and Reporter,
Comcast SportsNet/NBC Sports Philadelphia:

I remember my sister came to visit me in early summer or fall, and it was still warm out. I was living in Old City at the time, and we were walking across the Old City Bridge to get something to eat, and I must have stopped, like, three times within a block. She looked at me and was like, ". . . ?" It would happen when I go to a game. People were surprised: "Why are you going to a game?" Because I'm a sports fan, and I like to go to the games.

Rick Williams, Anchor, WPVI:
In Philadelphia, to be an on-air personality is no small thing. There was a part of it that you do become a celebrity, and I embrace that. I didn't take advantage of it. I always like to consider myself very approachable because I know that if you are going to work in Philadelphia and be on the air, then people, hopefully, are going to want to say hello and take a selfie or, with COVID, a distanced selfie. I've been flattered by the way folks in the Delaware Valley have embraced myself and my colleagues at 6abc and made us more than just people who do the news.

Marshall Harris, Anchor, Reporter, and Host,
Comcast SportsNet/NBC Sports Philadelphia:
Meteorologists, main anchors, sports people, and morning-show hosts: Everyone knows who they are. Even though they don't know who you are, they know you are a person on the news. The first year I worked there, I got called everything from Ron Burke to Keith Russell to Ducis [Rodgers]. I've been called every person in the city. It was funny because after three or four years, people knew my exact name.

Colleen Wolfe, Sports Reporter, WTXF:
I never realized what a soap opera Philly sports media really is. I left and saw it from afar. I always knew it was ridiculous while I was in Philly because John [Gonzalez] and I would sit around, and we would get home from media availability and talk about all of the funny stuff that happened. It gave us so much material. Every day, every single person in that room is a character. It's all of the same people for the most part that have been there for so long. You really get to know everyone. You are in tight corners in these locker-room scrums. You end up going through these shared experiences together. It's really like they become family. That's how I feel when I think of Philly sports media. It's like going to Thanksgiving with all of your crazy uncles and cousins and all of the drama because everybody has certain cliques and riffs that go down.

You know who has what reputation and where and who and why. It has just such a history to it. I just love that Philadelphia sports media has the reputation that they do of being in Philly sports media. It's like a Mafia, almost.

Matt O'Donnell, Anchor and Reporter, WPVI:
I don't know if we are celebrities or not, but the one thing about Philadelphia—and I'm talking broadly, the general area—it's the same things with athletes in town, the professional sports teams. There's a trial period, and they watch you. They want to see what kind of person they are, and they want to see if you are one of those people who slack off or give maximum effort every time. Once they see you are one of those people that give maximum effort, you are good. You pass the test, and they will be loyal to you forever. That's what's special about our viewers.

Art Moore, Publicity Director, WPVI:
It's the sincerity, the first-hand approach, the community involvement all of these people that have charities and projects they support and are out visibly helping. The collective viewers feel "These people are my people." It's almost like the Mummers. If you look at how that plays out generically, one passes it on to the next and to the next all of these years. It's a very strong, large, [tight-]knit group of people who participate. It's sort of the same thing. Families pass onto their kids to their kids to watch us, and they like what they see, and they stay.

John Clark, Sports Reporter and Anchor, WCAU and NBC Sports Philadelphia:
I think it's important that you are from here and you kind of get Philadelphia people. You get the passion and get the love for Philly sports and understand that the mood of the city on a Monday morning can kind of get dictated by whether the Eagles won or lost. The Sunday of an Eagles game is almost like going to church. The routine, the coming together of people and family—it's like a ritual in our town. I think it's really good to be from here and to understand where the people are coming from.

Larry Mendte, Anchor, WCAU and KYW:
I love Philadelphia television. I grew up in Lansdowne, and my parents watched local TV and knew everybody, and it's what got me the bug—

there is no question. I always said I wanted to be an anchor in Philadelphia, and that's all I wanted to be. I got that. My parents just watched every single night. We watched Mort Crim, Diane Allen. When I got my job at WFIL radio, I was nervous because I got to interview Vince Leonard, who is the nicest man in the world. I remember watching Jack Jones and Ralph Penza. My family watched all three stations. Most people in town watch PVI, and that lasted forever, 'til this day.

Adam Joseph, Meteorologist, WPVI:
Once I was out of the studio and doing these live reports at the shore in front of people and in the public, I could really show my personality. When you are out of the studio, you are more fun, and you can do things. I was doing "Adam's Adventure Down at the Shore." I think that really made people realize who I was because I kind of stood out while having fun, and we never did weather live at the shore. I started that. I think people really started connecting, and I started connecting with them. When we would see them on the boardwalk, people would come up, chat and take a picture, and that sorta thing. I think once I announced that I was having a son and I have a partner, and I really opened up my personal life to the public, that they really understood that I trusted them and that I cared about them, and I can be honest about anything in my life. I felt so comfortable, and I felt so strong. I remember my boss saying, "You are in such a great place that you created such a tremendous foundation in this market and in the station that no one can crumble your foundation. It's strong, it is tough, and you're only going to build from that." Even my current boss, [general manager] Bernie [Prazenica], saying, "You know, you were popular before you came out, but you are even more popular now that you've come out." I think it's, again, because of that trust factor there. I trust people to know about my personal life. No one really shares their personal life. I was the very first big on-air person to officially come out in Philadelphia television history. There was no one else who had done it before me who actually said it on the air and showed pictures of the same-sex family. No one had done it before. We didn't know what to expect. We had many meetings about it prior too.

It was great. I think that was my time here at Channel 6 to say who I really was and that I trusted everybody. I knew they had my back, and it's worked out so well ever since then.

Brian Taff, Anchor, WPVI:

This is a small business, so you have friends who work at other stations that you have worked with in other cities. When I got here, one of my friends who worked at a competing television station invited me out. I guess they were all getting together to go out that night. I was the lone representative from Channel 6, but I wasn't on the air yet, so no one would have known yet. Not fifteen minutes after I arrived did one person in that group from the other channel say, "I've been on the air for seven years here, and, in seven weeks, more people will know who you are than know who I am." I was impressed with the humility that he said that with. I think it spoke to what he perceived of the power and importance of Channel 6.

I will also say, if you get into this business because you want to be recognized, you will not last all that long in this market. I think the audience doesn't care for it. Ego and vanity are pretty easily called out here. People appreciate the genuineness of someone. That was an important moment in setting the table for what I was about to experience. Sure enough, weeks later, you walk down the street, and people know your name, they know who you are dating. When I got married, people would come up and say they knew what church we got married in. It was, like, that's next-level stuff. It's all good. To me, it's never felt strange or creepy for a moment. It's always felt that it comes from a real place, and people want to know you because they like you and they trust you.

Jim Donovan, Anchor, KYW:

I worked in three other TV markets before arriving in Philadelphia, and the day I moved here, I could tell that something was different. The viewers often refer to people on the various TV stations as if they are speaking about their friends or family members. It's a very unique relationship that I had never seen before. Many viewers are loyal to a particular network or news team, and there is not a lot of channel surfing.

The advent of social media opened a new avenue to reach out to those viewers in a much more personal way. We could engage with them personally, sometimes even daily, on Facebook, Twitter, and Instagram. Before that, we were just people that they saw on their TV set, or perhaps at an event or running errands. Now, we could do live chats, post pictures of our lives outside of TV, even broadcast breaking news outside of a newscast. For the news junkie, it was like they were handed the keys to the candy store.

Steve Capus, Producer, KYW:
These people [on air] become their neighbors and are treated like their neighbors. They carry themselves like they are their neighbors. The best marketing campaign, the best strategies are built around being so readily identified as a part of their communities.

Eliott Rodriguez, Reporter, WPVI:
Something that I think was brilliant that we used to do is that at the end [of a broadcast], they would show random people out and about in the street. That's brilliant. We would just shoot somebody out and say, "Wave hello, goodbye, you are gonna be on TV tonight." Those are extra viewers every night.

Jane Robelot, Reporter, WCAU:
People are very proud of their neighborhood. They are proud of their favorite cheesesteak, their favorite who's got the best water ice. They are proud of the culture of their neighborhoods. There's just something charming and wonderful about that. They are very, very loyal. They can pick on each other all day long, but anyone on the outside picks on them you better get ready for a fight. It's like having a big brother.

Steve Highsmith, Anchor and Reporter, WPHL and WCAU:
Being a member of the Philadelphia broadcasting community and having worked in it for so long, number one, I'm grateful—grateful to viewers and grateful to my colleagues. I think we have to understand that whatever good things happen to you, it's because other people wanted those things to happen to you. In other words, you can't believe your own press clippings. You have to be able to understand that there's a responsibility that comes with being on the air. That's one of my biggest concerns about the "trendlines." There were always people in television that looked at it as a form of entertainment or personalities as opposed to journalists, but there have always been a good number of journalists. The challenge is going to be, what is that definition of journalism? Are they [journalists] running those newsrooms, and are the consumers go-

ing to watch them? I never was someone that people wanted to follow from a personality standpoint. But I do think I tried very seriously, from a journalism standpoint, to be fair to people and report accurately. Those are the basics of what we do in a free society. Where Philadelphia journalism is important is being able to illuminate those things that need to be shown to prevent or catch abuses of power, to give voice to the voiceless. Those are things that are in danger of being lost in the rapid change to social media and other platforms. Some of them are very much still immature. There was a lot of truth said in the traditional era of television on television newscasts. There is a lot less truth being said on a lot of other platforms. It's hard for the consumer to know which is which, but we tend to devolve into groupthink and finding justification for our own beliefs in what we watch and read.

ACKNOWLEDGMENTS

Although my name graces the cover of this book, it would not have come to fruition without the help of many others along the way.

I thank my best friend and wife, Jodi Grzybowski, for pushing me to finish the manuscript. Since my last book, we have created our own family with the addition of my daughters, Quinn and Baby Grzy number two, who arrived in July 2024. Becoming a #GirlDad has been the most transformative and fulfilling experience of my life. It has filled my heart with a love so deep and pure, one that I never knew existed. My daughters have brought a new perspective to my world, teaching me patience, kindness, and the true meaning of unconditional love. My girls have forever changed me for the better, and I am grateful every day for the privilege of being their father.

I am grateful to the extended Grzybowski family—my parents, Danny and Joanna; my brothers, Johnathan and Jeffrey; Uncle John; and the Gilbert family—for their love and support. We lost my father-in-law and Mom in 2019 and 2020. Although we miss their presence, there's not a day that goes by when we don't think about them and how we wish they could hold and see their grandchildren light up the world. I will always work hard in their honor.

This book is my love letter to Philadelphia television. I am thankful to have worked at WPHL-TV (Philadelphia) and WNCN-TV (Raleigh) over the years as a producer, photographer, on-air reporter, and many other jobs that would be too extensive to list. Although I left the industry in 2017 and started my own marketing agency, I still miss and love storytelling. I remain a true news junkie at heart. I am forever a journalist and will always give a voice to the voiceless.

My research for this book sort of started when I caught the "post–writing my first book/becoming an author" bug. It was a few months after I wrote *Mr. All-Around: The Life of Tom Gola* (Temple). I was sitting in a shopping center parking lot in New Jersey talking to my editor and Temple University Press extraordinaire, Ryan Mulligan. We were discussing how I wanted to write another book, and we were tossing some ideas around. Ryan mentioned the ESPN book titled *Those Guys Have All the Fun: Inside the World of ESPN*, by James Andrew Miller and Tom Shales, an oral history of how ESPN became to be. He said something along the lines of "what about a book like that, but about Philly TV?" A light bulb went off in my head, and the book process started a few days after. It was go time!

I started this book on February 21 (my birthday ironically) in 2019, per my email records. I laid out chapters and ideas weeks prior, but if this book was going to work, I needed to have a really strong foundation of support from people to interview for the book. I interviewed over one hundred people for the Tom Gola book, and I wanted to crush that number with this one. I remember that same night I sent out about twenty-five emails to former Philadelphia reporters and anchors who were working in other markets. I received responses almost instantly from people wanting to talk to me for this book, and from that moment on, I never looked back. (Shout-out to Lori Wilson and Mike Dardis for being among the first few people to respond to my interview request, seconds after I'd sent my first email.)

This book should have been released sooner, but our world was flipped upside down in March 2020 due to the COVID-19 pandemic. Getting in touch with current Philadelphia television on-air talent with requests to participate in this book was a tedious process, but we made it. Interviewing certain folks from all four Philly TV station powerhouses took way too long for my liking, but I understood and respected the process in the end. Special thank yous to the following folks behind the scenes: from WCAU, Diana Torralvo and Sam Retamar; from WTXF, Jim Driscoll and Victoria Gurrieri; from WPVI, Elita Fielder Adjei, Mike Monsell, Mark Meany, and Bernie Prazenica; and from KYW, Sara Ahmad-Visomirski and Danielle Nick. All of these aforementioned individuals played a key role in helping me interview current on-air talent for this book. I greatly appreciate their time in responding to my multiple email requests and their scheduling help.

When I was getting into the television business, many people told me to find a mentor. I didn't know how or where to look for one, but I'm sincerely thankful Steve Highsmith came into my life. Thank you, Steve, for believing in me and pushing me to keep going in my career. I'm forever grateful for your guidance and friendship.

I am grateful to my dear friend and fellow author Jared Caracciolo. I love and appreciate our monthly coffee meetups, life, and book chats. You are a true friend!

To Anthony Mallamaci, my friend and La Salle University alum, thanks for always checking in on how this book was going, keeping me sane, and helping me keep my goals in order. I greatly appreciate you!

Thank you to Chris Blackman. I interned at WCAU my junior year of college and Chris was the news director at the station at the time. Chris has been a great friend and has always remained supportive of my work.

Thank you to my La Salle friends Justin Gick, Julie Wood, and Christina DeLullo for helping transcribe interviews for this book. Logging hour-long interviews is not an easy task, so I greatly appreciate their handwork and commitment.

To my Mummers family: my goal in my career was to work in Philadelphia television and annually be a part of the Mummers Parade broadcast. I'm proud to now be an executive producer and on-air host for the annual Mummers Parade since 2023. I'm extremely pleased to have witnessed the growth of the parade and its participants over the years. It's been extremely rewarding to work with Sam Regalbuto, Barry Fisher, Joel Keeler, Megan McFarland, Larry Mendte, Dawn Stensland, and others. Little Mummer fan David is still on cloud nine about being able to help market and change the parade for the better.

I had a few talented designers work on the first few phases of this book cover. Thanks to the following people for their time and interest in this book: Dhwani Saraiya, Woody Harrington, Alex Fine, and Jeremy Klinger.

I am forever grateful to Ryan Mulligan of Temple University Press. As Ryan knows, this book was tough to get over the finish line, but we made it. My deepest gratitude for all of your hard work and dedication in helping me bring my book to life. Writing two books would not have happened without Ryan's guidance, and I truly appreciate his friendship, phone calls, and more.

I also offer special thanks to the rest of the Temple University Press team: Aaron Javsicas, Gary Kramer, Karen Baker, and others. Special thanks go to copyeditor Heather Wilcox for her hard work on this book. Thank you to long-time Philadelphia television writer Neal Zoren for reviewing a few chapters of this book as well.

This book would not have been a success in my view if Jim Gardner hadn't been a part of it. It took quite some time to get Jim to sit down for an interview, but when we did, hearing his insight, wisdom, and detailed stories lived up to the hype. Special thanks to my friend and fellow Temple University Press alum Ray Didinger for the assist.

Finally, I thank the many people who graciously took time out of their busy schedules to answer questions pertaining to this book, especially Robin Mackintosh, Mike Strug, Nora Muchanic, Dick Sheeran, Chris Wagner, Pat Ciarrocchi, Larry Kane, Steve Highsmith, Justin Pizzi, Michael Barkann, Keith Jones, Paul Gluck, Brian Taff, Adam Joseph, Jamie Apody, and countless others. One phone interview led to the next, and I loved the countless hours interviewing individuals for this book.

The Big Story: The Oral History of Philadelphia TV News is the first of its kind in the city. I hope readers walk away with a great sense of appreciation and admiration for what it's like to work with our beloved Philadelphia television personalities and stations and watch them broadcast the news.

The world needs more journalism!

SOURCE LIST FOR CHAPTER INTRODUCTIONS AND STATION HISTORY

Books

Kane, Larry. *Larry Kane's Philadelphia*. Philadelphia: Temple University Press, 2000.

Shull, Bill. *Philadelphia Television*. Charleston, SC: Arcadia Publishing, 2015.

Shull, Bill, Mike Monsell, and John Morris. *WPVI Action News Celebrates Fifty Years*. Glendale, CA: Disney Enterprises, 2019.

Newspaper Articles

Associated Press. "Larry Kane Is Seen Returning to Philadelphia." *Lancaster New Era*, July 6, 1978.

———. "Philly Anchor Accused of Punching New York Police Officer in Face." *Sentinel*, December 17, 2007.

———. "TV Stations Trade Networks." *Standard-Speaker*, September 10, 1995.

———. "WCAU Dethrones WPIV News at 11." *Morning Call*, March 2, 2001.

Bianculli, David. "Ch. 10 Dominates MOVE Coverage." *Philadelphia Inquirer*, May 15, 1985.

———. "WCAU-TV Tops Nielsen Ratings Monday Evening." *Philadelphia Inquirer*, May 15, 1985.

Bittan, Dave. "WPVI Won Ratings War." *Philadelphia Daily News*, December 12, 1979.

Bruton, Mike. "Comcast's SportsNet Premieres." *Philadelphia Inquirer*, October 2, 1997.

Bunch, Will. "Alycia Tells Her Side in Suit." *Philadelphia Daily News*, June 20, 2008.

Bykofsky, Stu. "Bad Call: Bolaris Blows Another One." *Philadelphia Daily News*, March 12, 2001.

———. "Forecast Calls for Bolaris, Channel 10 to Split." *Philadelphia Daily News*, October 18, 2002.

———. "$100 Misunderstanding: Bolaris vs Byko in Charity Bet." *Philadelphia Daily News*, March 5, 2001.

Dale, Maryclaire. "Alycia Lane Gets the Ax." *Daily Intelligencer*, January 8, 2008.
Eichel, Molly. "Melvin Kampmann, Creator of 'Action News.'" *Philadelphia Daily News*, July 19, 2016.
Falk, Jeff. "New Philly Sports Network Debuts Today." *Lebanon Daily News*, January 23, 1997.
Fox, Tom. "N.Y. Chain Buys WFIL-TV, Radio Stations." *Philadelphia Daily News*, February 14, 1970.
Gray, Ellen. "CAU Brings Jim Back for an Encore." *Philadelphia Daily News*, February 22, 2001.
———. "Kane Breaks Story . . . of His Retirement." *Philadelphia Daily News*, November 27, 2002.
———. "TV Scored in Ratings: Local Station Benefited by Pre-empting for Storm Story." *Philadelphia Daily News*, January 9, 1999.
Gray, Ellen, and Christine Olley. "Cancer Takes Courageous Papa: Channel 6 Sports Anchor's Death Leaves Hole in the Hearts of Family, Friends and Fans." *Philadelphia Daily News*, June 20, 2009.
Guigar, Brad. "Hype King Bolaris." *Philadelphia Daily News*, March 7, 2001.
Harris, Harry. "Jim Gardner Will Take Over Kane's Anchor Assignments." *Philadelphia Inquirer*, April 5, 1977.
———. "Larry Kane Finds Action Is Really in New York." *Philadelphia Inquirer*, May 1, 1977.
———. "News Innovator to Leave Ch. 6." *Philadelphia Inquirer*, October 15, 1974.
Intelligencer Journal. "Dwyer Commits Suicide at Pa. News Conference." January 23, 1987.
Kane, Larry. "The Story behind the Kane Mutiny." *Philadelphia Daily News*, November 10, 2000.
Klein, Michael. "Alycia Lane off the Air Indefinitely." *Philadelphia Inquirer*, December 18, 2007.
———. "Larry Kane: 'I Have Had Enough.'" *Philadelphia Inquirer*, November 27, 2002.
Lawler, Sylvia. "Larry Kane New Anchor at 11 P.M. on Channel 3." *Philadelphia Inquirer*, April 21, 1994.
Lowry, Tom. "Coverage of Dwyer Suicide Spurs Broadcasters' Debate." *Morning Call*, July 21, 1987.
Madley, Grace. "On-the-Air Menswear: It's Subdued." *Philadelphia Inquirer*, July 19, 1971.
May, Marvin. "Forecast for WPVI: Not Quite So Young." *Philadelphia Inquirer*, July 4, 1971.
———. "WFIL Changing Name to WPVI—Here's Why." *Philadelphia Inquirer*, April 4, 1971.
———. "When Larry Kane, East Met Larry Kane, West." *Philadelphia Inquirer*, June 20, 1971.
Medina, Regina, Dan Gross, and Bob Cooney. "Anchor Lane Arrested in NYC." *Philadelphia Daily News*, December 17, 2007.
Nelson, Nels. "Young Man with a Voice." *Philadelphia Daily News*, June 8, 1977.
Nolan, Jim. "This Is No Hype: No Snow Job from Bolaris." *Philadelphia Daily News*, November 27, 2002.

O'Brien, Jim. "Gardner Wins Kane's Anchor." *Philadelphia Daily News*, March 9, 1977.

———. "Jim O'Brien (Not Me) Eyes Kane's Anchor." *Philadelphia Daily News*, December 9, 1976.

Philadelphia Daily News. "Snow Job: Now That the Hysteria Has Outdone 'The Storm' Who Overhyped It the Most?" March 6, 2001.

Philadelphia Inquirer. "Channel 6's New News Really Moves." April 20, 1970.

———. "KYW-TV Is on the Bottom and Looking Up." April 28, 1983.

———. "Marciarose to Join Newscasts." August 4, 1965.

Polak, Maralyn Lois. "Jim Gardner: The Anchorman Strikes Back." *Philadelphia Inquirer*, February 3, 1980.

Preston Lee, David, Paul Horvitz, and William W. Sutton Jr. "O'Brien's Colleagues Devastated, He Was the Best Friend Many of Us Had." *Philadelphia Inquirer*, September 26, 1983.

Shister, Gail. "Anchored to City for Three Decades, Larry Kane Is up for an Honor." *Philadelphia Inquirer*, September 30, 1996.

———. "At Ch. 6, Excitement over Major Merger." *Philadelphia Inquirer*, March 19, 1985.

———. "Ch 3's 11 O'clock News Is a Solid Second." *Philadelphia Inquirer*, May 3, 1985.

———. "Ch. 6's 11 P.M. News Loses Ground to Ch. 10 in Ratings Battle." *Philadelphia Inquirer*, January 12, 1983.

———. "Channel 10 Eclipsing Channel 6 as Ratings Leader for 11 P.M. News." *Philadelphia Inquirer*, March 1, 2001.

———. "Channel 10 Tries to Dig Out from the Storm That Never Was." *Philadelphia Inquirer*, March 6, 2001.

———. "A Distant Third in Sweeps, KYW Is Still Saying 'Hallelujah.'" *Philadelphia Inquirer*, May 31, 1999.

———. "For Angry Ch. 6 News Viewers, the Theme Was: 'Drop the Music.'" *Philadelphia Inquirer*, October 2, 1996.

———. "LaMay Leads the Charge of Channel 29's Good Day Philadelphia." *Philadelphia Inquirer*, February 19, 1996.

———. "Larry Kane Pulls the Plug Tomorrow on KYW." *Philadelphia Inquirer*, December 22, 2002.

———. "'Millionaire' Had No Spare Change for WPVI's 11 P.M. News." *Philadelphia Inquirer*, December 7, 1999.

———. "Ratings Seesaw Tips NACL to 'CAU at 11 in Latest Sweeps." *Philadelphia Inquirer*, March 7, 2005.

———. "What Did It Take to Get Don Tollefson back to TV? Ask Channel 29." *Philadelphia Inquirer*, April 11, 1995.

Smith, Jack. "The Anchorman as Victim . . . and Other Ploys for Making You Love Your Local TV News Team, Remember, in Advertising You Don't Sell the Steak—You Sell the Sizzle." *Philadelphia Inquirer*, November 20, 1977.

Tornoe, Rob. "But the Big Story on Action News: Ratings!" *Philadelphia Daily News*, March 6, 2018.

Winfrey, Lee. "Coming Home with Concessions." *Philadelphia Inquirer*, August 10, 1978, Page 55.

———. "Kane, Home Again and Happy, Dreams of a Team Back on Too." *Philadelphia Inquirer*, August 12, 1980.

———. "The O'Brien Style Was His—and His Alone." *Philadelphia Inquirer*, September 26, 1983.

Woods, Anthony. "Region Sighs with Relief over the Fizzled Blizzard." *Philadelphia Inquirer*, March 6, 2001.

York Daily Record. "NBC Settles Govt. Anti-Trust Suit by Agreeing to Sell Phila. Stations." September 23, 1959.

Online Articles

Akman, Terri. "Ten Questions: Terry Ruggles: Life after TV News." *SJ Magazine*, January 2014. https://sjmagazine.net/january-2014/terry-ruggles.

Brady, Jeff. "Three Mile Island Nuclear Plant to Close, Latest Symbol of Struggling Industry." *NPR*, May 8, 2019. www.npr.org/2019/05/08/721514875/three-mile-island-nuclear-plant-to-close-latest-symbol-of-struggling-industry.

Broadcast Pioneers of Philadelphia. www.broadcastpioneers.com.

Jones, David. "The Rise and Demise of Comcast SportsNet as Told by Those Who Worked There and Loved It Best." *Penn Live*, August 9, 2020. www.pennlive.com/sports/2020/08/the-rise-and-demise-of-comcast-sportsnet-as-told-by-those-who-worked-there-and-loved-it-best.html.

"Nuclear Disaster at Three Mile Island." History Channel. www.history.com/this-day-in-history/nuclear-accident-at-three-mile-island.

Rys, Richard. "The Stranger in Your House." *Philadelphia Magazine*, May 15, 2006. www.phillymag.com/news/2006/05/15/the-stranger-in-your-house/.

"The Stations of UHF." The History of UHF Television. https://uhfhistory.com/channels.html.

Tornoe, Rob. "Remembering 'Daily News Live': From Bad Eagles Guests to Christmas Eves with John Chaney." Inquirer.com, February 27, 2019. www.inquirer.com/sports/michael-barkann-daily-news-live-nbc-sports-philadelphia-philly-sports-talk-john-chaney-20190227.html.

Wood, Anthony. "30.7 Inches Fell upon Philly 25 Years Ago, and Snow Hasn't Been the Same Since." *Philadelphia Inquirer*, January 7, 2021. www.inquirer.com/weather/blizzard-philadelphia-snow-record-1996-winter-climate-change-weather-20210107.html.

Zoren, Neal. "Television: 'Action News' Changed Viewership and Continues to Do So 50 Years Later." *Delco Times*, June 14, 2020. www.delcotimes.com/2020/06/14/television-action-news-changed-viewership-and-continues-to-do-so-50-years-later/.

INDEX

David Grzybowski is a former television news reporter for WPHL in Philadelphia and WNCN in Raleigh, North Carolina. He is the founder and owner of the marketing production company Grzy Media Group and the author of *Mr. All-Around: The Life of Tom Gola* (Temple).